BARNSLEY LIBRARIES

BARNSLEY LIBRARIES

GW01513793

027

Return Date

21. MAY
23. MAY
24. 87
22. AUG 84
2. MAR 8
12. MAR 8
10. AUG
25. OCT 8
10. DEC
12. JUN 89.
10. DEC
5. APR 8
89
09. NOV 9
MAR 8
30. MAR 94
0. MAY
18·4·94
16. FEB 87
30. MAR 94
14. FEB

2 067330 02

The New Local Government Series
No. 14

THE PROCESS OF
LOCAL GOVERNMENT REFORM
1966-74

The New Local Government Series

General Editor: Peter G. Richards

1. A HISTORY OF LOCAL GOVERNMENT
   by K. B. Smellie
5. THE REFORMED LOCAL GOVERNMENT SYSTEM
   by Peter G. Richards
6. THE FINANCE OF LOCAL GOVERNMENT
   by N. P. Hepworth
8. TOWN AND COUNTRY PLANNING IN BRITAIN
   by J. B. Cullingworth
10. HOUSING AND LOCAL GOVERNMENT
    In England and Wales
    by J. B. Cullingworth
11. THE GOVERNMENT OF GREATER LONDON
    by Gerald Rhodes and S. K. Ruck
12. DEMOCRATIC THEORY AND LOCAL GOVERNMENT
    by Dilys M. Hill
13. THE LOCAL GOVERNMENT ACT 1972:
    PROBLEMS OF IMPLEMENTATION
    by Peter G. Richards
15. LOCAL GOVERNMENT AND EDUCATION
    by D. E. Regan

THE PROCESS OF LOCAL GOVERNMENT REFORM

1966-74

BY

BRUCE WOOD

University of Manchester

FOREWORD BY
LORD REDCLIFFE-MAUD

London
GEORGE ALLEN & UNWIN LTD
RUSKIN HOUSE   MUSEUM STREET

First Published 1976
by George Allen & Unwin (Publishers) Ltd

This book is copyright under the Berne Convention. All rights are reserved. Apart from any fair dealing for the purpose of private study, research, criticism or review, as permitted under the Copyright Act, 1956, no part of this publication may be reproduced, stored in a retrieval system or transmitted, in any form or by any means, electronic, electrical, chemical, mechanical, optical, photocopying, recording or otherwise, without the prior permission of the copyright owner. Enquiries should be adressed to the publishers.

© Bruce Wood, 1976

ISBN 0 04 350052 8

Photoset in English Times by
Red Lion Setters, Holborn, London
Printed in Great Britain by
Biddles Ltd, Guildford, Surrey

FOREWORD

BY LORD REDCLIFFE-MAUD

Academics played no distinguished part in the ten-year struggle between 1964 and 1974 to reform local government in Britain. Most of them seemed content to treat the reformers like candidates for doctorates and pick holes in their reasoning, rather than joining them in the search for practical solutions to grave democratic problems. This makes it the more pleasant to salute in Mr Bruce Wood an academic who helped the English Local Government Royal Commission of 1966/69 as a researcher, collaborated in a book describing the results, and has now written his own scholarly record of the battle for reform. I find his story fascinating and fair, and I hope many readers will get as much enjoyment from it as I have. But enjoyment is not the only profit to be got from Mr Wood's book: there is also wisdom and the stuff of which sound judgement is made.

We shall certainly need all the sound judgement we can get if local government in Britain is to survive the next few years. Already some advocates of devolution, especially those like Mr Derek Senior who are also dedicated critics of the English Local Government Commission report, have started urging us to scrap the 1972 Act and reorganise local government from top to bottom. Before we follow their lead, let us 'read, mark, learn and inwardly digest' what Mr Wood has written — in particular, his analysis of the 'missing debate' during the two gestation periods preceding delivery of the Labour and Conservative White Papers in 1970 and 1971. My guess is that, if local referenda had been required in Britain, as they commonly are in the United States, before changes in local government structure could be made, there would have been no substantial changes anywhere in the local government structure of the 1960s. When local chips are down, most people in Britain would, I believe, say 'leave us as we are'. Fortunately local government reformers in Britain do not yet have to win local referenda. But whether they think further reform is needed on democratic grounds or for the sake of more effective services or for both reasons, they ignore at their peril the appalling consequences of a second holocaust of local councils so soon after that of April Fool's Day 1974. This book is a salutary warning to the wise.

And it is more than that. It is a source of encouragement. It demonstrates, I dare to say, the great advantages Britain can still get from her traditional methods of achieving change: the long-established technique of an exploratory Commission, political decision-taking by the Cabinet, and Parliament's power to act decisively for the whole country.

In 1966 neither Labour nor the Tories knew what they wanted for the future of British local government, but they both knew that change was needed. The same could be said of all the local authority associations. This, then, was a classic case for Royal Commission inquiry. It became clear soon after the first meeting of the Commission that ten of the eleven Commissioners did not yet know what their own answers to the basic question would turn out to be. During the next two years or so we read the evidence, argued the toss, and ten of us reached broadly unanimous conclusions. Once our report, and Mr Senior's dissenting memorandum, had been presented, the issue rightly became political again. The Government took over the consultative and decision-taking process — and concluded, to my astonishment, that the Commission had got the answer nearly right.

Mr Wood discriminatingly tells us what happened next. As I personally remain an unrepentant believer in the Commission's 'unitary' plan, I stumped around the country trying to explain it throughout 1969. But once the Tories had won the 1970 general election on a platform committing them to 'two tiers everywhere', the Commission's basic proposal had no chance of acceptance by the new Parliament. Only one crucial question remained: whether or not the Tory plan was better than nothing. My own answer was 'yes', and about that, too, I remain unrepentant.

The present fashion is to denounce the 1972 Act as a disaster. It has grave faults, and most of them follow inevitably from the two-tier principle. The need to find work for the new districts in shire counties has fragmented planning, separated housing from other social services and made it absurdly difficult for citizens to pin down responsibility. Some of the new boundaries are indefensible on rational grounds. Nevertheless, it is inflation, not the 1972 Act, that is the real cause of current discontent with local government. For longer-term purposes it is a huge advantage that we have done away once and for all with separate counties and county boroughs, abolished rural districts and established the principle of metropolitan counties for great conurbations. Now we must grapple effectively with the remaining untouched part of local reform, namely finance. If we make progress there, and for some years to come refuse, either for devolutionary or any other reason, to attempt another major local government reform, the new authorities, county and district, will come to terms with one another and prove that British local government now has a future worthy of its past.

PREFACE

Whatever one's views of its contents, the Local Government Act 1972 cannot be dismissed as trivial or inconsequential. It represented only the second successful attempt this century to update our institutions of local self-government (the London Government Act 1963, which overhauled the built-up Greater London area, was the first), and history suggests that it is likely to remain on the statute book for several decades.

Local government reform — I use the word 'reform' throughout, though there is a strong case for shifting the emphasis to 'reorganisation' as the process unfolds — is a painful business. The local government world contains powerful vested interests in the form of councillors, paid officials, their associations and professional bodies. Often these groups had diametrically opposed objectives; on other occasions they were divided internally. This world is also closely linked with central government through the party system and the complex relationships between Whitehall and county and town hall. Finally, the limited amount of change in the twentieth century meant that the public had become used to traditional boundaries and structures and were often hostile to new plans, though they had little understanding of the reasoning behind them. There were many battles to be won before legislation could be achieved: Indeed it is sometimes hard to understand why successive Governments contemplated embarking on the stony path to reform.

The object of this book is to chronicle the process of reform from 1966 to 1974, and to assess the relative importance of concepts such as democracy and efficiency and of political strategies and tactics. The struggle for power between and within local government's vested interests and the opportunism of successive Governments provide the two central features of this process and account for the nature of the final legislation. Every issue is unique, but the basic model of Royal Commission-White Paper-Act of Parliament is a familiar one to students of British government. This book offers a detailed analysis of problem-solving by means of a traditional process and assesses some of the strengths and weaknesses of this process.

Most of the people who helped in the preparation of this study did so unwittingly, as I collected a great deal of material in the

1966-71 period without ever being quite sure to what purpose I would put it (until 1971 it was unclear whether there would be reform, though the omens seemed favourable). The reactions of students to lectures on which some of the chapters are based have been valuable. Chapter VI is partly based on documents kindly made available to me by Mr John Roper MP. More recently Professor P. G. Richards has been particularly helpful with both general encouragement and a host of perceptive detailed comments. I would also like to thank Marilyn Dunn who typed the bulk of the work with her customary accuracy.

BRUCE WOOD
Bury, Lancashire
October 1975

CONTENTS

FOREWORD		*page* 7
PREFACE		11
I	*The Decision-Makers and their Objectives* Background to the 1966 decision – the principal participants 1966-74 – democracy and efficiency – the scene is set	15
II	*The Redcliffe-Maud Commission 1966-69* Evidence – terms of reference and membership – research – reasons for establishment – concurrent developments – likely reactions – the problem of size – government by Commission	31
III	*The Report and its Reception, June 1969–February 1970* The main report – Derek Senior's memorandum of dissent – early reactions in Westminster and Whitehall – local authority and interest group attitudes – the 'missing debate' – meaningful consultations?	63
IV	*The Response of Two Governments, February 1970–February 1971* The Labour Government White Paper – the Conservative Opposition: a commitment emerges – new minister, new agenda – Mr Walker's White Paper – early reactions: the battle-lines emerge – two hectic years	91
V	*Wales* No Royal Commission – the 1967 White Paper – the impact of the Redcliffe-Maud Report	117
VI	*Implementation – (1) The Legislative Process 1971-2* The consultative process – the Bill and Second Reading – Committee Stage – Members and Committee Stage: a survey – from Committee to Royal Assent – the value of the legislative process	128
VII	*Implementation – (2) Preparing for the Appointed Day* Constitutional issues – the new areas – urban parishes – electoral arrangements – shared functions	161
VIII	*The Process of Reform 1966-74* Why handle a 'hot potato'? – policy-making – the objectives of reform	176
APPENDIX *A comparison of the various reform proposals 1969-72*		191
INDEX OF PERSONS AND PLACES		195
SUBJECT INDEX		199

Chapter I

THE DECISION-MAKERS AND

THEIR OBJECTIVES

Background to the 1966 Decision
Policy-making is a lengthy and complex operation in Britain. This is well illustrated by a study of the reform of the structure of local government in provincial England and Wales. In the eight-year period 1966-74 successive Governments, Parliaments, local authorities, civil servants, and professional, local authority and other national associations interacted fairly continuously. They took literally thousands of decisions which together constituted a policy on local government reform. Yet both dates are, to an extent, arbitrary. The process did not start from a vacuum situation in 1966 — reform had been on the political agenda throughout the twentieth century and almost continuously from 1945. As a result, those principally involved in this story began with a set of attitudes, values and objectives developed over a long period of time. Nor is 1974 an absolute end-point. It merely marks the moment when major changes to the structure of local government were implemented, when the provisions of the Local Government Act 1972 took effect. Further changes are certain to follow, whether of areas, electoral arrangements, or powers and duties. The debate about the organisation and role of local government is indeed endless.

If the choice of 1974 is reasonably obvious, that of 1966 as a starting-point is much more arguable. In that year a crucial Government decision to establish the Redcliffe-Maud Commission (The Royal Commission on Local Government in England) opened a new chapter in what had come to seem the endless debate about the structure of local government. But in order to understand both the Government decision and the subsequent activities of the Redcliffe-Maud Commission it is necessary to start the story rather earlier in the chain of decisions which eventually led to the 1972 Local Government Act. Events throughout the whole of the post-war period had helped to shape attitudes to local government which were important in the period 1964-6 when Mr Richard

Crossman, Labour's minister responsible for local government, was deciding on his best course of action.

The Labour Government — and Mr Crossman — came to power in October 1964. The election manifesto had included a broad commitment to administrative modernisation, and it was generally expected that both the civil service and local government would come under close scrutiny. In the case of the civil service early action was possible, and, indeed, was politically feasible following a critical report in 1964-5 by the House of Commons Estimates Committee. Early in 1966 Mr Wilson appointed the Fulton Committee to conduct a wide-ranging review.[1]

Mr Crossman's position was far more complicated. He became Minister of Housing and Local Government at a time when the Local Government Commission for England had already spent more than five years touring the country making proposals for boundary changes. The Commission — set up under the 1958 Local Government Act — had limited powers and a complex procedure to follow.[2] Only in five conurbations designated as 'Special Review Areas' could it do more than recommend a realignment of county and county borough (i.e. 'top-tier') boundaries. By late 1964 it had covered the midlands, the south-west, and the east of England from East Anglia to the Scottish border. It was at a fairly advanced stage in the north-west, but had hardly started work in the south and south-east. Government decisions on its recommendations lagged well behind even this slow rate of progress. Furthermore, these decisions had, in several cases, rejected what were often fairly modest proposals of the Commission (the most notorious rejection being that of the Commission's plan to merge the miniscule Rutland County Council with neighbouring Leicestershire).

Given the limited terms of reference of the Commission, and the still more cautious approach of the previous Conservative Government, Mr Crossman found himself in a difficult situation. Many local authorities would be very critical of a decision to wind up prematurely a Commission whose creation had been the result of an agreement between local authorities and the Government. Certainly no minister would relish an early confrontation with authorities and their powerful national associations.* Furthermore, the Commission had showed signs of approaching its task rather more radically as time passed. The major problem areas were the conurbations. In 1961 in the West Midlands (its first

---

*The Minister of Education took a similar view over the question of the organisation of secondary education. Anxious as he was to implement the Labour Party's commitment to comprehensive schools, he decided to adopt techniques of persuasion rather than of legislative control. He therefore 'requested' rather than 'required' schemes. See M. Kogan, *The Politics of Education* (Penguin, 1971), pp. 189-90.

inquiry) the Commission had been timid; in mid-1963 it took a more positive line in the north-east, with a proposal for a Tyneside County Council; by late 1964 it was pressing for major extensions to the two designated conurbations in the north-west and was clearly contemplating recommending the creation of at least one, and possibly two, further new urban county councils there. Perhaps a fair amount of reorganisation could, after all, be achieved through the established processes.

Within a few months Mr Crossman became disillusioned with these processes. A crucial decision which lay on his desk in October 1964 was that about the boundaries of the two 'Special Review Areas' in the north-west. In November 1963 the Commission had asked for these to be extended so that the Merseyside and Greater Manchester conurbations 'met' at the line of the M6 motorway. Such a request meant the addition of major areas of south Lanchashire and north Cheshire to the conurbations — Wigan, St Helens, Warrington and their hinterlands. County council reaction in Lancashire and Cheshire was extremely hostile, for such extensions placed these areas in jeopardy should the Commission seek new urban counties (as seemed likely, especially to the inhabitants of the two county halls).[3] Though the counties had put their case to the Conservative minister in January 1964, he had left the decision pending — further evidence of the sensitive nature of the issue.

Crossman's instinct was surely to allow the proposed extensions. After all, this increased the chances of the Commission producing a wide-ranging set of recommendations, and it could fairly be portrayed as no more than an intermediate decision designed to allow the 'expert' Commission to do its job as it thought best. Crossman could state that his decision implied no commitment to new urban counties on behalf of the Government (though others might interpret his action in a rather different way). Against this, however, there were political and administrative arguments which, in the end, he allowed to override his natural instincts. These related to the wording and intention of the 1958 Local Government Act, and to ministerial statements made during the passage of that Act. While these latter had no legal status, they, coupled with the text of the Act, did suggest that large extensions to Special Review Areas would not be undertaken unless the added areas were clearly urban extensions to the conurbation core. It was debatable whether much of the terrain which the Commission wanted included in the Merseyside and Greater Manchester Special Review Areas could possibly be described as urbanised extensions to the conurbations. Undoubtedly there must have been pressure on Crossman from civil servants and well as from the county councils. His decision to allow only very small extensions in April 1965 was one of the cautious minister bowing to precedent and to traditional procedures. Professor Ely Devons, a member of the Local Government Commission, resigned in disgust.

Further disillusionment with the established processes for reform also followed in 1965, though this time through Crossman's determination to overturn Commission proposals. He preferred the notion of a large Birmingham-sized county borough based on Newcastle-upon-Tyne to the proposed Tyneside urban county with four districts based on Newcastle, Tynemouth, South Shields and Gateshead at the second-tier level, and in July 1965 he announced that he intended to call a conference of Tyneside councils to consider this and the various alternative plans.[4] He soon found that, under the 1958 Act procedures, it was far easier for him to suggest a new plan than it was to get it actually implemented. Lengthy public inquiries were inevitable, and the possibility of actions in the High Court (already tried in the West Midlands) could not be entirely ruled out. The proposal effectively died with the decision early in 1966 to replace the 1958 Act procedure by a new Royal Commission, though it remained on the table until Crossman's successor, Mr Anthony Greenwood, buried it in May 1967.

If, as seems certain, Crossman became steadily disillusioned with the Local Government Commission era, he kept his views very much to himself throughout the first nine months of 1965. In April he told the Town Planning Institute's conference that radical reform would never be feasible in terms of practical politics and that he accepted the continued existence of county and county borough councils. To overcome problems of town planning he advocated the creation of sub-regional teams to produce plans which would not be binding on individual local authorities.[5] He repeated this approach at another widely reported conference in September,[6] and throughout 1965 he issued a steady stream of decisions on recommendations of the Local Government Commission. But astute observers noticed that he made no move to strengthen the Local Government Commission, which had lost one member through death, as well as losing Professor Devons. Nor did he offer much in the way of hope to the County Councils Association, which had been trying since early 1963 to get the Government to reconsider the terms of reference of the Local Government Commission (and, in particular, the presumption that a population of 100,000 made a town viable as a separate county borough, for this was leading to boundary extensions and to creations of new county boroughs at the expense of the surrounding county councils).[7]

The reference to 'practical politics' came, it must be remembered, at a time when the Labour Government had an overall majority in the Commons of only six. Local government reform is a sensitive issue which directly affects the lives of tens of thousands of elected councillors, and of far more local government officials. Indirectly it has repercussions throughout the grass-roots party organisations and for MPs when constituency boundaries are realigned to coincide with new council boundaries. Its impact on the voter is less easy to define, but there is a general feeling among politicians that this is a vote-losing rather than a vote-winning issue. Obviously no major legislation could be contemplated given the political situation in 1965. It would be equally dangerous for the minister to put up extensive proposals of his own for public consultation and debate — as was already becoming evident in the Tyneside case. Thus the alternatives to a continuation with the Local Government Commission were effectively narrowed down to only two: end the Commission and close the debate about the structure of local government altogether, or replace the Commission with another, but more powerful, intermediate advisory body. The party manifesto plus Crossman's natural instincts pointed to the latter course of action once the 'failure' of the Local Government Commission was proved to his satisfaction. No doubt his powerful permanent secretary, Dame Evelyn Sharp, with whom he developed a good, if sometimes stormy, working relationship, concurred also.[8] She was known from her limited public statements to be critical of the existing structure of local government.*

The new policy was first unwrapped in September 1965, when Crossman spoke to the annual conference of the Association of Municipal Corporations, a body which had, by and large, enjoyed the 1958 Act procedures as these had strengthened county borough government through both boundary extensions and new creations. The AMC was also sympathetic to the Labour Party, for its members come from the urban areas where that party receives the bulk of its electoral support. In his speech, Crossman was severely critical of the principle underlying the local government structure that town and country should be governed separately.[9] He indicated that he was unhappy with the 1958 Act procedures because they further strengthened this principle, and because of their time-consuming nature. He saw the alternatives as being either a radical reconstruction of local government or a further

---

*With hindsight this is very clear, as she became an important member of the Redcliffe-Maud Commission. But in an article in *Public Administration* in 1962 she had criticised the plethora of small councils.

erosion of council powers, and here traffic planning was cited as a likely example. A major problem facing him was 'the absence of any agreed first principles' and reform could only follow acceptance of these. Ministerial initiative in proposing a reform package was ruled out. His tentative suggestion was a new, powerful, small committee to establish new general principles about the structure of local government, and he intended to discuss the idea with the associations.

Crossman's criticisms were reiterated in the Commons in February 1966, when the creation of a Royal Commission was announced. But other aspects of his first scheme were altered following consultations within the Government and with the local authority associations. The 'small' committee became one of eleven members (whereas the earlier Herbert Commission on Greater London's local government had had only seven), and its terms of reference were not restricted to 'general principles'. The new Commission, chaired by Lord Redcliffe-Maud, began its work in May 1966 and reported in June 1969.

The Principal Participants 1966-74

As well as illustrating the reasons for choosing 1966 as a starting-point, this background to the creation of the Redcliffe-Maud Commission has also brought to our attention many of the principal participants in the policy-making process.

Democratic theory suggests that we all participate in government, if only through the periodic exercise of the franchise. That this exercise can be important has already become clear: the election of a Labour Government in 1964 led to the appointment of a new minister, Mr Crossman, with quite different values and philosophies from those of his Conservative predecessors. The minister is, or can be, the most important of all the proximate decision-makers,[10] and changes of minister due to government 'reshuffles' as well as to election defeats can have great consequences. For example, Mr James Griffiths, Secretary of State for Wales, took a quite different line in 1965. He chose to keep the issue within his department, and published his own proposals in 1967 — these proved to be much less radical than those of the Redcliffe-Maud Commission. The consequences of Mr Griffiths's decision are explored in Chapter V.

Vital to any minister is his immediate advisory staff, the senior civil servants. Like most people, they are happier at dealing with the known rather than the unknown. They also place a great deal of importance on precedent. Their influence was strong during the first six months of the Crossman regime, reaching a high-point in Spring 1965 with the announcement of the decision on the

North-West Special Review Areas. Later that year the minister was more firmly in the saddle, though his decision to create a Royal Commission can also be construed as one in keeping with the tradition of utilising advisory bodies, and was certainly not taken against civil service advice.

Members of Parliament are a third group of participants. On many issues they have little or no public impact — but when legislation is required, and when its details affect 'their' area (as is the case with local government reform), then they can have a considerable amount of influence. We shall see in Chapter VI that they helped to shape the Local Government Act at the margins. And they were active also in the 1964-5 period — Cheshire MPs, for example, lobbied privately against the Local Government Commission's request for extended Special Review Areas.[11]

Three further groups of proximate decision-makers represent the 'local government world'. First, there are individual councils — numbering about 1,400 in provincial England and Wales up to 1974. Their attitude to change is, of course, based first and foremost on its effects locally. The smaller authorities, the district councils, more than half of which contained a population of less than 20,000, naturally felt threatened throughout and were constantly on the defensive. Individual county and county borough councils found themselves in a more varied set of situations. Traditionally their interests clashed — the boroughs wanted larger areas through boundary extensions at the expense of surrounding county territory. The clash often continued in the 1966-74 period — in Lancashire, for example, the boroughs of Blackpool, Preston, Blackburn and Burnley rather liked the notion of city regions based on themselves, whereas the county saw this as fragmentation and preferred a larger, county-based unit. It is fair to say that individual councils react to proposals for change almost entirely in terms of self-interest. Sometimes they are criticised for behaving in this manner. Yet they are surely entitled to take such an approach.

So, too, are associations of local authorities. If all the urban district councils set up an association to look after their collective interests, that association surely behaves quite correctly in supporting the status quo. Indeed, were it to suggest the abolition of urban districts it would clearly be acting unconstitutionally (unless such a policy reflected the attitude of its member authorities). For the associations of urban and rural districts (UDCA and RDCA) the issue was a straightforward one, for only the merest handful of their members could hope to survive a major reform. It was the Association of Municipal Corporations and the County Council's Association which faced the greatest difficulties. Both had a mixture of members, some of whom were small and could only support the status quo, while others favoured change, if it were of a particular type. These varied attitudes of individual members caused both bodies to be extremely evasive about specific details from time to time. For example, when giving evidence (both written and oral) to the Redcliffe-Maud Commission, both tried to avoid publicly committing themselves to statements about either the desirable population size of a local authority, or how their proposals would look on a map. The AMC produced neither a population size nor a map, but the CCA did talk in round figures of 500,000 as the minimum size of a new top-tier unit.[12]

Finally, there are around one hundred further national organisations with an interest in local government reform. The large majority represent groups of professional workers in local authorities — either at senior levels only (e.g. Association of Chief Education Officers) or at all levels (e.g. NALGO; National Union of Teachers). Inevitably they, too, are concerned with members' interests. Sometimes these interests are less affected by the actual pattern of boundaries than by such matters as redundancy payments or compensation arrangements resulting from loss of work, or changed responsibilities due to amalgamations. In other cases areas can be of great importance and various ideas for reform could split these bodies — the Society of Chief Education Officers, for example, represented members from small and large education authorities, and from one- and two-tier systems. Its problems mirrored those of the AMC and CCA, except that it had less need to take up a clear position.

These six groups of proximate decision-makers collectively shaped the final policy on local government reform. In the initial stages they were joined by a seventh, the Redcliffe-Maud Commission. From 1969-74 there was no such intermediary to cushion the impact of direct confrontation between governments and those groups which either resisted or sought to modify the changes being proposed. At times it seemed possible to claim that one lobby or another was 'winning', and it is sometimes said that the final policy represented a 'victory for the counties'. In fact, as we shall see, the issue of local government reform was far too complex to be assessed in such simple terms. The collective wisdom of all these groups of decision-makers contributed to the final policy, and no one group could feel totally satisfied with the end-product of several years' hard work.

Democracy and Efficiency
Central to the debate about the structure of local government were the concepts of 'democracy' and 'efficiency'. The overriding objective of would-be reformers was to obtain changes which

would increase both the effectiveness and the democratic content of local government. Commissions (including those of 1945-9 and 1958-66), governments and oppositions, local authorities, their associations and other interest groups all worked within this framework. Yet this broad agreement about objectives did little to simplify the policy process. This was because there was no general consensus on the interpretation to be attached to such concepts in the context of the issue of local government reform. As a result, all the participants could and did claim to be advocating proposals consistent with the overall objectives, yet these proposals frequently conflicted with one another.

The Redcliffe-Maud Commission was given the task of proposing a structure within which functions could be 'most effectively exercised', and was also warned of the 'need to sustain a viable system of local democracy'.[13] But these were not new terms. They stemmed for the work of the 1958 Local Government Commission. Its proposals had had to be 'desirable in the interests of effective and convenient local government'.[14] This phrase also rang familiar to many, for the 1945-9 Local Government Boundary Commission had also had to seek 'effective and convenient units of local government administration'.[15] Not surprisingly, the Herbert Commission on Greater London government (1957-60) was also 'to secure effective and convenient local government'.[16] The civil service penchant for using what has been not unsuccessfully tried before is apparent!

The difficulty is that no one has ever decided just what words like 'effective', 'convenient', 'efficient' and 'democracy' mean in the context of the structure of local government. As a result everyone can be saintly, pursuing a goal laid down by governments without thought to self-interest. Or, more realistically, anyone can justify almost any comment or criticism about the structure of local government, and the whole debate can be one of everyone talking in a different language using the same words! While this semantic problem can lengthen the battle, it can also place the Government in a very strong position. Governments can, and did, justify almost any action (whether positive or negative) at least to the immediate audience, if not to the complete satisfaction of the academic philosopher.

During the long-drawn-out debate on the reform of local government the word 'democracy' was frequently used in four quite different ways.[17] At times it was given its electoral or representational meaning. Thus the Redcliffe-Maud Commission proposed single-member wards with no more than 10,000 constituents, a recommmendation which helped to sway the Commission towards the suggestion that a population of one million should be the maximum for a local authority as a council size of 100 members seemed quite large enough. A second example occurred when the Conservative Government in 1972 conceded to rural interests the case for single-member wards after having previously advocated three members per electoral division. The three-member plan was strongly opposed by the RDCA on the grounds that it would have resulted in large divisions covering numerous villages in sparsely populated areas. On several occasions the local authority associations all made great play of the 'undemocratic' nature of large authorities on the grounds of potential remoteness from the electorate, and it is certainly the case that under the pre-1974 structure around half the seats at county council elections were regularly filled without a contest.

A second, or geographical, meaning of 'democracy' also emphasised the value of 'smallness'. This suggested that a council should be physically accessible, and should represent a genuine community of interest. The Redcliffe-Maud Commission also paid attention to this notion by running a 'Community Attitudes Survey' which sought information about the size of area to which people felt most attached, and by mapping areas in terms of such factors as the journey to work, the circulation area of local newspapers, and bus routes. Yet, as Mr Derek Senior in his lengthy memorandum of dissent pointed out, there were several occasions on which this notion was abandoned by the Commission.[18] For example, it proposed several bi-polar units such as Bury and Rochdale, where the two main towns had little community of interest, and where some of the smaller towns such as Radcliffe, Littleborough or Milnrow would find the new administrative centre virtually inaccessible (which of these smaller towns would suffer in this way would depend on whether Bury or Rochdale were chosen).

Senior's criticism reflected the importance which the Commission attached to a third definition of 'democracy': that which embraces the idea of 'responsible' government. Professor Birch further breaks down this concept into three sub-classifications, two of which imply more than mere electoral accountability or physical accessibility.[19] 'Responsive' government is government responding to public demands, and 'accountable' government is government seeking judgement on its performance. Both imply that a council has goods to deliver, that it is responsible for the provision of reasonably important public services. Here there is a clear link between the ideas of 'democracy' and those of 'efficiency' or 'effectiveness'. A responsible local authority is one with clear choices to make about the nature of its outputs: it is not one which is too small to be entrusted with a reasonable range of functions by Parliament. Though the discussion about responsiveness and accountability frequently revolved around calls for 'participation', for local ombudsmen, for press and public access to meetings of council committees, beneath all this lies the clear implication that democracy and functional effectiveness are linked.

Finally, 'democracy' could be invoked in discussions about the allocation of functions between different tiers of government. Lip-service was frequently paid to the 'lowest level' principle. For example, the Conservative White Paper of 1971 stated that 'a genuine local democracy implies that decisions should be taken as locally as possible'.[20] This concept led to complicated decisions about responsibility for services like highways and planning as we shall see in Chapters VI and VII. Once again, it emphasises the link between democracy and efficiency.

Yet this link, present in two of the four interpretations of democracy, was often ignored during the process of local government reform, particularly by such bodies as the Urban and the Rural District Councils Associations. The latter launched a massive £40,000 publicity campaign against the proposals of the Redcliffe-Maud Commission — 'Don't Vote for R. E. Mote'. This concentrated on the concepts of smallness and electoral remoteness and suggested that large authorities of 250,000 population or more were undemocratic. To this the Commission would surely have replied, had it still been in existence, that smaller authorities, in its opinion, could not have been allocated a sufficient range of powers to make them truly responsible. In addition the Commission would have been unable to contemplate the one-tier or 'unitary' system, with its theoretical advantages of simplicity and of clear responsibility for all decisions about local priorities and the allocation of resources, for such a system required authorities of sufficient size to be effective providers of important services such as education.

It is interesting that successive commissions were asked to seek 'effective' rather than 'efficient' local government. The latter term is often considered to be inapplicable to local government, where the outputs are frequently of a personal nature (the activities of teachers or social workers, for example). This is because of the common association of 'efficiency' with industry and commerce where profits and sales are clearly measurable and performance can be quantified. In fact the terms were frequently assumed to be interchangeable by commissions, councils, politicians and other participants in the debate on local government. As with democracy, from time to time various different meanings were attached to the concept of 'efficiency'.

Sometimes efficiency was linked with decentralisation.

Sub-national government, it was claimed, is efficient because it is manageable, and because it can respond more easily than national government to the particular local situation. Again the link with responsible 'democratic' local government is clear, for the assumption is that decentralised government is in fact able successfully to take local circumstances into account in coming to decisions. In practice two difficulties occur. First, not all systems of decentralised government are constructed in a manner which guarantees this local sensitivity (single-purpose appointed bodies such as water authorities, gas boards and health authorities are suspect here). Second, the degree of central government control and influence over council activities may reduce the scope of local policy-making to an unacceptable level (for example, a council cannot hope to build all schools and no houses or roads in a particular year, because project approval is necessary and the ministries involved would refuse to sanction such a policy — they have fought at national level for the funds allocated by the Treasury for school, house, and road building).

In much of the debate from 1966-74 the idea of increased decentralisation played an important part, though the Redcliffe-Maud Commission's terms of reference only allowed it to look at local government's 'existing functions'. The Conservative Government in 1971 placed great emphasis on its proposals for a reduction in central controls. Mr Peter Walker opened his speech on the Second Reading debate of the Local Government Bill by claiming that this was an important Government objective (though, in the event, it proved to be something of an illusion as the key controls were retained). The Labour Government, too, claimed to be anxious to add to the powers of local authorities. The aim was to make the reform package as attractive as possible by holding out to councils the prospects of greater powers in the future.

The question of resource-allocation leads to two further notions of effectiveness which can conveniently be discussed together: the ability to co-ordinate and to control the provision of local services. At one level this is concerned with the choice of priorities, and at another with the adequacy of supervision of service delivery. The Redcliffe-Maud Commission paid considerable attention to coordination, and concluded that a single-tier structure of local government was theoretically the most satisfactory — a council could choose its priorities over the full range of municipal services, and could ensure that all services were provided in the right way at the right time. Others, however, took a different view. They argued that the case for large authorities on the grounds of technical requirements or economies of scale applied only to certain functions. Many services such as allotments, recreational facilities and footpaths could best be provided by small local second-tier authorities able to supervise their activities effectively. The single-tier unitary authority was either too small for some services, or too large for others, or, indeed, both.

These latter arguments paid relatively little attention to the question of resource allocation. They reflected a deep-seated mistrust in long administrative hierarchies, and a faith in the value of laymen inserted in such hierarchies at as local a point as possible in order to break them up. Elected members are there, it is claimed, both to ensure that bureaucrats treat their clients equitably and to push these same bureaucrats into action when local demands for an altered level of services are strongly articulated. A difficulty which emerges is that councillors are, as a result, playing many different roles — resource allocators, co-ordinators, local watch-dogs — which may not always be compatible. Furthermore, they may not always be feasible — the choice of priorities between services is more difficult when a council has a limited span of responsibility.

With so many different meanings attachable to the terms democracy and efficiency, it is now easy to see why throughout the period 1966-74 it was possible for all the participants to claim to have similar objectives in mind. It is also now clear why there can be no single 'correct' solution to the problem of creating a structure of local government. One-, two-, or three-tier? Large or small areas? Separate or joint units for town and country? All could be justified in terms of the long-standing charge to successive commissions to find an 'effective and convenient' system of local government. Frequently the view was taken that democracy and efficiency were conflicting principles (Crossman spoke of the need 'to resolve the conflict between local democracy which is inherently small, and efficiency, which is sometimes large'), though the discussion above has revealed that this conflict presupposes a restricted view of the meaning of both terms. In particular it was convenient for those hostile to radical change to dismiss proposals for reform as 'undemocratic' by implying that there was a distinction between representation and function.

The Scene is Set

The core of this book consists of more than a series of critical reviews of the various proposals for local government reform which appeared in the 1966-74 period and which are summarized for reference purposes in the Appendix on pages 191-4. These proposals were, of course, of great importance in shaping the complex policy-making process. They reflected the absence of a generally accepted solution to the problem: 'what is the best structure of local government?'. Though they are described as discussed in this book, the reader who seeks comprehensive comment on the several reform models must supplement the text here.[21]

The book is in fact about governmental policy-making and the process of implementation of public policy. This involved a series of decisions taken over a period of time which collectively may be said to add up to a 'policy'.[22] Key decisions required to be processed by Parliament before they could be translated into action, whereas supplementary decisions were processed only by civil servants and, through conventional channels for consultation, certain extra-governmental bodies such as the local authority associations. The nature of the political process frequently ensured that the resulting 'policy' was far from coherent. Compromises between the various proximate decision-makers resulted in government outputs containing numerous inconsistencies. To give a single example, the Government sought a distribution of functions between top-tier county councils and second-tier district councils which was 'clear cut'[23] (on the grounds of democracy — an intelligible system, and of efficiency — clear levels of responsibility). However, we shall see in Chapters VI and VII that the 1972 Local Government Act divided responsibility for planning, highways and cleansing, and encouraged further complicated sharing arrangements through a section which became known as the 'agency clause'.

In this chapter, three important background points have been introduced. First, the Government decided in 1965-6 to proceed by way of royal commission rather than by initiating proposals itself. This reflected the complex nature of the problem, the traditional strength of the local authority associations and deference paid to their views by earlier Governments, and the prevailing political situation nationally. The main consequence of this initial decision was that the initiative then resided for a period outside the Government and in the Commission. Though, as we shall see, the Government can attempt to 'steer' a commission towards a particular set of proposals (through factors such as the choice of members and the terms of reference), it cannot guarantee proposals which it will find acceptable.

Secondly, we have briefly introduced the main actors and mentioned something of their motives and objectives. Outwardly, all could claim to be seeking and supporting systems which were both democratic and efficient. Inwardly, their objectives reflected their constitutional and political environments — with councils, their associations and professional groups viewing the issue first and foremost in terms of their future role; with politicians weighing the political balance sheet; and with civil servants thinking very much in terms of administrative and legal feasibility, largely by drawing on precedent. All three worlds — those of the local authority, the politician, and the administrator — knew at the outset that reform was possible. The reform of Greater London government in 1963, when the Government withstood bitter attacks on its proposals from both the Labour Opposition and many local councils, was proof of this.

Thirdly, something of the complexity of the debate has emerged from the discussion of some of the more commonly employed meanings attached to the key words 'democracy' and 'efficiency'. Sometimes discussions about local government reform confused means and ends. The structure of local government is not an end in itself and this added to the problem of measuring the likely performance of various reform models. In the final analysis it is how the structure is made to work that really counts, and one reason for the delay in reforming local government was that the existing structure could often be adapted (e.g. by moving responsibilities from districts to counties) or even bypassed (e.g. by setting up quite separate health authorities).* Furthermore, there could be no certainty as to how a new structure would work in practice. London had had a new structure, but only since 1965, and this was a very short period over which to make a fair judgement.[24] The doubtful viability of alternatives to the status quo only added to the confusion in the debate about democracy and efficiency.

In Chapter II a close look is taken at the work of the Redcliffe-Maud Commission. Particular attention is paid to the problems with which it had to cope — problems which, in general, are common to all advisory committees. The importance of these problems or 'constraints' is that they can considerably narrow the possible range of recommendations, and that they therefore help to explain the outcome of the Commission's work. It was this outcome which generated and shaped the subsequent public debate.

*Mr Senior made this second point very strongly: 'The dominant political maxim of the post-war period: that if a service needs reorganisation, it cannot wait for local government reform; and if not, then local government reform can wait.' (*Cmnd 4040*, vol. 2, para. 288.)

NOTES

1 R. G. S. Brown, *The Administrative Process in Britain* (Methuen, 1970), p. 29.
2 For details of the Commission's work and a critical discussion see H. V. Wiseman (ed.), *Local Government in England 1958-69* (Routledge & Kegan Paul, 1970), Ch. 2.
3 See J. M. Lee and B. Wood, *The Scope of Local Initiative: A Study of Cheshire County Council 1961-74* (Martin Robertson, 1974), pp. 56-60, 76-7.

4 *Hansard (Commons)*, vol. 717, Written Answers, cols 67-8 (27 July 1965).
5 *Municipal Review*, July 1965, pp. 397-8.
6 J. Brand, *Local Government Reform in England 1888-1974* (Croom Helm, 1974), p. 60.
7 *Ibid.*, pp. 120-3.
8 Crossman discusses this relationship in his diaries. See the extract in *The Sunday Times*, 26 January 1975.
9 The speech was issued to the press and received considerable coverage. It was reprinted in its entirety in *Municipal Review*, November 1965, pp. 655-60.
10 The phrase 'proximate decision makers' comes from C. E. Lindblom, *The Policy Making Process* (Prentice Hall, 1968), Ch. 9.
11 Lee and Wood, *op. cit.*, pp. 79-80.
12 See below, Ch. 2, p. 34.
13 Royal Commission on Local Government in England 1966-9, *Report, Cmnd 4040* (HMSO, 1969), vol. 1, p. iii.
14 *Local Government Act 1958*, sec. 17.
15 *Local Government (Boundary Commission) Regulations 1945* (SI 1569), sched. 1.
16 Royal Commission on Local Government in Greater London 1957-60, *Report, Cmnd 1164* (HMSO, 1960), p. i.
17 For a comprehensive treatment of the concept see Dilys Hill, *Democratic Theory and Local Government* (Allen & Unwin, 1974).
18 See Cmnd 4040, *op. cit.*, vol. 2, Ch. 2 for Mr Senior's outspoken criticism of the main report's geography.
19 A.H. Birch, *The Idea of Responsible Government* (University of Hull Publications, 1962).
20 *Local Government in England: Government Proposals for Reorganisation, Cmnd 4584* (HMSO, 1971), para. 8.
21 References in succeeding chapters will suggest additional sources. Brand, *op. cit.*, provides a historical background. Jane Morton, *The Best Laid Schemes?* (Charles Knight, 1970) is an extremely readable account of the Redcliffe-Maud Commission.
22 John Dearlove uses this definition. See *The Politics of Policy in English Local Government* (CUP, 1973), pp. 2-6.
23 Mr Walker, when introducing the Local Government Bill 1971-2. *Hansard (Commons)*, vol. 826, col. 249 (16 November 1971).
24 Royal Commission on Local Government in England, *Research Study 2: The Lessons of the London Government Reforms* (HMSO, 1968) was an early attempt by the Greater London Group, London School of Economics, to assess the strengths and weaknesses of the new structure.

Chapter II

THE REDCLIFFE-MAUD COMMISSION

1966-9

Strong views have from time to time been expressed on the use made of Royal Commissions by British Governments. In his well-known critical essay, A. P. Herbert spoke of 'a failure to govern'.[1] At the other extreme, the American C. J. Hanser recently found no fault whatsoever with the concept, and advocated much greater use of such bodies in the United States.[2] Earlier H. F. Gosnell described Royal Commissions as 'the chief advisory bodies in the legislative and administrative process'.[3] Sir Kenneth Wheare, discussing advisory committees in general, placed great emphasis on their educative role ('their report is looked to as an exposition of the situation or problem'), and saw their investigatory work as being of at least equal importance to their actual recommendations.[4] It is a fact that governments do from time to time reject or modify proposals of commissions. But it would be wrong to think of a commission as more than an agent for change, and there are issues where a report has an impact on attitudes even though many or all of its recommendations fall by the wayside — the Redcliffe-Maud Report provides a good example. Writing in 1968, Professor Donnison suggested that 'a roll-call of recent committees and commissions . . . shows they can be a force to reckon with. What followed from their inquiries was not exactly what these committees intended, but their work generated and focused a reforming impetus which would have been difficult to mobilise in other ways.'[5] The sequence of events following publication of the Redcliffe-Maud Report in 1969 made this a prophetic statement.

Even the highly critical Herbert saw some 'possible' good reasons for establishing a commission. Among these were occasions when the topic was 'a delicate subject where the Government feels that impetus from a royal commission would be better'. Certainly the Redcliffe-Maud Commission would fall under this heading. Local government reform had for decades been treated by Governments of all parties as 'a delicate subject', and it seems reasonable to assume that the 1964 Labour Government was anxious to take some action about the long-established structure of local government. Crossman stated publicly that he wanted the Commission to have the maximum possible assistance through its own self-appointed research team, and that he hoped for a report within two years. He, at least, gave the impression of being anxious to proceed with a major piece of legislation, and this impression was accepted by most observers as being genuine.

Clear evidence of the reformist atmosphere generated by Crossman lay in the reactions of local authorities and their associations. They budged from their traditional position of root-and-branch support for the status quo when giving their views to the Commission. This contrasted sharply with the response in 1957 to the appointment of the Herbert Commission on Greater London government. In that case the Government had shown few signs of urgency, and witnesses to the Commission clearly had no idea that they were participating in the early stages of a major reform. The same local authority associations were in 1957 extremely conservative, all suggesting to the Herbert Commission either that the existing structure was perfectly adequate or that change should be along traditional lines.[6]

Evidence

'Here, surely, is an instrument with an assured reputation for the profound and rigorous examination of problems of public policy.' Andrew Shonfield, in the 1967 Gaitskell Memorial Lecture, went on from this opening remark to question the continued deservedness of this reputation which stemmed from the great reforming traditions of nineteenth-century Royal Commissions.[7] In particular, he questioned the habit of commissions of behaving like juries and listening to 'the whole nation'. He suggested that this traditional procedure required urgent modification in the interests of speeding up the period between creation and report. No doubt he would have had little time for the Herbert Commission, which took oral evidence in public from all the hundred-odd London councils (over a period of more than sixty days), and which visited as many as two-thirds of the authorities.

Obviously such a time-consuming procedure could not be adopted by the Redcliffe-Maud Commission. With 1,200 counties, boroughs, and districts (not to mention the 10,000 parishes), public oral evidence and visits, whether formal or informal, could not be contemplated. But a letter was sent to every authority requesting evidence within three months and an open invitation to the public was also made. In all, some 2,156 witnesses offered written evidence. Of these 1,269 were individual local authorities (including 594 parishes) and 536 were individual members of the public (a glance at the list of names reveals several academics and well-known local government officers and councillors). The remaining 350 or so included national and local political, amenity, business, professional and ratepayer associations.* Oral evidence was taken from only a dozen bodies — ministries, local authority associations, and NALGO. Visits to survey possible new boundaries were not undertaken, but the Commission did have several geographers among its supporting research staff.

The nature of the evidence received is a self-imposed constraint on the activities of a commission in the sense that it could decide, as Shonfield suggested, not to issue a request to all and sundry or to ask only for answers to specific questions. In this case, a restrictive policy would have been sharply criticised if it could be construed as preventing a council from putting its point of view on its own future. As it happens, the open invitation did not seriously handicap the Commission in its work, for the evidence received mostly fell into four categories which were already easily identifiable from the prevailing literature and past debate. These categories were Regional (or Provincial) Government — with about eight or ten regions usually favoured; City Regions — about thirty to forty based on the larger towns and covering the town and its hinterland; a strengthened two-tier system based on counties and districts but without the existence of autonomous urban county boroughs; or the status quo in an updated form to take account of post-war demographic changes.[8]

In the early stages of the Commission's life the Government Departments made much of the running. Their evidence solidly supported the creation of thirty to forty city regions as all- or most-purpose authorities.† The geography was left vague, but two sets of principles led the departments to take this view. First, the services provided by local authorities were, it was claimed, closely linked. It was desirable for the same council to provide the children's service, education, and housing. And the housing authority really should be the planning and transportation authority. Other services such as fire, police, libraries and public health were incorporated into the list as well. Second, the artificial and, indeed, harmful nature of the traditional distinction between

---

*The list (Annex 8 to the Commission's report) reveals some surprising witnesses including Prescot Town Football Club, the Association of Men of Kent and Kentish Men, and the Aylesbury and District Vigilante Committee!

†The Ministries of Transport and of Housing and Local Government also proposed an unspecified number of second-tier authorities, but these would not run any major services. In oral evidence it became clear that these ministries were extremely uncertain as to the nature of these second-tier units.

town government and country government was reiterated over and over again. In particular, this severely constrained councils as planning and transportation authorities.

The evidence from local authorities and their associations was particularly interesting because it reflected an acknowledgement on their part that reform was at last a political possibility. Individual councils naturally thought mostly of alternative patterns of authorities in their area, and many of their proposals were little more than minor modifications of the status quo. Because there was little support for a *completely* unaltered structure, the Commission was able to open its chapter analysing the evidence received with the following statement: 'It (the evidence) shows widespread agreement among witnesses on the need to change the present local government system.'[9] This alleged agreement was based on an analysis whereby any proposal for change, however limited in scope, was interpreted as acceptance of a need to change the 'system', and in the later stages of the policy process ministers from both major parties continued to reiterate the 'fact' that nearly all councils supported change. The Labour Government's White Paper, for example, alleged that 'the great mass of evidence to the Redcliffe-Maud Commission showed that an overwhelming body of opinion . . . believed that fundamental structural changes were required'.[10]

The local authority associations produced what, for them, were quite radical documents — with the exception of the UDCA, which was extremely vague about the number of tiers, the size of authority, and the urban-rural distinction.[11] Each association was faced with the problem that proposals for change would be interpreted by some of its members as being 'sold down the river'. The County Councils Association bravely suggested 'around 500,000 population' as a minimum size for its proposed top-tier authority, thus offending several of its members who would fall below this size even with the inclusion of county boroughs in the new unit. Part of the CCA's reasoning lay in the need to avoid the possible creation of additional counties centred on medium-sized county boroughs and bearing little relation to traditional county areas. The Association of Education Committees, which represented both county and county borough education authorities, acted even more bravely when it suggested 500,000 as a minimum size for an education authority. Many of its county borough members protested, and a motion to delete the figure was carried at a bitter special meeting on 3 November 1969. But the executive had already sent in its evidence by the deadline of 31 October, acting under delegated powers. The Rural District Councils Association suggested 30,000 as a rough minimum size for districts (or 60,000 if they were to be given responsibility for the Social Services), but could see some viable smaller ones (a let-out to reduce criticism from its smaller members). However the Association of Municipal Corporations, which represented boroughs with populations of from 1,000 to 1,000,000, understandably declined to suggest population targets for its second-tier units.

All three associations proposed two-tier systems (surprisingly in the case of the AMC, which had a record of support for single-tier local government dating back to 1942 and reiterated as recently as February 1965 in an important report on the 'Reorganisation of Local Government'), but with very different allocations of functions. The AMC wanted 'most-purpose' second-tier units, the CCA wanted the bulk of services at the top-tier level, while the RDCA hoped that its 60,000 population districts would be given added powers over and above those of existing district councils — if this were not possible, it suggested smaller (30,000) districts. All three seemed prepared to accept a system which ended the urban-rural dichotomy, but the UDCA was even slightly ambivalent on this point when giving oral evidence.

The evidence given to the Commission did not, in the event, act as a great constraint upon it. The views of councils, associations, interest groups, and individuals were varied. No one single solution emerged with overwhelming support. Furthermore, the Commission's decision to restrict severely the amount of oral evidence reduced its commitment in terms of time to the minimum commensurate with the pursuit of good public relations through the open invitation to the public to submit written views. But the little oral evidence that was taken was useful in two respects. First, it further revealed the internal difficulties of the associations due to the nature of their membership. Second, the uncertainty of Government Departments as to the viability of their city regions was apparent. There was concern about the concept of 'democracy' (one or two of them agreed that some sort of a more local second-tier might be necessary, but none had worked out the details) and about geographical practicality (what do you do in the West Midlands and other major conurbations, for example, where your city regional authority would need to be extremely large if it were to embrace both town and country).

Terms of Reference and Membership

If a commission can, to some extent, control the flow of evidence which it receives, then it has almost minimal influence over two further constraints on its freedom of action: its terms of reference, and its membership.* There are many examples in history of

*Its chairman may have some influence over the terms of reference as it is customary

commissions which have found either or both of these factors major barriers to their producing a strong, influential report.[12] The Redcliffe-Maud Commission also had its problems.

Crossman claimed that the Commission had been given very wide terms of reference, and, at first sight, his view seems reasonable, particularly if they are compared with the restrictive brief given to the 1958 Local Government Commission. The Redcliffe-Maud Commission was

> to consider the structure of Local Government in England, outside Greater London, in relation to its existing functions; and to make recommendations for authorities and boundaries, and for functions and their division, having regard to the size and character of areas in which these can be most effectively exercised and the need to sustain a viable system of local democracy.

This was quite a mouthful, and much could be read into it: did 'division' of functions imply a two-tier system, for example? Perhaps the most important general point was that for the first time since the basic structure of local government had been established in 1888 and 1894 here was a body with powers to look simultaneously at both areas *and* functions throughout the whole country. The 1945-9 Boundary Commission had only been able to look at areas, though in its 1947 report it refused to be so constrained and thus committed suicide.[13] The 1958-66 Local Government Commission had been able to look at both areas and functions in the conurbations, but only within very tight geographical limits.

On the debit side, however, there were certain restrictions on the Commission's freedom of action — either by explicit statement, or by implication. First, Greater London was excluded from the review. This would seem logical, for this area had only just been reformed. On the other hand, its outer boundary was already the subject of much criticism and it might prove difficult for the Redcliffe-Maud Commission to locate sensible local government areas around the metropolis if that boundary was to be deemed sacrosanct. Even more important was the implication of this exclusion should the Commission be interested in a regional or provincial government reform model: could Greater London be included in a proposed south-east province?

---

to consult him about these. This convention was proposed in *Report of the Departmental Committee on the Procedure of Royal Commissions, Cd 5235* (HMSO, 1910), para. 14.

A second restriction limited the Commission to 'existing functions'. The functions of local government have varied greatly over time. Never have they been consciously collectively established on a basis of principle. Instead they have emerged through a series of political decisions. For example, what principle lay behind the decision to have separate hospital boards and executive councils in 1948, with the resultant tripartite national health service? Did this principle apply to the decision to make councils responsible for the issue of driving licences, the collection of the road fund tax, and birth, marriage and death registration? By forcing the Commission to keep within the bounds of existing functions, the Government posed further problems for its commissioners — particularly in respect of the national health service, national parks, water-based services, and 'planning' (economic, physical and resource) — where the existing situation was a blurred division of responsibility between central government, *ad hoc* bodies, and local authorities. Again, this made it particularly difficult to look at a strong provincial model; the Commission could discuss 'regionalism from below' but not 'regionalism from above' through devolution of Whitehall powers.[14]

Mr Senior, in his memorandum of dissent, found this part of the terms of reference quite unacceptable. He took the view that there was no legal reason why he should not ignore them, stating that 'in my colleagues' view, to recommend that the hospital and general practitioner branches of the NHS should become a local government responsibility would exceed our competence. I know of no warrant for this opinion.'[15] Legally he was correct. The danger is political: the fate of the 1947 Report had shown that a commission's proposals could be side-stepped on the grounds that it had exercised its charge. But Mr Senior did acknowledge that it was not possible for the Commission to pronounce upon the organisation of the NHS as a whole 'without calling for much more expert evidence than had been volunteered'. In his view, the 1968 Green Paper (see pp.50-1) constituted 'the necessary expert inquiry' and committed the Government to a policy of unification of the health service. 'It is surely inconceivable that we should go to all the trouble of reshaping the structure of local government and yet still leave it unfitted to serve as the administrative framework for a unified NHS.'[16]

'The need to sustain a viable system of local democracy' was a phrase which the local authority associations had been particularly anxious to have incorporated in the terms of reference. It constrained the Commission from proposing alternatives involving the abolition of elected councils (not that such a recommendation had the remotest chance of acceptance anyway). Much more important was the handle which it gave to the associations and their members — hundreds of whom reminded the Commission of the phrase when giving evidence. Furthermore, we have already discussed the multiple meanings which were attached to the word 'democracy'. Most prevalent from among council witnesses was the view that this meant small authorities and areas. The UDCA, for example, reminded the Commission of Crossman's statement that one problem facing the commissioners was how 'to resolve the conflict between local democracy, which is inherently small, and efficiency, which is sometimes large'. The RDCA made the phrase a separate chapter heading in its memorandum of evidence, and emphasised the close links between councillors and electors in small communities. The CCA rejected regional governments on the grounds that 'such units are too large to be considered as local government' in a section headed 'Needs of Democracy'. The UDCA concurred, and, in oral evidence, the chairman of its executive council stated that 'for democratic representative government to have real meaning, the local unit . . . must be one which has a sense of community and a prospect of creating a sense of pride and loyalty. Communities in this sense are on the whole small.'[17]

Two additional constraints following from the terms of reference concerned the internal organisation and the finance of local government. Neither was in fact mentioned, which suggests that the Government had no wish for the Commission to concentrate its efforts on these subjects. Internal organisation was already under review by two further advisory committees which had been set up in 1964 at the request of the local authority associations (party in order to suggest that local government was by no means as blind to its own shortcomings as observers were increasingly suggesting): the Maud and Mallaby Committees were, by 1966, coming towards the end of their investigations. Several of their members (including Maud himself, of course) were appointed to the Royal Commission. Presumably this overlapping membership was designed partly to ensure that the Maud, Mallaby and Redcliffe-Maud proposals were consistent with one another. However, it could not help to make acceptable recommendations which councils refused to implement, as happened in the case of the Maud Committee's concept of a Management Board. The fate of the Maud Report made it necessary in 1971 to appoint a further committee on 'management structures' (the Bains Committee) to advise the new councils. Finance was not mentioned presumably because the Government was in the process of reorganising the vital aspect of central grants through the Local Government Act 1966. This established the Rate-Support Grant as a more sophisticated successor to the former General Grant. In addition, the Government made it clear in a White Paper in 1966 that it saw a reform of local government finance as being appropriately undertaken only after a new structure had been established: the new structure 'should provide a more promising context for drastic reform of local government finance'.[18] But the Commission did have among its members one 'expert' in this field — Dr Hedley Marshall, former city treasurer at Coventry and author of a standard text on the subject. In the event, the Commission not surprisingly found it necessary to devote two chapters in its report to management and finance. After all, its proposed structure was designed to provide services to the public, and both management and finance are crucial facilitators of council outputs.

It will be recalled that Crossman's first intention had been to appoint a small committee to seek general principles. Obviously the Commission would seek such principles, though within limits — given its terms of reference. It was also asked to deal with boundaries, which suggested that the Government wished it to produce principles which were of clear practical application. The danger here was that geography would come to dominate the procedure, although this was averted at the outset by the natural desire of the major witnesses (Government Departments and local authority associations) to avoid at all costs committing themselves to detailed statements about individual areas. Such issues were highly sensitive.

If Crossman had gone some way towards achieving his 'general principles' committee, he certainly had not made it small. The Herbert Commission on Greater London government had had seven members; the 1958 Commission had also begun its life with seven; the 1945 Commission had had only five. In sharp contrast, the Redcliffe-Maud commissioners numbered as many as eleven. The number alone has important consequences, for the initial aim of every commission chairman is to obtain a strongly-worded unanimous report and this objective is likely to become increasingly difficult to achieve as the number of members rises. A united report not only shows that he has done his job well, it also adds strength to the recommendations when they are publicly debated. In general terms, a unanimous set of proposals is more likely to be accepted by government than one from a body divided — it was often alleged that a great strength of the 1960 Herbert Report lay in its united approach.[19]

If numbers alone made unanimity difficult to achieve, the make-up of the Commission made it virtually impossible. It is always difficult to know on what grounds members should be appointed. In particular, the question of expertise is highly problematical. Ideally, a commission needs a core of 'expert' members, but a difficulty is that most experts bring with them a set of values and beliefs developed over a long period of time. When these values have been translated into commitments to particular sets of proposals the situation is especially problematical.

Only two of the eleven members could be classified, in terms of knowledge about the structural problems of local government, as completely 'non-expert'. Mr John Bolton and Mr Victor Feather had business and trade union backgrounds respectively. Such appointments are 'normal' to most commissions and they represent government use of patronage powers. Bolton, a former Chairman of the Council of the British Institute of Management, was Commission Vice-Chairman. Feather, Deputy General Secretary of the TUC, played only a limited role because he soon had to act as General Secretary due to the lengthy illness of George Woodcock.

The remaining nine were all well known in local government circles. Sir John Maud (he became Lord Redcliffe-Maud in 1967) was already chairing the Committee investigating the internal organisation of local government, and his interest in the subject could be traced back to 1932 when he wrote a textbook entitled *Local Government in England and Wales*. He later had a distinguished career in the civil service (Permanent Secretary at the Ministry of Education) and diplomatic corps (Ambassador to South Africa) before re-entering academic life as Master of University College, Oxford. Three important characteristics made him a good choice as Chairman. He knew the subject but had no known strong opinions about a desirable solution, he was an experienced chairman well used to the task of seeking a consensus, and he was an experienced drafter of papers who could be expected to produce a readable report. The first two were particularly vital if the Commission was to have any chance of success.

Dame Evelyn Sharp's role in the background to the Commission's appointment has already been discussed. She was known to be a powerful Permanent Secretary at the Ministry of Housing and Local Government until she retired early in 1966. She was also known to be in favour of local government reform and a reduction in the number of small authorities. Her strong personality ensured that she would be an influential commissioner, though, like the Chairman, she was not identified with any particular alternative structure of local government. In September 1966 she became a life peeress, Baroness Sharp of Hornsey in Greater London.

Three further members had been associated for long periods of their lives with county borough government. Sir Francis Hill had been a city councillor at Lincoln for more than a quarter of a century and Chairman of the Association of Municipal Corporations from 1957 to 1966. He could be expected to be a supporter of single-tier government, or of the new AMC approach of most-purpose second-tier authorities of which Lincoln and its surrounds could constitute a clear example. Dr A. H. Marshall was not clearly committed to the AMC approach, despite his background as Treasurer of the City of Coventry (a post from which he had retired some years earlier — he was in 1966 at the Institute of Local Government Studies, University of Birmingham).

Nor, by 1966, was Mr T. Dan Smith committed to the AMC approach. He had risen rapidly to power in Newcastle-upon-Tyne at the beginning of the 1960s, and had been Leader of the City Council at a time when it undertook a tremendous amount of urban redevelopment. But in 1965-6 he nailed his colours to a new mast by resigning altogether from the city council in order to concentrate his efforts on the new Northern Region Economic Planning Council, of which he had been appointed Chairman. This was one of eight advisory planning councils set up in 1964-5 by Mr George Brown, Secretary of State for Economic Affairs. Their creation had been accompanied by statements that the powers of local authorities would not be affected, in order to meet criticism from councils and their associations that the move represented a further undermining of the status and responsibilities of local government. Smith was one who viewed the experiment with enthusiasm, for he was convinced that a city like Newcastle was physically too small a unit to create or stimulate growth in the depressed north-east, and that a system of regional authorities was the only solution for the area. He came to the Commission after several times publicly expressing this conviction, the most recent occasion having been at the 1965 AMC conference at which Mr Crossman made his major speech. His questions during oral evidence were mostly about the prospects for regional government, and this was the model of reform which he favoured.

County government was represented by two members. Sir Peter Mursell was Chairman of the West Sussex County Council and was prominent within the County Councils Association. His first instinct was to support the notion of strong counties of which, he could claim, his own was an example. To persuade Mursell and Sir Francis Hill both to sign a report proposing anything more than a modified status quo was not going to be easy. Mr (later Sir) Jack Longland was probably the most widely known of the commissioners after Feather, through his chairmanship of radio panel games such as 'My Word' and 'Round Britain Quiz'. This did not qualify him as a commissioner as much as his lesser-known post of Chief Education Officer for Derbyshire County Council. He brought with him a faith in the value of large education authorities with considerable resources and case-loads to exploit. This, in his view, allowed for an excellence of provision, particularly of a specialist nature such as schools for the handicapped and advisory services. Size of authority was important to him.

The final two members of the Commission were also 'experts' in their own particular way, though neither had had a career within local government. Mr Reginald Wallis had recently retired after thirty years as Labour Party regional organiser for the north-west. As such he had been closely involved with both councillors and MPs from that party, and with the management of their election campaigns. He was likely to be closely concerned with the political implications of local government reform — not just with the question of political control of any new authorities, but also with the future implications for parliamentary constituency boundaries (which tend to follow local government boundaries wherever possible). He did not join the Commission with any known strong views about alternative structures.

Mr Derek Senior, however, did. As planning correspondent of the *Manchester Guardian* he had built up a reputation both as a specialist journalist and as a knowledgeable critic of town and country planning. This latter had led him to study closely the structure of local government, as he had observed at close quarters the problems generated by conflicts like that between Manchester and Cheshire on 'overspill' housing.[20] This type of conflict had made him aware of the weakness of the existing structure of local government, and of the inability of councils effectively to control land-use in their areas. The great expectations of the post-war planners who had pushed through the 1947 Town and Country Planning Act remained expectations.

Senior had gone beyond mere analysis of the problem, and had formulated an alternative structure of local government based on the 'city region'. He claimed to be able to delimit around thirty city regions — areas based on a large town or city and embracing its surrounding suburban and rural terrain. Boundaries between city regions would be placed where the travel watershed was most clearly apparent — this could be mapped by an analysis of statistics relating to travelling to work, shopping, entertainment and leisure (where such statistics were available). And Senior was on public record as strongly supporting such a solution. This was clear from an important article he had written in *Political Quarterly* in 1965,[21] though its message had also appeared in other journals and newspapers. Soon after the Commission began its work he published a book entitled *The Regional City* in which he further elaborated his views on the course of editing a set of conference papers. So committed was he that, unless he was prepared to modify his views considerably, the Commission would find a unanimously agreed report difficult to obtain should other members not accept the city region model. In the event the Commission chose an alternative approach and Senior did not agree to modify his approach — instead he produced a mammoth 'memorandum of dissent' in favour of city regions.

Way back in 1910 the Balfour Committee on the Procedure of Royal Commissions had stressed both the advantages of a unanimous report and the need to select 'persons who have not committed themselves so deeply on any side of the questions involved in the reference as to render the probability of an impartial inquiry and a unanimous report practically impossible'.[22] With hindsight it is, of course, apparent that Senior fell within the category of problem members. But in 1966 it appeared that several of his colleagues were also potentially in dispute. Hill and Mursell came from the opposing camps of AMC and CCA.* Longland was a 'large authority' man, and Smith was known to support regional government. Up to a point all four were prepared to participate in the process of seeking compromise — though Hill (supported by Wallis) and Longland both wrote short 'notes of reservation' favouring more smaller, and fewer larger, authorities respectively. The Redcliffe-Maud Report therefore consisted of a main report signed by ten of its eleven members (three of whom disowned small parts of the detailed geographical proposals) and a memorandum of dissent (published as volume 2) written by Mr Derek Senior. The text of Senior's memorandum was a little longer than that of the main report — a notable achievement in authorship given that he had little or no help from the secretariat under the Balfour Committee recommendations, and that he was suffering from severe eyesight problems (which caused him to enter hospital for an operation soon after publication of the report in 1969). Had Senior not been a paid member of the Commission and able to devote a large proportion of his time to its work, it is unlikely that he would have been able to produce such a lengthy and sustained account of his views.

Research

The Redcliffe-Maud Commission was the first Royal Commission to produce a memorandum of dissent longer than the main report.

---

*They were appointed as individuals and not as representatives of these associations. This was made clear by Mr Crossman following a complaint from the associations of district councils that they had not been represented on the Commission.

It was also the first to have its own permanent self-appointed research team. Previous commissions had sometimes contracted with universities and individuals for pieces of research. The Herbert Commission, for example, reproduced a study of London service centres written for it by a research officer at the Ministry of Housing and Local Government. The (Donovan) Commission on Trades Unions and Employers Associations (1965-8) spawned several research reports and one of its members acted as research director. The Redcliffe-Maud Commission, in addition to publishing a series of sponsored Research Studies, was also able to produce a separate volume (volume 3) of research studies undertaken by its own team.

Research was directed by L. J. Sharpe of Nuffield College, Oxford. He was supported by ten geographers, planners, sociologists and political scientists — some seconded from government departments, others recruited direct from universities and research institutes. Research comes under the list of 'constraints' on the Commission for two main reasons. First, because of the misplaced importance attached to it by Crossman (and others) at the time the Commission was established. In several speeches the Minister placed great emphasis on the role of researchers and the impression was given that research would 'prove' things — which may occasionally be the case in the natural sciences, but is certainly rarely so in the social sciences. In oral evidence the UDCA, in particular, seized on this impression and openly challenged the Commission to prove that larger authorities were superior through 'research in depth'.[23] Later, those continuing to defend the smaller authorities made much of the alleged 'failure' of the research to illustrate any clear connection between size and efficiency in the performance of important functions such as education and housing. The RDCA, for example, gleefully quoted from the Commission's report where it was openly admitted that 'size cannot be statistically proved to have a very important effect on performance.'[24] It is true that the Commission did make a major attempt to undertake research into the question of size, but it is equally true that at the outset it was clear that 'proof' could only result from a series of value judgements.*

A second constraint on the Commission can result from the findings of its researchers. To give a hypothetical example first — what would the commissioners have done had it emerged from the research that only councils of below 10,000 population were efficient? How could this have been incorporated into its

*See pp. 55-9, for an illustration of the numerous value judgements which must be made in order to draw conclusions on the desirable size of a local authority.

recommendations when the public debate had been revolving around the idea of councils much larger than those existing at the time?

Actual examples are less dramatic, though they still illustrate the point. First, a survey of parish councils suggested that a goodly proportion of such authorities were 'active', and this was used as evidence in support of the creation of local councils.[25] But critics could both challenge the definition of 'active' as being pitched at a low level, and point to the fact that another considerable number had had to be classified as 'inactive'. Secondly, a research report was claimed by the Commission to show that the West Yorkshire conurbation differed from the other conurbations in terms of 'many of the characteristics examined', and this was part of the justification for not giving the area a two-tier metropolitan system.[26] A study of the actual research report in fact reveals that on only three counts (density of population, level of rateable value, proportion of nineteenth-century schools) did the West Riding differ. Finally, because level of education was found to correlate closely with interest in local government, the Commission concluded that 'on the fairly safe assumption that more people will reach a higher level of education in the future, we may expect that interest in local government will steadily increase rather than fall off'![27] To be fair, few other sentences in the report matched this for slapdash thinking.

Despite these misgivings it would be wrong to conclude that research and Royal Commissions should be kept apart. A strength of many recent reports has been that their 'evidence' has not been confined to the 'opinions' of interested parties acting as witnesses. The provision of 'intelligence' is a valuable function of a support team, and it should be noted that L. J. Sharpe was styled 'Director of Research and Intelligence'. But sophisticated research into quite new areas of exploration is unrealistic given the constraint of time and the inevitably tentative and uncertain nature of the findings. A major value of the research on the effects of size on outputs was in fact to point the way for further, more sophisticated studies in the future. [28] A secondary value was that pitfalls emerged which the commissioners knew they must avoid in their report. Of least value were the few positive conclusions, and there were occasions on which the commissioners wished to ignore these.

Reasons for Establishment
Any commission is certain to review at an early date the reasons for its establishment. Most commissions are anxious at the outset to produce proposals which will eradicate the problems that led to their creation. Furthermore, it is only natural to start an

investigation by looking carefully at what one knows before proceeding into the unknown. Hence a further constraint appears through the attempt to formulate a solution which removes the weaknesses and keeps only the strengths of the prevailing situation.

The Redcliffe-Maud commissioners did not have to look far to find the weaknesses of local government. Every textbook and most previous reports contained lengthy diagnoses of the ills of the existing system (the 1947 Report of the Local Government Boundary Commission was particularly strong in this respect, and it had barely dated at all in the succeeding twenty years). Weaknesses could be placed under six main heads (excluding those relating to finance and internal organisation as they were not clearly within the Commission's remit).

(1) In a two-tier system shared functions can be a recipe for conflict and delay. In London by 1966 this was already becoming apparent in the case of town planning and highways. Generally there was a growing problem of relations between housing and welfare authorities over homelessness.

(2) Delegation from one tier to another could also lead to conflict and delay. The Herbert Commission had made this point strongly in the case of Middlesex. A Ministry-sponsored study of development control (1967) was also critical; so, too, was the Institute of Education in a research study for the Commission on school governors and managers.[29]

(3) The division between town and country severely restricted the activities of planning and transportation authorities. This had been hammered home by academics for many years, and 'officially' underwritten by Crossman in the 1965-6 period leading up to the Commission's appointment. The Ministries of Housing and Local Government and of Transport concurred in their evidence.

(4) Many authorities were very — or too — small to be effective. This, again, had become a 'normal' criticism. It should be recalled that more than half the existing councils served populations of below 20,000.

(5) The structure was remarkably inflexible. It had become virtually impossible to obtain boundary changes by agreement largely because of the problem of the separation of town and country. The situation was commonly known as the 'Cold War' between councils, and the experience of the 1958-66 Commission was living proof of the accuracy of this label.

(6) For all its financial importance and breadth of service provision, local government provoked little public interest and enthusiasm. Election statistics and survey findings suggested that most people viewed their authorities as being of little relevance and importance.

Obviously the Commission was going to have difficulty in overcoming this last weakness — that of public apathy. But the other five were all structural features which might be avoidable. There would be difficulties in formulating a view about the size of local authorities, but the principle of town-country amalgamation seemed a logical one to accept. Provisions could, hopefully, be made to ensure greater flexibility and adaptability to changing conditions in any new structure, and if more than one tier proved necessary then a clear-cut division of functions might avoid the problems of delegation, overlapping powers, and the like. That this diagnosis had an effect on the Commission is very apparent from a close study of the majority report — though Derek Senior's alternative proposals did contain some complex suggestions for the division of powers between his city regions and districts.

Concurrent Developments
Commissions have to cope with a changing world. While they sit, public affairs continue. Frequently events over which they have little or no control alter the environment within which they are working. Furthermore, many of the incidents which do occur may have a considerable impact on the thinking of commissioners. This is partly because such incidents reflect current government policies and attitudes with which a commission will be anxious to appear to be in tune in its report, and partly because events tend to have a short-term impact which often seems unwarranted when assessed from a historical perspective. Looking back in 1975, for example, a public dispute between the Redcliffe-Maud Commission and the Ministry of Health about responsibility for the ambulance service seems trivial. At the time it appeared to raise an important issue of principle.*

An important aim of the Commission was to strengthen local government. It was, therefore, particularly concerned with concurrent developments which had clear structural implications for local government. With no fewer than ten Government Departments responsible for services and activities which impinged on local

---

*In 1966 the Minister of Health proposed to transfer responsibility for the service from local authorities to Regional Hospital Boards. In a public exchange of letters in January-February 1967 the Commission protested that this decision should not be taken in advance of its report. The Minister, although annoyed that the Commission refused to give detailed reasons, later agreed to drop the plan.

authorities, and in a political situation in which a reformist government had been returned to power after more than a decade in opposition, it is not surprising to find that the commissioners had to digest a considerable number of events. The following carried the clearest implications for its work.

First, the Home Secretary, Mr Roy Jenkins, decided in 1966 to embark on a policy of reducing the number of *police* forces to between forty and fifty. The background lay in the recommendation in 1962 of the (Willink) Royal Commission on the Police that the optimum unit, from the point of view of efficiency, was a force of 500 men or more, which would require a population of at least 250,000.[30] In 1966 fifty-six forces were smaller than this, most of them in county boroughs. A further twenty-eight had 500-1000 men and fell below the Home Office's preferred minimum, as given in evidence to the Redcliffe-Maud Commission.[31] The Police Act 1964 gave the Home Secretary wider powers to initiate amalgamations into joint forces, and these he intended to use. In the main the 1966 policy involved joining a county borough force with that of its neighbouring county (e.g. a Derby and Derbyshire combined force), which also had the advantage of ending the distinction between town and country that caused forces to work within boundaries unrecognised by most criminals. Even the large borough forces, Birmingham and Bristol apart, were not to be spared — Manchester joined with Salford, Liverpool with Bootle, Sheffield with Rotherham. In the event one or two were reprieved when Mr James Callaghan replaced Jenkins as Home Secretary, for he chose to be less rigid in his implementation of the policy. But this was much later in the life of the Redcliffe-Maud Commission, which clearly had to create a structure of local government capable of catering for this new policy on the size of police forces if it was to be confident that policing — one of the oldest of local authority functions — would remain under local authority control.

Second, White Papers in July 1966 and December 1967, followed by the Transport Act 1968, proposed the creation of new bodies to deal with *public transport* in the major conurbations.[32] The second White Paper proposed the eventual title 'Passenger Transport Authority'. The Government was anxious to strengthen the complex structure whereby local transport services were being planned, financed and operated by several authorities (including British Rail, private and nationalised bus companies as well as municipal bus undertakings) independently of one another in large urban areas when an integrated service was desirable. The PTAs were to be set up 'without prejudice to the work of' the Commission and the Government intended that they would be sufficiently flexible 'to allow their absorption in the long-term pattern of local government, whatever this might be'.[33] This was important not just because of the need to placate hostile councils critical of the concept on the grounds that it compromised the Commission, but also because ultimately the aim was to integrate passenger transport into 'the general planning of conurbations'.[34]

The Commission was certain to be heavily influenced by this new policy. Transport, highways and planning were basic local authority services and of fundamental importance to the concept of local government.* The proposals could be construed as a threat to all three unless the commissioners came up with a structure which could accommodate the new interim arrangements. And the Government was not beyond giving the Commission a push in the right direction in its second White Paper: 'Indeed, it is clear that one of the major factors making for the reorganisation of local government is the need to create local authority units big enough to tackle the sort of problems, like transport, which they ought to tackle if local government is to survive as an effective force.'[35]

The White Papers were followed by the inevitable squabble over the boundaries of the PTAs, with councils on the edge of the conurbations seeking to be excluded, partly because of the fear that inclusion in a PTA area might later be used as evidence for their inclusion in what were now a near-certainty; new conurbation-based local authorities. There is every chance that the Redcliffe-Maud Commission would have proposed such bodies in any case; the Government's transport policy merely helped to ensure this. But the outer boundaries of the conurbations, or metropolitan areas as they were later known, continued to be a contentious and sensitive issue.†

Third, the Government was also in the process of formulating a policy about the structure of the *National Health Service*. Since 1948 this had been organised on a tripartite basis, with countries and county boroughs responsible for the provision of ambulances, clinics, and domiciliary nursing services (home nurses, health visitors, district midwives). Hospitals and the family practitioner services (doctors, dentists, opticians) were under the control of two separate

---

*Two other reports had stressed the links between these services; the Buchanan Report 'Traffic in Towns' (1962) and the Report of the Planning Advisory Group (1965).

†The arguments that the Redcliffe-Maud Commission's work could be prejudiced by the creation of very large PTAs did persuade the Government to keep to fairly tight boundaries, despite its policy of including all areas with 'substantial movements' of commuters' into the conurbation centres (*Cmnd 3481*, p. 34). Later, in 1970-2, the argument was again used by councils, this time to justify their exclusion from the proposed new metropolitan countries on the grounds that they were not part of the PTA which covered the effective transportation area.

sets of appointed bodies, Regional Hospital Boards and Hospital Management Committees, and Executive Councils.

The case for integration was strong. It made little sense to divide responsibility for a single service in this way, and the original decision had reflected political pressures, notably from the doctors who were unwilling to work under the guidance of elected local authorities, rather than any rational analysis of desirable organisational arrangements. Any new decision to integrate the NHS closely affected local government and the Redcliffe-Maud Commission: the personal health services were an important part of the work of county and county borough councils. The loss of these would be a blow, the gain of the other parts of the NHS a major triumph. If a new structure capable of accommodating the NHS could be created there would be pressure on the Government to move towards making the new local authorities responsible for the health service. If it could not, the chances of retaining the personal health services were slim.

A Government statement in 1967 paved the way for the publication of a Green (i.e. discussion) Paper in 1968.[36] This proposed the creation of new area health authorities, numbering about forty to fifty, to run all three branches of the service. No final decision was made as to whether these area authorities would be the local authorities, and various alternatives were spelled out. Though the Government seemed likely to support non-elected health authorities (especially given the inevitable pressure from the doctors, who remained unprepared to work under elected councils), the door was not finally closed. If the new local government structure were technically suitable, the case for transferring the NHS to local authorities would not be easy to dismiss.*

We have already seen that the Redcliffe-Maud Commission was only to look at 'existing' local government services. This made it difficult for the commissioners to say much about the NHS without running the risk of being criticised (by health service staff as well as by the Government) for exceeding its brief. Nevertheless, the Green Paper could not be ignored. The majority report spoke of the close links between the health and the social services and attempted to allay the two fears of many who opposed council control of the NHS by stressing that the financial problems could be overcome if councils were given new sources of revenue, and that council control would not mean that doctors and nurses were so closely supervised by elected members that their traditional professional freedom would be placed

---

*It was, in the end, dismissed, and the NHS Reorganisation Act 1973 created appointed regional and area health authorities. The latter — the operational units — are coterminous with the new county and metropolitan district councils, so the case for winding up the AHAs and for a local authority take-over is certain to arise again in a few years.

in jeopardy. The Commission pointed out that under the 1968 Transport Act the PTAs were complemented by Passenger Transport Executives (PTEs) — boards of officers. By law these had a good deal of freedom from councillor control, and a similar relationship could be legally created in the NHS.[37]

Derek Senior, in his memorandum of dissent, went much further. We saw earlier that he felt able to disclaim the view that the matter was beyond the Commission's brief. To him the publication of the Green Paper 'completely transformed the situation with which we had to deal. The question was no longer whether the existing local government health services should be integrated into the NHS, but how; and this was most emphatically a question for us to answer, for the personal health services are the cornerstone of local government's system of community care.'[38] He went on to claim that his proposed structure was well able to cater for the administrative requirements of the NHS. The Green Paper's forty to fifty units for England and Wales, or about thirty-five for provincial England 'precisely corresponds to my regional level of local government'.[39] The lower operational level, based on the district general hospital, 'precisely corresponds to my district level'. Against this, claimed Senior, the majority report's proposed unitary authorities with populations between 250,000 and 1,000,000 were too small to cope with hospital planning (the Green Paper suggested units of at least 1¼ million population for this) but too large for the 150-200,000 optimum district general hospital catchment area. 'It would hardly have been possible for them to pick a scale more equally unsuitable for either purpose.'[40]

A fourth event with structural implications for local government was the publication in 1968 of the Seebohm Committee's report on the *personal social services*. This important document paved the way for the amalgamation of local authority children's and welfare departments into a single social services department under the Local Authority Social Services Act 1970. Because of the close links between the work of the Committee and that of the Redcliffe-Maud Commission, the two bodies had a series of informal exchanges, so the proposals of the Seebohm Committee, which carried clear structural implications, were known to the commissioners in advance of publication in July 1968. There were two such proposals or recommendations. First, the new social services departments should operate through teams of a dozen or more social workers, each team serving a population of between 50,000 and 100,000 (a figure which could be lowered later if the number of social workers was increased).[41] Teams should be based in the field rather than at headquarters, and should be able to call on the more specialised resources of the departmental headquarters. Though the Committee declined to discuss directly the desirable minimum size of a social services authority, this would clearly be well above that of the smaller counties and county boroughs existing in the 1960s as there would be 'a number of' teams of social workers.[42] In a parallel Scottish report a minimum figure of four teams was considered enough to keep the headquarters busy. The Redcliffe-Maud Commission saw this as a clear justification for its proposed minimum population of 250,000, but Derek Senior argued that when there were more trained social workers available four teams could operate in units of down to 100,000 (the size of his smallest districts).[43]

The second set of proposals concerned the links between various services. The Seebohm Committee's theme was the need to provide a 'comprehensive service', and its proposed amalgamation of departments was central to this. But it also emphasised the closeness of links between social services and other services — the NHS and, most important to the Redcliffe-Maud Commission, the education and housing services. Here the Committee was positive: 'We have arrived at the firm conclusion that a family service cannot be fully effective until the social services department and the housing, education, and health departments are the undivided responsibility of the same local authority.'[44] The Redcliffe-Maud Commission accepted this view in allocating services to its proposed metropolitan districts as well as in its advocacy of the concept of all-purpose unitary authorities wherever possible, but Derek Senior argued that co-operation between education and social services did not require that the two be run by the same council. He allocated the former function to his regions* and the latter, along with housing management, to his districts.

These were the four most important concurrent developments during the Commission's lifetime. Several other events also had implications for the Commission, though not as clearly as the main four. A separate Committee of Inquiry into the *fire service* was established in 1967. It was able to inform the Commission that it had concluded this should remain a local authority service.[45] The implication behind the Committee's establishment was, once again, that existing authorities were too small. They were also too small to each contain one of the twenty-five to thirty new *polytechnics* announced in 1966,[46] and there was a danger that these might ultimately be removed from council control and given a university-type status.

On the other hand the future of *regionalism* remained in doubt. The Regional Economic Planning Councils were busy producing their strategies, but these seemed to be in the nature of somewhat

---

*Though with district officers, advised by a committee of district councillors, playing an important role in the detailed administration of the service.

optimistic sets of proposals unlikely to be implemented by the Government. Mr George Brown, the inspiration behind the REPCs, became Foreign Secretary and their parent ministry, the Department of Economic Affairs, declined in status. True, the Queen's Speech of autumn 1968 contained a promise of a new commission to consider proposals for devolution, but this was seen at the time as little more than a political move designed to avoid further embarrassments to the Government like those in Carmarthen and Hamilton in 1966-7, when Welsh and Scottish Nationalists won parliamentary by-elections: 'Mr Wilson's constitutional commission looks uncommonly like a device for delay' concluded the main editorial in the *Guardian*.[47] In any case, by the time the Commission on the Constitution was formally established in 1969 the Redcliffe-Maud Commission was putting the final touches to its report.

Finally, the reports of the Maud and Mallaby Committees on the *management* and *staffing* of local authorities had to be taken into account.[48] Though neither committee made specific statements about the structure of local government, both were evidently thinking of the larger authorities when making their recommendations for committee and departmental structures and for the training and recruitment of local government officers. Also important was the immediate hostility shown by most councils to the Maud Committee's proposal for a Management Board supported by advisory committees rather than the traditional executive ones. The commissioners diplomatically played this proposal down in their report, referring instead to the need for a 'central committee'. Other committees 'would continue to be at the heart of affairs and their relations with the officers would be much as at present',[49] a statement which was close to an abandonment of the Maud Committee blueprint.

That the commissioners sought to indicate how their proposals could cater for these and other contemporary developments is apparent from a reading of the report. On many occasions the events outlined above offered strong supporting evidence for particular proposals — the links between services stressed above under the 'social services' and 'transport' headings, for example, were strongly emphasised by the Commission as being a factor supporting the concept of the unitary authority. On other occasions concurrent events were more difficult to incorporate — how far to discuss the NHS and how to cope with amalgamated police forces which made for strange geography in certain areas. Other developments offered negative evidence — the limited impact of regional economic planning councils made the objective of those advocating a regional model for local government that much more difficult to argue. Whatever the case, commissions have to live with a political situation over which they have no control, and have to take into account the contemporary mood of governments and people. In this way current developments are an important constraint on their freedom of manoeuvre.

Likely Reactions

A further constraint on their freedom of action concerns their assessment of the likely reactions to their report. Presumably commission members, who have invested a large amount of valuable time and energy in their work, are anxious to see their report accepted — preferably in its entirety or with only a limited number of amendments. Though they may not meet collectively to consider in general terms the political consequences of various possible sets of recommendations, this must from time to time be at the backs of their minds. Certainly those involved in the detailed drafting of the report — normally the secretary and chairman in the first instance — will be very much concerned with the reactions of readers to individual phrases and sentences (hence, possibly, the decision to use the phrase 'central committee' instead of 'management board' in the chapter on 'Local Government Management', following the hostile reception accorded to this aspect of the Maud Report). Other members may be more concerned with the likely fate of the general principles and broad recommendations.

In the case of the Redcliffe-Maud Commission the target was, first and foremost, the Government. Some commissions produce reports which require limited government action (Maud and Mallaby, for example). Others are seeking legislation as the sole means of implementation, and the Redcliffe-Maud Commission fell within this latter category. At the same time the reactions of the other groups of proximate decision-makers were also important. Proposals acceptable to the CCA but not to the AMC, for example, could be doomed, for successive governments had avoided changes of this type. Proposals which divided the local authority associations and other groups would have the value of reducing the pressure on the Government. In Chapter III we shall see that the Commission's report did, in fact, pose problems for both the CCA and the AMC.

But it is never easy to assess the reactions of the major political parties to a report, particularly when the assessment has to consider the degree of priority which will be attached to an issue. A Bill to reform local government was certain to be one of the four of five major pieces of legislation in any session — a major commitment on behalf of any government. Furthermore, no commissioner could be sure of the political composition of the Government. It was clear that no legislation would be possible under after the next general election, due in spring 1971 at the latest. In 1967-9 the Labour Government was at the height of its unpopularity, yet it might still be re-elected in two years' time. So the proposals could not safely be aimed too much at any one party. Finally, though the Labour Government seemed reasonably likely to legislate (several statements and documents — such as those on transport, discussed above — carried an implied commitment to action), the attitude of any Conservative Government was much less certain. This suggested a need for a strongly worded report stressing the urgency of the problem.

In very general terms, then, most commissioners would be thinking of the political consequences of their report. Mr Reg Wallis, for one, would no doubt be weighing up the Labour Party's chances of taking political control of any proposed new authorities (an exercise which would immediately be undertaken at all party headquarters following publication of the proposals). Other members would be thinking in broader terms than this. All would be anxious to produce a saleable commodity and the prevailing political atmosphere could well influence commissioners in their selection of what was and was not saleable.

The Problem of Size
The interplay of most, if not all, of these several constraints on the Commission is well illustrated by a study of one major issue confronting it — that of the desirable size of reformed local authorities. We have already seem that discussion on this point led the commissioners to divide into four camps and resulted in the important memorandum of dissent from Derek Senior as well as two notes of reservation from three other members.

The case for multi-purpose local authorities assumes that services can be effectively provided by a composite body, and that areas can be created over which such provision is technically and administratively feasible. Some deny this and claim that each service has its own peculiar technical requirements which demand a unique structure of authorities. In the case of certain services such as water supply, drainage, river pollution prevention, national parks and railways, the case for special areas is at its strongest. But for most local government services particular *geographical* requirements are less clear — except perhaps that of combining town and country in the interests of effective planning, transportation and policing. The concept of merging town and country was not an issue of principle between commissioners. Further, it was known to be a concept which alleviated a major alleged weakness of the existing structure, and which was likely to prove acceptable to central government given concurrent events in the planning, transportation and police services.

The detailed application of the town-country concept caused more difficulty than the concept itself, and led directly to the rift between Senior and his colleagues. Senior considered that social geography should be the prime determinant of size of authority, whereas the other ten commissioners placed their main emphasis on the criterion of *population* as a measure of the potential effectiveness of a local authority.

The use of population as a measure of size stems directly from the history of local government. There has long been a magical quality in certain levels of population. After 1888 a town which reached 50,000 qualified for county borough status; this figure was raised to 75,000 in 1926, and to 100,000 in legislation in 1945 and 1958. In the post-war period, district councils of 60,000 were entitled to receive delegated powers in the case of parts of the education, health, welfare, and planning services. For food and drugs administration 40,000 was sufficient. And so on. Keeping to tradition, witnesses frequently cited population figures and the influential evidence of the several government departments spoke of 300,000-500,000 as a desirable minimum for an education authority, 250,000 for a children's authority, 500,000 for a police authority, and 150,000-200,000 for a local health authority. A feature of all these suggestions was that they represented large increases on the figures bandied about a few years earlier when the 1958 and 1963 Acts were being debated.

Population alone is, in fact, a very crude measure when the aim is to create effective administrative units. It is of most value in the case of functions like education, libraries, housing and the social services, where resources and case-loads are important. Yet the use of population totals can in practice mask very large differences in both resources and case-loads. Take two extreme examples. In West Sussex the two largest towns of Crawley and Worthing both had populations of 60-80,000. In Crawley 22 per cent were of school age and 5 per cent were pensioners; in Worthing 31 per cent were pensioners and only 10 per cent of school age. In Lancashire a penny rate in Blackpool (151,000) raised £33,000 in 1967-8; in Bolton (157,000) only £21,000.

Constrained by history and tradition, by the nature of the evidence, by concurrent developments, and by what little research there had previously been on the question of size, the commissioners embarked on a close study of the population requirements of various services. Evidence from ministries rarely reflected lengthy rational analysis, though the Home Office did offer detailed reasons for its choice of 250,000 for a children's authority (approximately 250 children in care and 100 in residential care were deemed necessary to justify an establishment of at least twelve child care officers, the alleged minimum requirement for effectiveness). This evidence from Whitehall ministries was, in any case, claimed by some within local government to be an agreed package between civil servants designed to steamroller the Commission towards city regions. We saw earlier that the UDCA in particular challenged the Commission to prove the oft-cited need for large authorities. Not surprisingly the Commission turned to its research director for assistance.

The problems facing those who undertook studies of the relation between size and performance were immense. Statistics could frequently be interpreted in several ways (for example, do low unit costs per visit of a child care officer indicate efficiency, undesirably short visits, a lack of trained and highly paid staff, or what?). In particular it was exceedingly difficult to measure *quality of performance*. The inputs — visits, books, expenditures — were normally measurable, the outputs were intangible in the case especially of services where quality depends on personal communication (teaching, social work).

Assuming that statistical problems could be overcome, the statistical findings of any research still required interpretation through a series of value judgements which could be challenged. At least five such judgements were necessary. First, if it is shown statistically that larger councils provide better services than smaller ones, then the question arises as to what level of service is deemed satisfactory. Is it that provided by the average council of 100,000 population? Or 250,000? Or 500,000? With no definite criteria as to quality of service laid down by law, such a decision must reflect the judgement of individuals. Second, if one analyses a service by dealing with each component part, what weight is to be attached to each part? For example, the Local Government Operational Research Unit studied twenty-seven measures of educational provision. In only five was there a size-performance relation (in two of these the smaller LEAs did the best). Should the size of education authority depend on a handful of specialist aspects?

From this comes a third judgement — the importance to attach to each separate function. If the Home Office was correct in stating that police forces covering a population of under 500,000 were second-best,* and the Ministry of Health was happy to see health authorities more than twice as small, what does one do? Should the requirements of the service needing the largest unit dictate the size

---

*It failed to give detailed reasons and acknowledged that 'any assessment of this sort must to a considerable extent be a matter of judgement.' RCLGE, *Minutes of Oral Evidence 3* (HMSO, 1967), Q. 294.

of new authorities at the cost of possibly creating unnecessarily large authorities for other services?

Fourth, the statistical evidence relates to the services today (or, more realistically, last year!). Given the tremendous advances in service provision in recent years, are the findings relevant to tomorrow when there may be new and different demands made on local authorities? Finally, who is to say whether new, possibly quite differently constructed councils will perform in similar manner to current ones — is today's (yesterday's) performance valid as a pointer?

The researchers and the commissioners ran headlong into these problems. The statistical evidence, the Commission had to admit, showed 'that size cannot be proved to have a very important effect on performance'.[50] Though 'research' was classed earlier as a constraint on the Commission, in this case it gave the commissioners complete freedom of manoeuvre,* though at the cost of giving critics grounds to attack the Commission's conclusions. For support for its view that 250,000 was a desirable minimum population for an authority providing major functions like education and the social services, the Commission had to rely on the Seebohm Report, the evidence of government departments and of certain other witnesses such as the Association of Education Committees, and the findings of surveys of the education and children's services carried out by the relevant Her Majesty's Inspectors. These latter consisted of a quantification of the views of the Inspectors presented as two 'research appendices' in volume 3 of the report. This gave them an undeserved status. Other contrary evidence such as that of the Department of Education and Science (which suggested 500,000 as a minimum size) was incorporated by giving it less credence than that cited above, and the Commission acknowledged that joint police forces in some areas would be necessary.

When it came to consider whether there was a desirable maximum size of authority, the Commission also found its freedom of manoeuvre restricted. Research was unhelpful here because only a handful of existing authorities were really large. The vast majority of witnesses in evidence stressed the phrase 'a viable system of local democracy' in terms of smallness, accessibility, and community of interest. But others — the Ministry of Housing and Local Government and the Institute of Housing Managers, for example — proposed authorities with populations of three million

*Research on size would have been a major constraint had it clearly indicated, for example, that councils needed to have a population of 100,000-200,000 for social services; 400,000-500,000 for education; and 750,000-1,000,000 for police. For the commissioners such results would have been disastrous!

or more. Several commissioners were certain to be hostile to the creation of massive authorities, though others would press for a fairly high upper limit if a positive recommendation as to a maximum population size was being contemplated. Finally, under the existing structure the problem of apathy seemed particularly marked at county hall level, and counties were, by and large, a good deal bigger than county boroughs and districts.

The Commission's report reflected these difficulties. The section on 'Maximum Size of Authority' is one of the least strongly worded, though the concluding recommendation is neat and clear. A million population was deemed to be a good upper limit — beyond it there 'could' be managerial problems, and 'democratic control' (by which was meant control over the organisation by the councillor) would be 'difficult'.[51] It was also 'doubtful' whether individual citizens would feel part of a larger authority. The figure of one million was a good round figure but the commissioners had to admit that 'there can be no firm rule about the maximum size of an authority.'

Every one of the constraints discussed earlier restricted the Commission when it came to deal with the issue of size of authority. At least five important value judgements had to be made during the course of the debate on this point, and to maintain a united front among members while proceeding along such a tortuous path required a massive exercise in diplomacy and a set of commissioners anxious and prepared to moderate their views in the interests of the report as a whole. The members were divided. The terms of reference gave support to the notion that 'smallness' was desirable (that at any rate was the way the phrase about 'a viable system of local democracy' was frequently interpreted by witnesses). Evidence to the Commission offered a wide variety of views. Concurrent developments were not entirely helpful. The research foundered in the mire of statistical problems, difficulties of interpretation and incorporation of value judgements. This part of the report was, as a result, open to attack — though a decisive attack, in fact, never got off the ground because both major parties declared the issue of population size to be non-debatable by firmly accepting the Redcliffe-Maud Commission's preferred population range of 250,000-1,000,000.

Government by Commission

We saw in Chapter I that the Government in 1965 was in no position to take the initiative on the issue of local government reform. The most it could do was to indicate a broad commitment to a more marked reorganisation than that being slowly effected by the 1958 Local Government Commission. Crossman's proposed small high-powered committee would, he hoped, produce some guidelines fairly quickly. In the event, the Redcliffe-Maud Commission sat for a little over three years before it reported in June 1969. This prevented the 1966 Labour Government from legislating before a further general election was due.

Yet the Commission served a valuable purpose in maintaining a reform momentum and in creating a new agenda for public debate. The contents of this agenda were more radical than at any previous time. In 1969 local authorities and their associations were forced to participate in a public debate which threatened to lead to changes which would make the administrative map of England almost unrecognisable. Naturally this posed problems for them. The Government and the Opposition were also parties to this debate, and they, too, would not find it easy to cope with dramatic proposals affecting large numbers of key public services, thousands of local politicians, and more than two million local government officers. It was the Government which had to take the lead, a Labour Government committed in broad terms to administrative change. But, by opting for 'government by commission', the Government was handed an agenda in June 1969 over which it had had only limited influence. This influence, through choice of terms of reference and of members back in 1966, and through the impact of its policy statements on such matters as transportation in 1966-8, should not be underestimated, though few in 1966 could have predicted with any certainty the outcome of the Commission's work. Its recommendations went beyond the expectations of most observers.

Commissions are agents of change. Their success or failure lies in the extent to which they generate an atmosphere of reform, and this is not necessarily dependent on the atmosphere surrounding their establishment, as the Herbert Report and its aftermath had shown. The success of the Redcliffe-Maud Commission lay in the attraction of its report to the Government (and in the hostile reactions which produced an alternative approach attractive to the Opposition). The Government was able to adopt a set of proposals as its own which, it could claim, had emerged from an impartial, expert inquiry. It could continuously quote this 'expert advice' as a defence to its proposals.[52] History suggests that it is doubtful whether the Labour Government could have initiated such a radical set of proposals itself without attracting a storm of abuse which would have forced their withdrawal.

NOTES

1 A. P. Herbert, *Anything But Action?* (Hobart Paper 5), (Barrie & Rockliff, 1960).
2 C. J. Hanser, *Guide to Decision: The Royal Commission* (Totawa, New Jersey, The Bedminster Press, 1965).
3 H. F. Gosnell, 'British Royal Commissions of Inquiry', *Political Science Quarterly*, vol. 49 (1934), p. 85.
4 K. C. Wheare, *Government by Committee* (OUP, 1955), pp. 68-9.
5 D. V. Donnison, 'Committees and Committeemen', *New Society*, 18 April 1968, p. 558.
6 See G. Rhodes, *The Government of London: the struggle for reform* (Weidenfeld & Nicolson, 1970), pp. 36-7.
7 A. Shonfield, 'The Pragmatic Illusion', *Encounter*, vol. 28, no. 6 (June 1967), pp. 8-10.
8 See Royal Commission on Local Government in England 1966-9, *Report*, *Cmnd 4040*, vol. 1, ch. 4. Another analysis is I. Gowan and L. Gibson, 'The Royal Commission on Local Government in England', *Public Administration*, vol. 46, no. 1 (1968), pp. 13-24.
9 *Cmnd 4040*, vol. 1, para. 109.
10 Ministry of Local Government and Regional Planning, *Reform of Local Government in England*, Cmnd 4276 (HMSO, 1970), para. 5.
11 All written evidence was published in a series of volumes — one for the associations, one for county councils, etc.
12 One was the Ullswater Commission on Local Government in Greater London. This sat from 1921-3 and produced two minority reports. See Rhodes, *op. cit.*, pp. 4-6. Another was the 1945-9 Local Government Boundary Commission, which decided to go beyond its terms of reference.
13 Local Government Boundary Commission, *Report for the Year 1947* (HC Paper 86, 1947-8), para. 39.
14 The distinction is made by L. J. Sharpe, 'British Politics and the Two Regionalisms' in W. D. C. Wright and D. H. Stewart (eds), *The Exploding City* (Edinburgh UP, 1972), pp. 131-46.
15 *Cmnd 4040*, vol. 2, para. 287.
16 *Ibid.*, para. 296.
17 RCLGE, *Minutes of Oral Evidence 9* (HMSO, 1967), Q. 1053.
18 Ministry of Housing and Local Government, *Local Government Finance in England and Wales*, Cmnd 2923 (HMSO, 1966), para. 6.
19 For example, Rhodes, *op. cit.*, p. 86; W. A. Robson, *Local Government in Crisis* (George Allen & Unwin, 2nd edn, 1968), p. 148.
20 For a discussion of this classic conflict see J. M. Lee and B. Wood, *The Scope of Local Initiative: A Study of Cheshire County Council 1961-74* (Martin Robertson, 1974), Ch. 2.
21 D. Senior, 'The City Region as an Administrative Unit', *Political Quarterly*, vol. 36, no. 1 (1965), pp. 82-91.
22 *Report of the Departmental Committee on the Procedure of Royal Commissions*, Cd 5235 (HMSO, 1910), para. 15.
23 RCLGE, *Minutes of Oral Evidence 9* (HMSO, 1967), Q. 1065, 1069, 1117, 1126, 1128.
24 *Cmnd 4040*, vol. 1, para. 217. Quoted in Rural District Councils Association, *The Democratic Alternative to Maud* (RDCA, 1969), para. 12.
25 *Cmnd 4040*, vol. 1, paras 239, 373; vol. 3, Appendix 8.
26 *Ibid.*, vol. 1, para. 207; vol. 3, Appendix 4.
27 *Ibid.*, vol. 1, para. 241.

28 'In an attempt to avoid these disadvantages (i.e. of the methodology used), the LGORU evolved an alternative method which would enable the Commission to evaluate alternative forms of local government. Owing to the amount of research work involved in it, the method was not in fact employed, but it is detailed here as it is felt that it could be adapted to aid in the implementation of the Commission's findings.' RCLGE, *Research Studies 4 — Performance and Size of Local Education Authorities* (by the Local Government Operational Research Unit), (HMSO, 1968), pp. 166-8.
29 RCLGE, *Research Studies 6 — School Management and Government* (by the Research Unit, Institute of Education, University of London) (HMSO, 1968), ch. 11.
30 Royal Commission on the Police, *Final Report, Cmnd 1728* (HMSO, 1962), para. 280.
31 RCLGE, *Written Evidence of the Home Office* (HMSO, 1967), pp. 6-9, 46-8.
32 Ministry of Transport, *Transport Policy, Cmnd 3057* (HMSO, 1966); *Public Transport and Traffic, Cmnd 3481* (HMSO, 1967).
33 Cmnd 3057, *op. cit.*, para. 60.
34 *Ibid.*, para. 56.
35 Cmnd 3481, *op. cit.*, para. 14.
36 Ministry of Health, *National Health Service: The Administrative Structure of the Medical and Related Services in England and Wales* (HMSO, 1968).
37 *Cmnd 4040*, vol. 1, paras. 359-67.
38 *Cmnd 4040*, vol. 2, para. 290.
39 *Ibid.*, para. 413.
40 *Ibid.*, para. 298.
41 *Report of the Committee on Local Authority and Allied Personal Social Services, Cmnd 3703* (HMSO, 1968), paras 568-94.
42 *Ibid.*, para. 681.
43 *Cmnd 4040*, vol. 2, paras 277-8.
44 Cmnd 3703, *op. cit.*, para. 676.
45 *Cmnd 4040*, vol. 1, para. 352.
46 Department of Education and Science, *A Plan for Polytechnics and Other Colleges, Cmnd 3006*, (HMSO, 1966).
47 *Guardian*, 31 October 1968.
48 Ministry of Housing and Local Government, *Report of the Committee on the Management of Local Government* (Maud Report) (HMSO, 1967); *Report of the Committee on the Staffing of Local Government* (Mallaby Report) (HMSO, 1967).
49 *Cmnd 4040*, vol. 1, paras 486, 493.
50 *Ibid.*, para. 217.
51 *Ibid.*, paras 270-6.
52 Gerald Rhodes concludes that this is one of four major reasons for resorting to the appointment of an advisory committee. See G. Rhodes, *Committees of Inquiry* (Allen & Unwin, 1975), pp. 191-3.

Chapter III

THE REPORT AND ITS RECEPTION,

JUNE 1969-FEBRUARY 1970

From mid-1968 (the orginal target date set by Crossman) until actual publication on 11 June 1969 rumours about the content of the Redcliffe-Maud Report were rife. *The Times, The Sunday Times* and, most of all, the *Guardian* all offered their readers an advance list of the major proposals. On 14 February 1969 the *Guardian* actually led with this under the headline '1000 Councils Swept Away in Maud Report', causing a parliamentary row and requests from several MPs for a Select Committee to investigate the alleged leak. The article did indeed prove to be a fairly accurate account, though by June it had been forgotten. In May *The Sunday Times* was also accurate, even to the point of the title of the proposed new councils — 'unitary authorities', though most of this article dealt with the future of regionalism. These and other rumours all helped to maintain the climate of reform.

The forebodings of many were fully realised on 11 June. Both the main report and Derek Senior's alternative blueprint spelled extinction for many existing councils. Inevitably there were bitter reactions from all points of the compass in the days following publication. Before we assess these reactions and consider the impact of the report on the various groups of proximate decision-makers identified in Chapter I, we must first take a brief but close look at the proposals of the commissioners.

The Main Report[1]
The key recommendation of the majority was the concept of the 'unitary authority', an all-purpose council covering both town and country and with a population of between 250,000 and 1,000,000. The concept came out of many of the constraints, influences and pressures surrounding the commissioners' work and discussed in Chapter II. It was justified in terms of some of the meanings attached to the terms 'democracy' and 'efficiency' in Chapter I.

The strength of the all-purpose authority was alleged to lie in its recognition of the close links between services, and in its sheer simplicity.[2] There was great potential for efficiency because responsibility for the allocation of resources lay with a single council, as did responsibility for the co-ordination and supervision of service provision. Democracy was possible as this was a structure which the public could understand and with which it could easily identify itself. In addition councils had the ability to take definite choices and could be accountable for their success and failure to deliver effective services. The merging of town and country into geographically cohesive units added to the democratic strength of the concept, reflected the technical needs of the planning and transportation services, and abolished a traditional structural weakness.[3] Finally, the population size recommendations allegedly further supported the notions of democracy and efficiency — all councils would have sufficient resources but none would be so large as to be inaccessible, remote or unmanageable.

Four problems confronted the Commission at this point, and in each case its preferred solution weakened this major principle. First, around the major conurbations based on Birmingham, Liverpool and Manchester a town-country unitary authority would have a population well in excess of one million. The three principles of function, geography and population size were here incompatible. The Commission decided to drop the notion of all-purpose government in these areas, and opted instead for a modified 'Greater London model' of county plus districts. The London structure was taken as a starting point, but was strengthened in three ways. First, the Commission's proposed 'metropolitan' counties embraced large areas of the rural hinterland, whereas the GLC did not. Second, metropolitan districts would fall within the 250,000-1,000,000 population range, whereas several London boroughs were a good deal smaller than this. Third, the proposed division of powers was, with the exception of housing, clear-cut, whereas in London several functions were shared in such a manner that responsibility was often blurred. The districts would be responsible for education, libraries, social services and consumer protection, the county would be responsible for planning, transportation, police and fire.[4]

A second problem lay in the future of parish councils. A genuine unitary approach would mean their abolition. But there was a good deal of pressure on the Commission in favour of their retention and, possibly, of their being strengthened. The National Association of Parish Councils had argued strongly for their retention both in its written and in its oral evidence (where, led by the articulate and humorous Professor Bryan Keith-Lucas, the Association provided just about the only interesting session for the handful of members of the public who observed proceedings).

Almost 600 parish councils and meetings had submitted written evidence. The research team had produced a study which suggested that many councils provided valuable minor local services such as seats, allotments, village halls and recreation grounds, and that they could be effective translators of local opinion to higher authorities. Finally, several commissioners came from rural areas and could be expected to provide a strong internal lobby in favour of their retention — notably Sir Peter Mursell from West Sussex. These reasons all pointed to the retention of parishes. They were supplemented by the thought that offering parish council status to many of the small doomed municipal boroughs and urban districts might make the central concept a little more palatable. From all this was born the notion of the 'Local Council',[5] which was later criticised by many as a poorly constructed attempt by the Commission to illustrate that its recommendations did constitute 'a viable system of local democracy'. Regardless of whether this was the case, the proposal for local councils meant that the total concept of the unitary authority would not be realised should the whole report be adopted: there would be two levels of elected councils, the unitary and the local council.

The future of regional government constituted a third problem. Already under the old structure there was some regional-level machinery such as the Advisory Councils for Further Education and, in several regions, regularised conferences of local planning authorities (for example, the Standing Conference on London and South East Regional Planning). The Regional Economic Planning Councils were producing strategies which, if implemented, would be major determinants of future land-use patterns in many areas (despite the original Government statements that these Planning Councils would not affect the work of local authorities). A full-scale review of devolution was in progress following the establishment of the Commission on the Constitution. Either the Commission could ignore these developments, or it could attempt to incorporate them in its proposals. It chose the latter course of action and recommended the creation of eight indirectly elected 'Provincial Councils'. *Inter alia* these would draw up a strategic land-use plan and co-ordinate the planning of aspects of the education and children's services. They would not be executive bodies.[6] Once again the total concept of the unitary authority was being modified by the introduction of an additional tier, however functionally weak it might be.

Finally, there was sometimes incompatibility between the Commission's criteria of geography and of population size. In many places a geographically cohesive area falling within the population limits could not be found. This led to the proposed creation of some new local government areas which fell outside the upper and lower limits, and of others whose geography was supect. Thus five of the fity-eight unitary authorities and four of the twenty metropolitan districts had populations of under 250,000, and four more of the seventy-eight were larger than 1,000,000. Geographers could take their pick from a considerable choice of examples when criticising the commissioner's map. In an entertaining but acid Chapter II Derek Senior spoke of 'artificial misalliances such as Bury-Rochdale, Birkenhead-Chester, Stafford-Tamworth, and Kidderminster-Redditch'; of the Northumberland unit being 'devoid of coherence', and of 'unnatural forced marriages [which] are not merely lacking in coherence: they are positively fissile. They make the worst of all possible worlds.' Here he was referring to double-headed districts based on Eastbourne-Hastings, Salisbury-Swindon and Aylesbury-High Wycombe.[7]

In order to 'solve' the geography-population incompatibility the Commission included a fourth criterion, that continuity with the past should be preserved where possible.[8] This, it was argued, meant that new councils could build on the historical strength of their predecessors, and that the transition to the new system would be administratively more straightforward. It also enabled units like Eastbourne-Hastings to be justified as being a continuation of East Sussex, while Salisbury-Swindon was Wiltshire, the Aylesbury-High Wycombe was Buckinghamshire.

The main councils, then, were to consist of fifty-eight unitary authorities, three metropolitan areas (around Birmingham, Manchester and Liverpool), and twenty metropolitan districts. These would be supplemented by provincial and by local councils. But in two separate notes of reservation, three of the ten commissioners proposed several detailed alterations to the fifty-eight unitary and twenty metropolitan district authorities.[9] Sir Francis Hill and Reginald Wallis sought five additional unitary areas (Chesterfield, North Nottinghamshire, Southend, the Medway towns, and Bath). Jack Longland wished to reduce five West Riding unitary authorities to two based on Bradford and Leeds, four Lancashire unitary councils to one probably centred on Preston or Blackburn, and four Black Country metropolitan districts to one centred on Wolverhampton. He also recommended the amalgamation of Southport and Liverpool, of Bedfordshire and Buckinghamshire (with High Wycombe going to Berkshire), of East and West Hertfordshire, East and West Kent, East and West Surrey, and of Brighton and East Sussex. His county background, plus his anxiety to avoid the creation of more 'small' (250,000-500,000) education authorities than was absolutely necessary, emerged strongly here and his proposals resulted in fifteen fewer major authorities than the eighty-one recommended by the majority of his colleagues. But he, Hill and Wallis all supported the unitary principle and the broad criteria of geography and population size. Their reservations well illustrated the difficulties of translating principles into practice.

Derek Senior's Memorandum of Dissent[10]

It takes courage to write a memorandum of dissent as comprehensive as Derek Senior's, not just the courage needed to produce a document the length of a book without the assistance of administrative and research staff, but also the courage required to defy one's colleagues over a lengthy period of time. The author of such a memorandum probably has two or three different objectives: to offer the world a set of principles sufficiently at variance with those of his colleagues to be non-negotiable; to illustrate the practical application of these; and, possibly, to reduce the chances of his colleagues' proposals being acceptable. He has the advantage of being able to produce a report which is his, and not an amalgam of views suitably watered down during the search for the maximum possible amount of consensus. He also does not need to open with the traditional chapters about the Commission's procedure, and the nature of the evidence presented by witnesses which often make a tedious start of a Royal Commission's report. There are reasons why memoranda of dissent and minority reports*
are frequently clearer, more concise and more readable than those of the majority of commissioners.[11]

The Senior plan was based on the concept of the geographical city-region, covering a central city and the surrounding town and rural areas falling within this central city's sphere of influence. Thirty-five regions were identified through socio-geographic analysis, ranging in population size from Carlisle (312,000) to Birmingham (nearly four million). Directly elected regional councils would be responsible for police, fire, public transport, libraries, education, water, housing policy and the structure plan. They would be complemented by 148 directly elected district councils which also embraced both town and country (apart from those near the centre of the major conurbations). Their populations ranged from 97,000 (Hexham) to 908,000 (Birmingham) and they were to be responsible for the social services, environmental health, refuse collection, local planning, housing management and local recreational facilities. Beneath the districts there would be

*The distinction between the two is constitutional — a minority report must be signed by a quorum of commissioners who are entitled to rather more assistance from the secretariat than are individuals writing a memorandum of dissent.

grass-roots 'common councils' for villages, small towns and communities within large towns. These would not run any statutory services, but would be consulted by regional and district authorities and would be free to spend money on those local amenities where no other authority had a statutory duty to provide facilities.

City-region, town-district and common council were each to be directly elected. At provincial level, though, Senior joined with his colleagues in recommending indirectly elected authorities, except that he suggested five rather than eight. However, Senior made it clear that he made this proposal on the assumption that provincial councils would only be concerned with existing local government functions. Should the Government be prepared to devolve important Whitehall functions to new provincial councils, then his blueprint was rather different. In this case there should be twelve to fifteen directly elected councils which would provide the services allocated to the thirty-five regional authorities as well as undertake devolved functions. Thus Derek Senior in effect proposed two new local government structures: indirectly elected province/region/district/common council; or, alternatively, province/district/common council.

Derek Senior's report is certainly readable and frequently entertaining, particularly when he is critical of his colleagues. His chapter on 'Statutory Functions' also contains a lengthy analysis of the requirements, in terms of size of authority, of the major services that is superior in construction to that of the main report (whether or not one agrees with all its conclusions). But the strength of his proposals lay, first and foremost, in their geographical sense. Though he claimed that his colleagues' recommendations failed 'to answer functional needs, democratic demands or geographical realities throughout the greater part of England', it was the last of these three points on which he placed most emphasis.[12]

History shows that Derek Senior's detailed proposals had little impact on the debate about reform, though in principle their espousal of a two-level system was attractive to the anti-unitary authority lobbies. Why was this? There were two good reasons for their failure. First, they were even more radical than those of his colleagues. Though he proposed more major authorities (183 compared with 81) than the majority — superficially potentially attractive to existing local authorities as more meant smaller in most areas — these bore little relation to existing areas over much of England. He openly professed early in his report that he found the concept of geographical continuity to be 'unacceptable . . . it seems to me that to distort the new pattern in order to resurrect as many as possible of the old boundaries can only prejudice both the acceptability of the new authorities and the prospect of their making a clean break with obsolete management practices.'[13]

Second, when the memorandum began to outline the operation of the scheme it became clear that it lacked simplicity. Indeed it is fair to say that Derek Senior's blueprint was extremely complex. Geographically, four regions would contain no second-tier of districts and two others had only two each, while five around Greater London posed particular problems in that they fell in effect within the London city region. The solution here was a set of special arrangements for the planning service through the creation of a Metropolitan Planning Area. Functionally the division of responsibilities between region and district was far from clear-cut and several services were to be shared. This was deliberate as Senior sought 'articulation' between the two levels in three ways. First, through a joint organisation of a region and its constituent districts. This would deal with capital programmes and would execute certain aspects of some services. Secondly, through district advisory committees to supervise some specified actions of decentralised regional officers, and thirdly through districts acting as agents for the region in the execution of parts of other functions.[14] To many the attraction of the geographical analysis was lost in the complicated nature of the functional conclusions. Furthermore, the concept of 'articulation' appeared to depend on region-district relations which would be very different from the tradition of conflict between tiers, and this gave the report the appearance of being an academic rather than a practical or realistic solution to the reform problem. The presentation of proposals can be as important as their contents, and Senior's package was too complex to be readily communicable (particularly when contrasted with the stark simplicity of the unitary concept), and too radical to be readily acceptable.

Early Reactions in Westminster and Whitehall
We can only speculate on the attitudes to the report of the small number of senior civil servants concerned with the problem of local government reform. Ten years earlier they would have been justified in assuming that such far-reaching proposals for local government reform would have been destined for the more inaccessible of Whitehall's numerous pigeon-holes, there to gather dust alongside the 1947 Boundary Commission's report and other redundant advisory committee proposals. But 1960-3 had shown that local government reform was both politically and administratively feasible. Further, the Government had at least given the impression of seeking a modern administrative structure in its statements and actions since 1964, and had accepted several

key proposals of the 1968 Fulton Report on the Civil Service.

Most civil servant swould welcome proposals to reduce the number of local authorities. Dealing with 1,200 or more individual councils inevitably posed simple administrative problems, and close supervision of council activities was virtually impossible. Learning their geographical locations was a major task, let alone developing an understanding of their individual political and administrative behaviour and attitudes. To this extent reform was welcome, though many would hope that it did not result in the creation of too many highly influential councils with the ability to challenge successfully central government administrative decisions.

Evidence of this view came earlier, when the government departments gave evidence to the Commission. The Treasury argued that a regional level of government was unnecessary. One reason was that 'there is also the danger that such a course would lead to the disintegration of broad national policy, and to very great difficulties for Whitehall in arbitrating between the claims of the regional authorities.'[15] The Department of Economic Affairs also foresaw conflict between regional councils and Whitehall.[16] While the Regional Economic Planning Councils had a 'rather special' character and relationship with the ministry, elected councils would pose problems, said Permanent Under-Secretary Sir Douglas Allen in oral evidence. 'We cannot envisage a situation in which the Government is advised how to discharge its function by a different body; we think it would be the source of endless confusion and friction.'[17]

Major reform, however, meant extra work. A civil service view of different sets of proposals would take into account the administrative ease of implementation. It was here that Derek Senior's report fell down badly. Its geography bore scant resemblance to existing units, and its allocation of functions would require skilled legal draughtsmanship and a large amount of administrative advice and supervision through consultations, circulars and statutory instruments. The majority report, on the other hand, was attractive for two reasons. First, it made an attempt to utilise existing boundaries where possible — thus making the transfer of property, and of staff, and the work of local joint committees preparing for change that much more straightforward. Second, in its three metropolitan areas it used the structure in Greater London as a model. The administrative precedent of the 1963-5 transition would be available as a starting point, and this was naturally an attraction. Many parts of this precedent (for example, the use of a Staff Commission to safeguard the interests of local government officers) could be used in any case, regardless of the model to be implemented, and this helped to make the general notion of reform acceptable to many senior civil servants.

The chances of massive administrative hostility from within Whitehall to reform, then, were slim. It was administratively feasible and, in the long run, it was attractive. Several government departments had expressed themselves in favour of change when giving evidence back in 1966 and 1967, and several had subsequently drafted and processed documents which strengthened the case (such as those discussed in Chapter II when concurrent developments were being reviewed). The right atmosphere for change existed in Whitehall.

Immediate Government reaction to the report maintained the impetus of reform which had been built up by Crossman in the 1965-6 period. The Prime Minister told the Commons that the Government accepted 'in principle' the main recommendations, which he defined as 'that a major rationalisation of local government is called for, that there should be a very marked reduction in the number of units with executive responsibility and that the anachronistic divisions between town and country should be ended'. 'We intend to press ahead quickly', he said, and consultations followed by legislation were promised.[18] Questioned by Mr Heath, the Leader of the Opposition, Mr Wilson made further remarks which helped to define the boundaries for the coming public debate. First, he said that it was 'unduly pessimistic' to assume that a new system could not be fully implemented before 1974 (implying that, on the basis of the London experience as a model timetable, he foresaw legislation in either the 1970-1 or the 1971-2 parliamentary session). Second, he elaborated on the meaning of the phrase 'in principle', stating that 'it does not mean acceptance in detail of, for example, all aspects of the three-tier structure.' In particular he spoke of likely controversies about the position of the proposed local councils, and about the allocation of responsibility for education in the metropolitan areas (the Commission had preferred this to be a district council function).

The Government's haste was quickly further underlined when Mr Anthony Greenwood, who had succeeded Crossman as Minister in 1967, requested views on the report by the end of October 1969. Observers like Peter Jenkins in the *Guardian* felt that it was Wilson rather than Greenwood who was making the running,[19] and Greenwood had said privately in 1968 that legislation before the next general election (due in spring 1971 at the very latest) would not be possible.[20] Wilson was probably anxious to make the Government's position clear before calling an election. The image of the party as one determined to modernise

Britain would then be maintained, and Wilson was shrewd enough to realise that the traditional view that this was a vote-losing issue had not been proved in the case of London where, despite bitter opposition in 1961-3 from the Conservative outer suburbs, the evidence that Tory candidates had lost a significant number of votes as a result in the 1964 election was extremely scanty.

We cannot be sure of the reasons for the urgency which the Prime Minister attached to this issue. There are several possibilities and the truth is probably a mixture of them. Peter Jenkins ascribed it to Wilson's 'reforming zeal' and to his being 'an incurable activist'. Michael Steed concluded that the new boundaries were favourable to Labour in terms of local political control in that party's very good or very bad years, though unfavourable in an average year.[21] No doubt Transport House had performed similar analyses. A further point concerns the attitude of local Labour parties. Many would be hostile to the Commission's proposals, but Government acceptance of them in principle as part of its election manifesto would temporarily silence or at least quieten the dissident group, and would commit MPs to acceptance of legislation during the first session of the new Parliament. Finally, and probably most important of all, promised early action on the report could be a valid reason for delaying the implementation of recommendations from the Parliamentary Boundary Commissioners which would cost Labour several seats in an election.[22]

The period from mid-June 1969 to early 1970 (the White Paper was eventually published on 4 February after suggestions earlier by Mr Wilson that it would be available before the end of 1969) saw not only Labour but also the other major parties undergoing lengthy internal debates. At the Labour Party Conference in September delegates voted, on the advice of the executive, against a motion totally opposed to the Redcliffe-Maud proposals. In the debate much opposition to the remoteness of the proposed new authorities was expressed, and Mr Arthur Skeffington (Joint Parliamentary Secretary, Ministry of Housing and Local Government) denied that the Government was totally committed to the report. He took the view that 'the Government is absolutely free to make up its own mind on what reforms it will put forward. It will do so in the light of discussions, and in the light of the report the National Executive will prepare.'[23]\ Regional conferences with party members were promised for October. Not unexpectedly these did little more than underline the fact that the proposals divided the party because of the varied political repercussions they would have on different areas. When Labour MPs debated the proposals in early December the divisions of opinion again emerged. Mr Anthony Crosland had just become Minister of Local Government and Regional Planning, and he told members that the Government intended to press ahead with reform. Several MPs criticised the Commission's report as creating unnecessarily large authorities, but Crosland claimed that its proposals must form a starting-point for the Government as it had created the Commission in the first place.[24]

The Labour Party National Executive Committees's report did not appear until 28 December 1969. A month earlier the *Guardian* had again led with the issue of local government reform, this time alleging (again correctly) that the Cabinet was contemplating broad acceptance of the report, but with the addition of two further metropolitan areas — for West Yorkshire and South Hampshire. A third, for Lancashire, had been considered but rejected, it was claimed. The NEC report did little to challenge this view.[25] It suggested that there should be five or six further metropolitan areas — Tyneside, Teesside, South Hampshire, Leeds/Bradford, Sheffield, and a second one in the West Midlands to cover just the Black Country. The case for Lancashire was stated but, on balance, rejected. Most of these proposals reflected grass-roots party pressure from several large towns which were faced with absorption into extensive unitary authorities within which they might have limited influence. Similar pressure elsewhere led the NEC to recommend the creation of 'a very few' more unitary authorities. This time no specific cases were mentioned but areas with 'a wide geographic scatter of population' or with 'rival urban centres' worried the NEC. The report went on to recommend that education be a metropolitan county function, that the concept of elected regional councils be left on one side until the Commission on the Constitution reported, and that local councils should not be involved in the running of major services as this would weaken the unitary principle. It was claimed that 'the recent eight regional conferences . . . showed that there was widespread agreement on many aspects of local government reform amongst Labour Party members in England' and that 'the proposal for unitary authorities received wide support.' While the NEC's proposals were designed to reduce criticism within the party, there remained more divisions than these statements suggested.

For the Conservative and Liberal Parties the problem of taking a clear line on the issue was less pressing. Both could snipe at obvious weaknesses in the Commission's plan, and the Government's haste could be criticised without a detailed alternative being offered. The Liberals controlled no more than a couple of councils and had few vested interests adversely affected by the Commission's proposals. At their September 1969 conference in Brighton they busied themselves with attacking the concept of indirectly elected regional councils, scarcely central to the report. These were 'a sham form of regional government'.[26] The inadequacy of the Government's consultation procedures was also criticised, but there was no debate of substance on the core of the report. The Liberals continued to lack a clear policy throughout the 1969-74 period. They preferred to concentrate their attention on the prospects for devolution and on the work of the Commission on the Constitution, and played little part in the parliamentary debates on the Local Government Bill of 1971-2.

The Conservatives in 1969 were in an unusual political situation. Nationally they were in Opposition but with good prospects of winning the next general election (the opinion polls gave them a substantial lead over the Government and by-election results confirmed this). Locally they were in control of a record number of councils, with Labour hanging on to only its rock-hard areas. These included fewer than ten of the eighty-three county boroughs. Official local authority reactions to the report were thus largely Conservative reactions from a new regime of councillors who in many cases had gained power only in 1967, 1968 or 1969 after years in the local political wilderness. Conservative MPs soon found themselves under pressure to oppose the report should the Government seek implementation, but opposition alone was not enough in a situation where the party could be in power within a matter of months. A clear line was needed, whether it be to shelve reform, to implement the report or to propose an alternative model.

There was no urgency about unveiling such a line, and the shadow spokesman, Mr Peter Walker, took good care not to commit himself publicly during the second half of 1969. Instead he, like the Labour Party, embarked on his own series of regional conferences — probably with a fairly open mind at the outset. These conferences — reported as being well-attended and hostile to the Commission's plan — coupled with massive support for a critical motion at the October 1969 party conference persuaded Walker that no Conservative Government could hope to implement the report. But, significantly, speakers at the party conference several times suggested that *some* change in the structure of local government was necessary if councils were to survive. Alderman Frank Marshall from Leeds (at the time also AMC Chairman) suggested that without change all that would be left for local authorities to do would be 'sweeping the streets and emptying dustbins'.[27] He attacked those who argued that the whole of the report was bad. Mr Roger Moate,* moving the motion regretting

*Mr Moate's chances of winning Faversham at the 1970 General Election would have been seriously jeopardised by the RDCA's 'Don't Vote for R. E. Mote'

the over-hasty acceptance by the Government of the principles of the report, also accepted that the structure needed to be altered, but he preferred to build on 'the traditional pattern of community life', whatever that may have meant. In his reply to the debate, Walker refused to disown the report completely. Furthermore, he now appeared definitely to favour change of some kind, claiming that 'we must examine these reforms, because if we don't, the drift from local government to Whitehall will continue.' If the Opposition felt unable at this stage to offer a clear alternative, they were at least showing signs of moving towards acceptance of local government reform as an issue with some priority for any incoming Tory Government. Certainly this was clearly recognised in the north-west, where Cheshire County Council pressed ahead with its own 'Alternative to Maud' during the run-up to the 1970 election campaign in order to be able to offer a viable set of proposals to the incoming minister (Walker) as quickly as possible.[28]

Local Authority and Interest Group Attitudes
The political and administrative barriers to reform at national level seemed to have been swept away for the first time for many years. Anyone who had seen the creation of the Redcliffe-Maud Commission as a delaying tactic by the Government increasingly had to admit that a major piece of legislation in the early 1970s was very much in prospect when Wilson, Greenwood and Crosland all stressed the urgency of the matter, and when Walker, too, seemed to be suggesting that the future for local government was 'change or die'. Local authorities, their associations and the many other professional bodies and interest groups concerned were well aware that their actions could affect their successors for many years to come. For associations and groups this meant the start of lengthy and intensive internal discussions and, frequently, the establishment of small groups of negotiators to act on behalf of the full membership when undertaking consultations with the Government (the Royal Town Planning Institute, for example, nominated three of its members to act thus, while the AMC and other associations set up rather larger committees).

Most individual local authorities found it reasonably easy to agree to a unanimous or near-unanimous view on the report. Their interest naturally tended to be first and foremost in the geography of reform. Urban and rural districts, in particular, were hostile as every one of them was faced with amalgamation into large units, normally along with towns which were larger than themselves. Hence they viewed the proposals as a 'take-over' by their neighbouring large

campaign but for the local rural district council's decision not to participate in it because of this problem of names.

city or borough. 'One can't help wondering what Sussex has done to deserve such very brutal treatment' remarked the Chairman of the Cuckfield Rural District Council in a typical statement coming from council chambers during the summer of 1969.[29]

But the impression must not be given that all councils were disenchanted by the report. In many areas there were authorities with a clear interest in the adoption of the Commission's blueprint. Among counties, Cumberland, Salop, Derbyshire, Nottinghamshire, Leicestershire, Dorset, Wiltshire, Norfolk and West Sussex all formed the basis of unitary authority with boundaries which were barely disturbed. Many county boroughs, too, formed the core of a unitary authority within which they would be the dominant area — Plymouth, Bristol, Southampton, Leeds, Bradford, Halifax and Huddersfield. Others found themselves as the core of a metropolitan district, and this was often acceptable as the district would retain responsibility for the bulk of council services including education, the social services, and housing.

The most common pattern was for opinion in a region or sub-region to be divided. On Tyneside, for example, the Newcastle City Council supported the notion of a large unitary authority embracing the whole conurbation and some rural areas beyond its urbanised limits — this was very close to the abortive Crossman plan in 1965 when the minister sought to overthrow the proposals of the 1958 Commission.[30] But South Shields preferred to resurrect the 1958 Commission's plan for four most-purpose boroughs and to amend it by turning these into all-purpose unitary authorities. Tynemouth and Gateshead were also unhappy at the prospect of a Newcastle unitary authority, and some other councils in the area preferred a two-tier system with a Tyneside metropolitan county paralleling the structure proposed for the north-west and West Midlands conurbations — several Labour-controlled boroughs and districts were particularly partial to this solution, which, it will be recalled, received the support of the Party's National Executive Committee.

In Greater Manchester there were few ardent supporters of the concept of a new county, but, equally, few were prepared to deny the case for such an authority. Manchester City Council diplomatically kept its reactions in low key, but Salford City Council was bitterly opposed to the recommendation that it should amalgamate with Manchester to form a single metropolitan district. Bury and Rochdale county boroughs were outspoken in their criticism of the proposed marriage between the two. Many Lancashire and Cheshire districts towards the edge of the metropolitan area began to press for their exclusion from it and in Cheshire several of them, including Congleton and Northwich, began talks with the object of putting up a scheme for an additional unitary authority based on Crewe (under the Commission's proposals Crewe would have formed part of the Stoke unit and south Cheshire would, as a result, have become the northern end of the West Midlands region). Fear of domination by Manchester lay at the root of much of the criticism, and this same fear was apparent in areas adjacent to other large cities. When unveiling a scheme for three unitary authorities based on Birmingham, the Black Country, and Stoke-Stafford the Chairman of the Staffordshire County Council was quite clear about this: 'In common with other local authorities we are completely against a metropolitan area dominated by Birmingham.'[31]

Voicing criticism was not difficult; offering practicable alternative schemes posed a much greater problem. By accepting the report 'in principle' the Government had attempted to establish consultations on a fairly narrow front. This was clear when, on 2 July, the Minister wrote to the associations requesting their views on the report. Comments on 'the general structure' would be welcome. In an appendix it was made clear that this meant comment on the *concept* of the unitary authority, rather than on the *application* of this concept. Proposals for extra unitary or metropolitan areas were discussable, along with detailed criticisms of boundaries. But those councils seeking universal two-tier government were taking two gambles: first, that the Government would interpret 'in principle' to cover such an alternative, which seemed unlikely when the Prime Minister was its spokesman, but just possible when some of his colleagues made statements or speeches (notably when Arthur Skeffington accorded the Government complete freedom of action at the autumn party conference). The second gamble concerned the political future of the Government. If it were to lose the next election any alternative to the Redcliffe-Maud plan might well prove acceptable to a new Conservative administration. Lancashire, Cheshire and the West Riding took this gamble and sought an agreed package with sympathetic district councils — usually at the cost of acknowledging that new stronger county districts could be given additional functions over and above those currently exercised by second-tier councils, though with no specific assurances or promises being made. As time went on, however, the opinion polls suggested a Government recovery in popularity, and Cheshire's county clerk attempted to open discussions privately with senior civil servants about a further alternative, an additional unitary authority based on Chester and incorporating a large proportion of the existing county at the expense of Merseyside and Greater Manchester.[32]

The national associations were faced with the same two gambles as those confronting individual councils. The two most important associations, the County Councils Association (CCA) and the Association of Municipal Corporations (AMC), were also faced with a deep division of opinion among their members. For the Urban District Councils Association (UDCA) and the Rural District Councils Association (RDCA) the situation was much more straightforward — they had to oppose the Commission's plan. The UDCA attacked it as destroying the balance of representative local government. At a special meeting to approve the Association's views the deputy chairman said 'deep down, there is in all of us a firm conviction that British representative local government, which has been taken as a model in so many parts of the world, is endangered by the Maud proposals' in probably one of the least rational of statements made during the process of reform.[33]

The RDCA decided not only to oppose the concept of unitary government, but also to launch a massive publicity campaign in an attempt to elicit the support of public opinion.[34] The slogan 'Don't Vote for R. E. Mote' was emblazoned all over the countryside at a cost of £40,000 — it reflected the Association's emphasis on the definition of democracy as equalling smallness. Mr R. E. Mote was a cartoon bureaucrat with his head in the air, ignoring the public he served. The detailed proposals were entitled 'The Democratic Alternative to Maud'. The positive proposals of the Association claimed to build on the concept of the metropolitan area in the hope that this would make them discussable. In fact its two-tier system was quite different in terms of geography, size of second-tier councils (smaller than the 250,000 minimum) and distribution of powers (with education as a county function).

In an effort to keep within the limits of discussable alternatives the CCA claimed to accept the broad principles of the Redcliffe-Maud Report. We have already seen that its members were divided, and the division came through very clearly in its proposals. It made three main points. First, unitary authorities should have a minimum population of 500,000 in order that they might be effective (the smaller ones were judged to be 'totally inadequate'). Second, 'the democratic basis of the unitary authorities must be strengthened by ensuring the greater participation of elected members in the administration of services.' This, said the CCA, could be achieved through the adoption of decentralised administration and district committees (on which unitary authority and local council members would serve) covering parts of unitary areas. Thirdly, a two-tier system should be created to cover the whole of Lancashire, Cheshire, West Riding, Hampshire and possibly other parts of the south-east.[35] The first and last of these proposals were aimed at the unitary authorities of central Lancashire, industrial West Yorkshire, Southampton, Portsmouth, Bedford and East Surrey and would have resulted in new counties much like the old (with the addition of the county boroughs). The second proposal could be interpreted as an attack on the remoteness of unitary authorities and as an olive branch to the associations of district councils. Though the CCA had modified its original evidence to the Commission to the extent that it was now prepared, if necessary, to accept the unitary concept, its proposals when mapped indicated that it had gone a long way towards preserving the interests of its individual members. Their diverse reactions to the report had almost all been accommodated.

In September 1969 the UDCA and RDCA requested informal talks with the CCA in an attempt to reach an agreement. The two districts associations accepted the CCA's olive branch and, as in the discussions in the mid-1950s which ultimately led to the 1958 Act, reached a tripartite agreement on a further set of alternative proposals. They issued a joint statement in November 1969 announcing a scheme for two-tier government everywhere.[36] The CCA's 500,000 minimum population for a top-tier authority was supplemented by the RDCA's plan for districts of 100,000 or more (though this figure might go down to 60,000 — the UDCA's plan — in some areas). The scheme favoured some additional but unspecified metropolitan areas, but the threat to county services through such additional creations was reduced by the suggestion that education be a top-tier function everywhere. The CCA's district committees were retained in the joint scheme. The tripartite agreement represented an astute move on behalf of the three associations. History had shown that joint approaches could be effective — a similar one had been influential in the pre-1958 Act consultation process. The plan went along with the views of many members of the Labour Party that additional metropolitan areas were desirable, views reflected a month later in the NEC report. Emphasis had been placed on the remoteness of giant authorities, and it was known that many MPs were concerned about this. The essential points raised by each association in its individual response had been incorporated. The majority of district councils were disappointed at the proposed size of second-tier units, but not to the extent of rocking the boat: they had been persuaded by events in the summer and autumn of 1969 that their complete survival was only possible if no reform took place, and that total governmental inaction was unlikely.

Division of opinion on the report was greatest among members of the AMC. That association represented all boroughs from the smallest, with populations of little more than 1,000, to the largest cities. The majority of its members were small and medium-sized towns similar in size to urban districts and with reactions close to those of UDCA members. The minority were the large towns, many of whom were content with the report, though others were not. Numerically, then, the association was dominated by elements hostile to the Redcliffe-Maud blueprint, and a resolution in favour of a two-tier system was passed at the 1969 annual conference. But the distribution of power within the Association's executive (where the small boroughs had only limited representation) and the parameters of the debate set by the Prime Minister ensured that the Council of the Association acted against the interests of its junior members (just as it had done in 1966 in an identical situation when formulating its evidence to the Commission).[37]

The attraction of the unitary concept to the AMC was obvious — it was based on the Association's much-valued county borough system, and the Association itself had proposed that such a system be adopted universally as long ago as 1942. Its 1969 reactions were favourable in terms of broad principles: 'The Association accepts the Royal Commission's diagnosis of the present problem and, with certain reservations, the consequent application of the general principles enunciated by the Commission.'[38] The 'certain reservations' turned out to be numerous and potentially fairly far-reaching. First, the minimum population of 250,000 was challenged, and although Derek Senior's blueprint was heavily criticised on grounds of the complexity of its distribution of functions his comments on the case for rather smaller authorities were endorsed. The AMC did not offer a neat alternative population figure. Instead it claimed to be able to divide England into 130-140 'coherent socio-geographic units' which would not be unduly large and inconvenient.[39] The possibility of creating an additional 50-100 unitary authorities was, of course, very acceptable to a similar number of AMC members!

AMC proposals for the division of functions in metropolitan areas were equally clearly based on the self-interest of its members. The aim was to make the metropolitan district as near to a unitary authority as possible. The Commission's distribution of functions gave a number to the county which, the AMC claimed, could be effectively exercised by the districts — notably several aspects of planning, slum clearance and development, transportation and highways. The need to keep education and the social services at district level was emphasised. The adoption of such proposals would have left the county boroughs with the vast majority of their powers as the centres of districts (and many had expressed a preference for universal unitary authorities in their individual reactions), and would have made amalgamation into metropolitan districts much more palatable for the non-county boroughs. For them there was the prospect of having more influence over the provision of important services than under the existing structure, where they were often remote members of large counties based on Preston, Chester, Worcester or Stafford.

Though we have concentrated on the reactions of local authorities and their associations to only the key proposals of the Commission, many of them also reacted to several of the other less central recommendations. Of particular interest was the general acceptance, with reservations, of the local council but the critical response to the notion of indirectly elected regional councils. On the subject of local councils the UDCA was sceptical, seeing the plan as no more than a sop to its members, while the AMC envisaged problems in giving effect to a concept which in principle had merit. In particular the Commission's view that local councils might participate in the running of some parts of major services was seen to be undesirable. It would 'detract from the standing and efficacy of the unitary authorities'.[40] The use of existing council areas, especially in the case of the large towns, was also questionable. Instead the AMC proposed the creation of 'Community Trusts' staffed by unitary authority officers. Later the Association produced further proposals jointly with the National Association of Parish Councils — one of the most unlikely of inter-association alliances.

The need for regional councils was accepted by the AMC and the CCA, but only if such bodies were consultative rather than executive. In the aftermath of the report there was, in fact, little debate about this particular proposal. The Commission on the Constitution was currently reviewing the possibility of devolution, which made proposals for strong regions more or less *sub judice* unless given in evidence to that Commission. The Redcliffe-Maud brand of regions did not seem central to the report and the recommendations had little impact — though occasionally they were attacked as 'undemocratic' because of the proposals for indirect elections. The Liberal Party, for example, spent a good deal of time at its 1969 annual conference on this point, perhaps because it had no firm line on the central issues of unitary and metropolitan authority models.

The Government received more than 2,000 comments on the Redcliffe-Maud Report,[41] a number close to that received by the Commission following its public request for evidence in 1966. As well as the views of councils and their associations, there were also observations from several of the hundred or more other bodies with an interest in local government. Few challenged the report as strongly as the Council for the Preservation of Rural England, which openly criticised the principle of councils embracing town and country on the grounds that the growing interdependence of the two and the growth of commuter travel and suburbanisation made it all the more important to distinguish between the identity and character of each. Professional bodies tended to restrict their attention to the proposals for their particular service. Often they mirrored the local authority associations in having members from a wide range of size and type of authority. The Association of Chief Education Officers, for example, included virtually all education officers and could not easily decide on the appropriate size of an education authority, or on whether the service should be at top-tier or second-tier level in the proposed metropolitan areas. Various sets of proposals affected the status or ambitions of individual members of the Society in diverse ways. Such difficulties led to most professional bodies prevaricating in 1969. When the Government produced clear proposals to which it was committed, the time for action would come, and the professional associations reached the peak of their activity in the 1971-2 period when reacting to a definite and detailed set of Government plans.

The 'Missing Debate'
All these groups of people — civil servants, politicans, councils and their associations, and professional and other bodies — had one thing in common, a clear vested interest in the issue of local government reform. The public, too, had an interest, for councils provided a wide range of public services and spent large sums of constituents' money, whether collected through the rates or through central taxation systems. But in 1969 public reaction to the Redcliffe-Maud Report seemed slight.

Fifty or a hundred years ago a set of proposals as radical as those of the commissioners would have led to a torrent of letters in *The Times*. In 1969 there was only one in the immediate post-report period. The 'Don't Vote for R. E. Mote' campaign was the one major nationwide attempt to elicit public support. Although it became quite well known, there is little evidence of it leading to mass pressure on Governments and MPs. Most people were apparently content to leave it to their councillors to represent their points of view, and the national press scarcely reported a single public meeting to discuss the report. Academics gave their lectures when asked, but the author, for one, detected little in the way of a concerted reaction among the audiences.* Public opinion may have been happy with the existing structure of local government

*There was criticism of proposed amalgamations, but, in most areas, little sign that this would be organised in an attempt to make an impact on MPs and the Government.

(57 per cent told Redcliffe-Maud's survey team that they favoured 'no change' and a further 20 per cent didn't know or didn't care)[42] and wary of suggestions that improvements would result from change, but it did not seem prepared to fight for its beliefs. Again, at a later stage, when there were definite Government proposals on the table, public opinion became vocal in a few areas such as Poynton (Cheshire) and Great Ayton (North Riding). Typically, these were small communities at the edge of a proposed new authority and anxious to move the boundary from one side of their area to the other.

To be fair, public response could hardly be expected. Surveys had shown massive public ignorance of the existing organisation of local government. For example in 1964 in a survey for the (Maud) Committee on the Management of Local Government, 26 per cent of electors could not name a single service provided by their borough or district council. For county council services the figure was a staggering 49 per cent. One voter in five thought the town clerk was elected (and a further 23 per cent didn't know).[43] In 1969 the Redcliffe-Maud survey revealed that about one in three thought the hospital and electricity services were provided by local authorities.[44] Any public expression of support for or concern with the Commision's proposals would not have been based on a close knowledge of the topic.

Journalistic comment on the proposals was also limited. After the initial and generally indecisive editorials, *The Times* and the *Guardian* provided little for their readers apart from frequent reports of the reactions of the proximate decision-makers. The *Guardian* had leading articles about local councils[45] (by Lady Sharp, a commissioner) and about the 'R. E. Mote' campaign (or, rather, about its author — a local journalist in West Sussex). *The Times* published a major article by J. K. Boynton, Clerk of Cheshire County Council, questioning many aspects of the proposals though not entirely condemning them.[46] Jane Morton in *New Society* contrasted the report with that of the (Wheatley) Royal Commission on Local Government in Scotland (which unveiled a two-tier plan in September 1969) in a piece entitled 'Commissions in Conflict'.[47] The journal had, within a week of publication of the report, produced first reactions from three academics to the report's geography, to the plan for local councils, and to the political effects of the changes in terms of party control of councils.[48] By no stretch of imagination could it be said that a clear line of approach came out of these journalistic reactions, though they and the academic reactions pointed clearly to some of the weaknesses of the report.

A final 'missing debate' lay in the almost complete lack of

public discussion about Derek Senior's alternative. The local authority associations attacked the proposal for a complex distribution of functions (though the AMC supported the geographical analysis of the existence of 140 or so cohesive areas). Individual councils sometimes liked the second-tier areas, but rarely those of the thirty-five regions. Probably few people read the memorandum of dissent thoroughly and there was no neat summary of the proposals. The Commission had achieved yet another 'first' in persuading the Government to allow it to publish, as a separate Command Paper, a shortened version of its report, but this contained less than two pages of explanation of the Senior plan.[49] Though Derek Senior himself spoke at several conferences and meetings, he was unable to generate much support. After publication of the February 1970 White Paper his memorandum of dissent was scarcely ever mentioned. Only in a negative sense can it be argued that the Senior plan had some impact in that it stimulated reaction to the 'unitary principle' through its advocacy of a two-tier system.

Meaningful Consultations?
Despite the Government's claim[50] that it had 'carefully weighed the views expressed in the consultations', there is little evidence to suggest that the reactions discussed above were influential. The February 1970 White Paper endorsed the main proposals of the Commission, though three major amendments were proposed. The creation of additional metropolitan areas in the West Riding and in South Hampshire, the removal of responsibility for education from metropolitan district to county level, and the concept of district committees in unitary areas were all ideas which could be traced to the reactions and proposals of the CCA. On the other hand the transfer of education had deeper origins. It had been mentioned as a likely area of controversy by the Prime Minister when he welcomed the report in June, and endorsed in the December 1969 NEC report. The creation of additional metropolitan areas had also been proposed by the Labour Party's National Executive Committee. Only the plan for district committees seemed to have definitely emerged from the 2,000 or so documents which had been received in Whitehall.

The district committee scheme was the most interesting of the three changes in that it reflected the buffeting which the report had received from all sides over the potential remoteness of the large unitary authorities. The Government was having to contend with a great deal of use of the word 'democracy' in this context. Many of its own back-benchers had joined with Opposition members and with outside groups like the RDCA in criticising the geography, size and lack of accessibility of many of the Commission's units, particularly those in the more sparsely populated areas. In his *Times* article Boynton had spelled this out bluntly: 'The mere fact that the unitary system works for the 81 square miles of Birmingham does not mean that it will work when transplanted to the 2,227 square miles of Exeter and Devon.'[51] He took the extreme example of the largest new unit, but an appendix to the Commission's report listed the proposed units in order of size and showed that eighteen covered more than 1,000 square miles and only twenty less than 500 square miles.[52]

Up to a point the Commission itself had acknowledged this problem, implicitly if not explicitly. Its recommendation that local councils should have 'powers to take part in some of the main local government services, responsibility for which must be exercised primarily by the main authorities and in parts of their areas exclusively by them' was a recognition that useful knowledge might not always be available to the unitary authority.[53] The Commission went on to speak of housing improvement work which 'might perhaps be better done by the larger local councils than by the much bigger unitary authorities, since it needs both local knowledge and local determination' and development schemes where 'any local council should be able to carry out local improvements of little or no interest to the wider area'.[54]

We have already noted that these proposals could be interpreted as undermining the neat simplicity of the all-purpose approach. The Government accepted this criticism as valid,* but for it to deny any local council involvement in the administration of major services without proposing an alternative would have increased the protests of those who were criticising the unitary concept as 'undemocratic', and their number included many Government supporters. The creation of additional unitary authorities might have been one solution, but this would have entailed a move away from the 250,000 minimum population recommended by the Commission. We saw in Chapter II that there was no clear evidence to support the figure. This meant that it was convenient for the Government to endorse it and foreclose debate. If it really wanted to introduce legislation, a reopening of the complex and insoluble question of population size was something to be avoided at all costs. The result was certain to be an interminable and indecisive debate during which the reform momentum could be lost.

The value of the period of consultation should not be judged solely in terms of its impact on the contents of the White Paper.

*When introducing the report in June 1969 the Prime Minister referred to the plan as being 'three-tier'. In its July letter requesting observations on the report the Ministry of Housing and Local Government described it as 'a system at three levels'.

Its greatest importance was in giving an indication to Government and Opposition of the extent to which reform legislation was politically feasible, and of the major areas of controversy where pressure could be expected to be continuously exerted during the period between White Paper and Bill, and during the passage of legislation through Parliament. That further changes, usually in the form of concessions to powerful lobbyists, would be made could scarcely be in doubt given the inevitable complexity of the legislation and the wide range of interested parties. The reform of London government provided a perfect precedent: there concessions had been made on both boundaries and functions.[55]

Boundaries were once again a sensitive issue, though one where the national associations did not normally play a leadership role when particular cases were involved. The associations concentrated on general principles, individual authorities on the detailed local application of potential legislation (though councils also expressed views on principles). In many localities pressures for boundary changes were apparent — particularly towards the outer edges of the proposed metropolitan areas. These were primarily Conservative Party strongholds where a Labour Government might be able to resist major alterations, but there were also many traditionally Socialist areas protesting at the proposals, and here concessions might prove necessary. Salford, for example, strongly resented the plan to merge it with Manchester. In the north-east there was a strong Labour lobby in favour of metropolitan area status for Tyneside. Even if Labour won the coming election its majority could be quite small and pressure from groups of back-benchers might in those circumstances be effective. The Government recognised the situation, and the White Paper accepted the Commission's unitary and metropolitan areas (plus an additional two of the latter) in broad terms. There were to be further consultations on the details of the map, and Crossland spoke of these taking about a year. But the agenda would be restricted to detail — the Government was not prepared to contemplate the division of a unitary area into two (though amalgamations were possible), nor would the creation of extra metropolitan areas be open to negotiation.[56]

Discussion about functions did not really get off the ground until the period after publication of the White Paper except, perhaps, on the question of responsibility for education. The allocation of functions in unitary areas was, of course, absolutely clear and this probably helped to delay the debate. In metropolitan areas there were certain to be arguments about details, particularly in cases where responsibility for a service might be divided between county and district. But the education service, which accounted for more than 40 per cent of all local authority expenditure, was the centre of the main argument of principle. The Prime Minister himself raised the matter when presenting the report to Parliament, which suggests that there were members of the Government and senior civil servants who were disturbed at the plan to create numerous small and financially weak metropolitan district education authorities.* The local authority associations took different views, reflecting their areas of interest, but there were no constructive additions to the discussion points raised in the Commission's report. Later there were, with the establishment of a 'Campaign to Save Education in the Conurbations' whose aim was to persuade the by then Conservative Government to implement Labour's policy of making the service a top-tier function.

During this period from June 1969 to February 1970 the debate was again concerned with the concepts of democracy and efficiency. The Commission claimed to have recommended a system which paid attention to both, but critics were quick to point to flaws. Planners, for example, were unhappy at the limited geographical size of many of the unitary authorities — particularly in areas like central Lancashire, west Yorkshire and south Hampshire where planning problems clearly affected a group of proposed unitary authorities. Close collaboration between new councils would be essential but could not be guaranteed (especially as the Commission's regional councils were to have so few teeth). Such areas were, in one way or another, under severe pressure. Parts of Lancashire (around Preston with a new town in the offing) and all south Hampshire were either expanding or about to expand. North-east Lancashire and west Yorkshire had different problems — of dereliction and decay, and of a dwindling industrial base. The pattern of unitary authorities could be criticised for isolating such areas and leaving them to fend for themselves. Some educationalists saw this as a problem for their service too, and Longland's proposal to amalgamate several such unitary authorities received support from them.

The alternative criticism was that the proposals created unnecessarily large authorities for the effective provision of certain services — local amenities, highway maintenance (where a research study for the Commission had found the small councils to be economical,[57] though, of course, quality of provision could not

*This had also been the case in London, where pressure from the London Teachers Associaton and from the London County Council for the preservation of the LCC education service and opposition to its division through the creation of borough LEAs had found support in the Ministry and the Government, and had led to the creation of the unique Inner London Education Authority. See G. Rhodes, *The Government of London: the Struggle for Reform* (Weidenfeld & Nicolson, 1970), pp. 96, 103-4, 106-10.

be measured), housing management and other examples were quoted. We have seen that the Commission itself fuelled this criticism with its comments about the desirability of local council involvement in these areas.

The reactions to the report in terms of its effect on democracy centred to a large extent around attitudes about smallness and remoteness. This had an appeal to the general public, particularly when it could be portrayed in terms of the loss of ancient dignities like the mayoralty and other ceremonial aspects of local government, or in terms of a 'take-over' by a larger neighbour. But there was also a real case to answer. The creation of physically extremely large areas would alter patterns of representation very dramatically and many MPs and civil servants acknowledged this (MPs in their speeches and statements, civil servants in their written and oral evidences to the Commission in 1966-7). The Hill-Wallis note of reservation also had its supporters.

What did emerge in the 1969 consultations was a new approach to the concept of 'democracy', and one which the Conservatives later utilised when selling reform to councils and their associations. This was an emphasis on the totality of powers of councils, and on the relationship between strengthened local government and the relaxation of central controls. The Prime Minister said on 11 June 1969 that reform 'would open the way for more devolution in decision-making on issues which at present fall within the decision of central government'. The Commission had called for this and he saw it as a real possibility, 'particularly in the case of the conurbations'.[58] However, the local authority associations were not asked specifically to comment on this when consultations were formally opened by Greenwood in the circular letter on 2 July 1969, and the February 1970 White Paper made only one or two specific proposals (though the statements of intent in it were very positive — 'the Government believe unequivocally in greater freedom for local authorities within the framework of national policies laid down by Parliament').[59]

Commitment to this kind of 'devolution' widened the debate about democracy. That debate had focussed on existing councils and traditional levels of responsibility in accordance with the Commission's terms of reference, whereas new authorities would (or might) have rather more sovereignty. Meanings of democracy associated with service delivery — accountability and responsibility — became of greater importance in this new context, and the link between democracy and efficiency became more explicit. Greater freedom of action for local authorities had to be placed alongside the concern with inaccessibility and remoteness. If the Government really meant what it said (and sceptics recalled a long history of statements of intent about reductions in central controls which had resulted in little positive action) then the case for reform was that bit stronger on ground of both democracy and efficiency. In the pre-White Paper period this debate did not get under way. 1970 dawned with the emphasis still on the links between democracy and accessibility or size.

NOTES

1 Royal Commission on Local Government in England 1966-9, *Report*, Cmnd 4040 (HMSO, 1969), vol. 1.
2 *Ibid.*, para. 253.
3 *Ibid.*, para. 243.
4 *Ibid.*, paras 255, 290-2, 324-46, 358.
5 *Ibid.*, Ch. 9.
6 *Ibid.*, Ch. 10.
7 *Cmnd 4040*, vol. 2, paras 39, 44 and 52.
8 *Cmnd 4040*, vol. 1, paras 279-80.
9 *Ibid.*, pp. 148-60.
10 Royal Commission on Local Government in England 1966-9, *Report*, Cmnd 4040 (HMSO, 1969), vol. 2.
11 There are several recent examples which illustrate this. One was the dissenting volume produced by two members of the Kilbrandon Commission (Lord Crowther-Hunt and Professor A. T. Peacock): Royal Commission on the Constitution 1969-73, *Volume II — Memorandum of Dissent*, Cmnd 5460-1 (HMSO, 1973).
12 *Cmnd 4040*, vol. 2, para. 2.
13 *Ibid.*, para. 16.
14 *Ibid.*, paras 361-70.
15 RCLGE, *Written Evidence of H. M. Treasury* (HMSO, 1967), para. 5.
16 RCLGE, *Written Evidence of the Department of Economic Affairs* (HMSO, 1967), para. 14.
17 RCLGE, *Minutes of Evidence 1* (HMSO, 1967), Q. 66.
18 *Hansard (Commons)*, vol. 784, cols 1461-4 (11 June 1969).
19 *Guardian*, 8 July 1969, 'Enter Maud in Strange Haste'.
20 J. M. Lee and B. Wood, *The Scope of Local Initiative: A Study of Cheshire County Council 1961-74* (Martin Robertson, 1974), p. 78.
21 *New Society*, 19 June 1969, pp. 951-2.
22 The Government made much use of this promise during parliamentary debates on constituency boundary changes. See Janet P. Morgan, *The House of Lords and the Labour Government 1964-70* (OUP, 1975), Ch. 6.
23 *Guardian*, 30 September 1969.
24 *Guardian*, 4 December 1969.
25 Labour Party, *Principles for Local Government Reform*, (Labour Party, 1969).
26 *Guardian*, 22 September 1969.
27 *Guardian*, 11 October 1969.
28 Lee and Wood, *op. cit.*, p. 81.
29 *Mid-Sussex Times*, 19 June 1969.
30 See above p. 18.
31 *Guardian*, 18 September 1969.
32 Lee and Wood, *op. cit.*, pp. 78-9.
33 *Guardian*, 23 October 1969.

34 RDCA, *The Democratic Alternative to Maud* (RDCA, 1969).
   For an interesting profile of the creator of the 'R. E. Mote' campaign, see *Guardian,* 29 November 1969.
35 CCA, *Memorandum of Views on the Report of the Commission,* (CCA, 1969), paras 77, 80, 87.
36 J. Brand, *Local Government Reform in England 1888-1974* (Croom Helm, 1974), pp. 125-6.
37 *Ibid.,* pp. 89-90, 127-8.
38 *Municipal Review,* Supplement, November 1969, Part III, para. 6.
39 *Ibid.,* para. 11.
40 *Ibid.,* para. 43.
41 Ministry of Local Government and Regional Planning, *Reform of Local Government in England, Cmnd 4276* (HMSO, 1970), Appendix A, para. 1.
42 RCLGE, *Research Study 9 — Community Attitudes Survey: England* (by Research Services Ltd) (HMSO, 1969), pp. 127-9.
43 Ministry of Housing and Local Government, *Report of the Committee on the Mangement of Local Government* (HMSO, 1967), vol. III, Ch. 1.
44 RCLGE, *Research Study 9, op. cit.*, 83-5.
45 'Parish Pump in the 70s', *Guardian,* 16 December 1969.
46 'After Redcliffe-Maud: Looking Beyond Self Interest', *The Times,* 22 August 1969.
47 *New Society,* 2 October 1969.
48 Michael Steed, Professor Bryan Keith-Lucas and Professor Peter Hall, *New Society,* 19 June 1969.
49 RCLGE, *Local Government Reform: Short Version of the Report, Cmnd 4039* (HMSO, 1969).
50 Cmnd 4276, *op. cit.*, para. 9.
51 *The Times,* 22 August 1969.
52 *Cmnd 4040,* vol. 1, p. 308.
53 *Ibid.,* para. 386.
54 *Ibid.,* paras 387, 389.
55 For details see G. Rhodes, *The Government of London: The Struggle for Reform* (Weidenfeld & Nicolson, 1970), Appendices 2, 3.
56 Cmnd 4276, *op. cit.,* paras 36, 39.
57 RCLGE, *Research Studies 3 — Economics of Scale in Local Government Services* (by S. P. Gupta and J. P. Hutton, University of York) (HMSO, 1968).
58 *Hansard (Commons),* vol. 784, cols 1462, 1471 (11 June 1969).
59 Cmnd 4276, *op, cit.,* para. 60.

Chapter IV

THE RESPONSE OF TWO GOVERNMENTS,

FEBRUARY 1970-FEBRUARY 1971

The pattern of responses to the Redcliffe-Maud Report — the use of arguments about democracy and efficiency to disguise a concern for self-preservation and motives of self-interest — continued to establish itself in the 1970-1 period. There continued to be no real lobby in support of the report, nor was there a build-up of strong pressure against any reform whatsoever. The debate continued to be about 'how' to reform rather than about 'whether'.

The lack of a pro-report lobby is common. After it completes its work, a commission or an advisory committee normally disbands (there are a few exceptions by way of more permanent commissions like the Royal Commission on Pollution), and this makes it difficult for the members to offer leadership collectively to a campaign for implementation of the proposals. In any case we saw in Chapter II that the contents of a report are likely to represent a compromise of views and that many commissioners will find parts of it more acceptable to them as individuals than are other parts: few will support unreservedly the whole package. Further, a report is likely to be attacked from all sides. Radical reformers will say that the proposals are insufficiently progressive; traditionalists will argue that the report goes too far in its call for change. A reform lobby which supports the principle of change may be able to absorb these varied attacks by avoiding too specific a commitment. One which has nailed its colours clearly to a detailed scheme is less able to rebuff criticism.

More surprising was the absence of an organised anti-reform lobby. There is no doubt that large numbers of individuals were against the changes proposed in their local area — either instinctively because of the apparent effect on traditional local customs and ties, or because of a personal interest in local government, as a councillor, an officer, or a member of a closely related body such as a civic society or ratepayers' association. That this hostility was never organised reflected to a large extent the atmosphere created by the Government in 1969. Change was in the air, the report was accepted 'in principle', and the intended timetable seemed a short one.* In addition, the leadership of the national associations was important. Although all four were unhappy with the report, they could not ignore it. Nor could they easily turn upside-down their 1966 policies of supporting reform in principle. Though they could express opposition to the specific proposals of the Commission, they were in no position to head an anti-reform campaign even if they had wanted to do so. Opposition to any change remained fragmented and completely ineffective.

The attitude of the Conservative Opposition was also important in this context. In 1970 the move to reform could easily have come either to a complete standstill or at least to a temporary halt following the June general election and the defeat of the Labour Government. But shadow minister Peter Walker had worked hard on the issue after the report appeared in June 1969. We saw in Chapter III that he approached it with a fairly open mind. It was not until after he took office as head of the new giant Department of the Environment that he produced a detailed policy of his own. But his actions in the run-up to the election paralleled those of the Government in that he, too, indicated a broad commitment to reform. An atmosphere conducive to reform was one created by both major parties.

The Labour Government White Paper[1]

The specific proposals contained in the February 1970 White Paper were touched upon in Chapter III. The Commission's areas were accepted with two modifications — the creation of additional metropolitan areas in the West Riding and in south Hampshire. The division of functions in the metropolitan areas was accepted with one important modification, the proposal that the county, and not the district, be the education (and, as a result, also the rating) authority. The Commission's proposed indirectly elected provincial councils had been overtaken by events with the creation of the (Crowther) Commission on the Constitution, and the Government planned to await that report before considering further this part of the Redcliffe-Maud package. Local councils were accepted, but would not participate in the running of major services. Instead district committees would advise on local service provision along the lines suggested by the CCA.

These were the most important details. In addition the Government, in the White Paper, made further statements designed

*On 8 June 1969, in *The Sunday Times*, John Whale predicted that 'a familiar fate awaits the report ... a brief period of argument will be followed by a long and probably permanent period of Governmental neglect.' He did not return to that theme!

once again to restrict the discussion, just as it had successfully done after June 1969. The 'great mass' of evidence to the Commission had shown 'that an overwhelming body of opinion . . . believed that fundamental structural changes were required'[2] (a myth which was taken up later by the Conservative Government and which made it hard to oppose change during private consultations and public debates at national level). Without the creation of large enough units local government's 'power must diminish, and with it the power of local democracy',[3] a threat which at that time was very apparent with the publication of a second Green Paper on the National Health Service within days of the appearance of the local government White Paper.[4] The first Green Paper (1968), it will be recalled, put local authority control of the NHS as one possibility among several. This second discussion paper firmly ruled out this prospect and plumped for the creation of appointed health authorities, though their boundaries would be coterminous with those of new local authorities.

The White Paper was to be followed by a further round of consultations on a range of topics such as electoral systems, allowances payable to councillors, detailed central controls (with a positive Government commitment to reduce these), and the size of councils. But consultations on boundaries would be restricted to a set agenda.[5] First, no further metropolitan areas could be proposed. Second, the pattern of metropolitan districts, as well as their detailed boundaries, was discussable (though the Commission's proposed minimum size of 250,000 was Government policy). Third, proposals for additional unitary authorities through a division of those recommended by the Commission were not discussable, though a merger of two unitary authorities could be contemplated. The exact siting of boundaries was also open to negotiation, but the outer boundaries of the metropolitan areas would, apart from details, be retained: 'The Government are satisfied that the Commission were right to draw wide boundaries for these areas.'[6]

Finally, as regards boundaries, 'lengthy inquiries based on forensic procedures would not be appropriate.'[7] Consultations and public conferences would not be excessively formal and could not be used to reopen arguments about the main structure. The Government considered reform to be a matter or urgency, and intended to legislate in 1971-2. Consultations had to be thorough but could not be slow, and delaying tactics of those hostile to the White Paper would not be brooked.

Given that the White Paper did not dramatically depart from the Commission's proposals, most of the reactions to it were predictable. Most councils were treated in the proposals just as they had been by the Commission. Hampshire County Council was, to an extent, reprieved in that the proposed south Hampshire metropolitan area covered the bulk of the county (though not the Basingstoke-Aldershot and Christchurch-Lymington areas), but the new West Yorkshire metropolitan area bore comparatively little resemblance to the existing West Riding county. County boroughs within the West Riding were less than delighted at the prospect of no longer forming the core of a unitary authority: 'Maud has been jilted' was the *Huddersfield Daily Examiner*'s headline over a long critical article by a prominent town councillor.[8] Elsewhere the only noticeable difference from the reactions of individual councils to the Commission's report in summer 1969 was that the terminology became more extreme as legislation loomed nearer.

The national associations also became more worked up. The CCA welcomed the addition of extra two-tier areas, the concept of district committees, the allocation of education to the metropolitan county and the policy of resisting any proposals for the division of unitary authorities. But the fragmentation of central Lancashire into four unitary authorities, the wide-flung boundaries of metropolitan areas resulting 'in the domination of a number of small towns and rural areas by enormous urban interests', and the removal of the health service ('inconsistent with the Government's stated intention to strengthen local democracy') were all deeply regretted.[9] While district committees were acceptable, the association considered that the submission which it had earlier made jointly with the UDCA and RDCA proposing elected district councils merited further exploration. Problems over the allocation of functions were admitted, but the two-tier concept, it was claimed, would sustain 'a viable system of local democracy'. The association would be 'disappointed' if this alternative was not 'carefully explored' by the Government and the associations during consultations on the role of district committees.

Of the main associations the CCA had been given most concessions by the Labour Government. At first sight this is rather surprising, for the association represents areas of traditional Conservative strength. However, it was noted earlier that on closer examination only the district committee concept is traceable solely to the CCA. Many educationalists, the Labour Party NEC, and, almost certainly, several civil servants within the Department of Education and Science were unhappy at the prospect of fairly small and, equally important, financially poor metropolitan district education authorities. The additional metropolitan areas were a response to planning and development problems rather than to the desire of the two shire counties to remain in existence. The decision not to discuss divisions of unitary authorities into two was designed, first, to underpin the acceptance of 250,000 as a minimum size and, second, to prevent long-drawn-out discussions on the AMC's alternative of around 130 smaller unitary authorities. If the Government was to proceed reasonably quickly it could not afford to include the proposals of any major association on its consultative agenda. This was particularly true in the case of the one association traditionally dominated by Labour councillors from the large cities. As it happens, in 1970 the vast majority of AMC members were Conservative, but this situation was unlikely to be permanent and local electoral swings to Labour were a near-certainty in May 1970 and May 1971 — the pre-legislation period — as seats which the party had lost on dramatic, indeed, in some cases, incredible swings in 1967 and 1968 again became vacant.

The White Paper, then, ruled out of order the preferred alternatives of all the main associations. For the AMC leaders this created problems. If the association continued to press for many additional unitary authorities it risked sterile consultations in which no concessions were achieved. But in 1969 it had had a good deal of trouble internally in its search for an alternative. To reopen the search would lead to further difficulties for its officers and leaders, and the chances of finding proposals which were both acceptable to members and discussable under the terms of the White Paper were slim. Much of the AMC's reaction to the 1970 White Paper was, as result, couched in fairly negative terms.

At a special meeting of the Association on 12 March 1970 the Chairman of the General Purposes Committee (Alderman — later Sir — Frank Marshall of Leeds) strongly condemned the White Paper in his opening remarks introducing a draft 'memorandum of comments'. The mood of the meeting was hostile and he sensed the need to accept an amendment strengthening the Association's criticisms by saying: 'It may be the view of some at this meeting that the wording of the paper is not sufficiently strong. I suppose we could have put in some more condemnatory expressions of disgust at some of the proposals included in the White Paper; we could have used more extreme language.'[10] He urged members to 'submit alternative patterns of new authorities' to the Government, and to resist attempts to amalgamate unitary authorities so that they come to resemble existing counties. He later accepted an amendment which produced a more strongly worded paragraph of conclusions condemning the White Paper for being 'on many matters quite vague and unspecific', for proposing authorities which did not bear 'some reasonable regard for the concept of "locality"', and for creating an 'administrative muddle' through the district committee concept. The reduction of many great cities to a status inferior to that of an existing non-county borough was described as 'astonishing' and the local council proposals were 'unsatisfactory and absurd'. The AMC scheme for a two-level system of provinces and most-purpose authorities was again put forward as a preferable solution.

Much of the AMC's memorandum was concentrated on the absence of any Government proposals for provincial councils. Without these the AMC's case for many additional unitary authorities was weakened, for it (and, as it pointed out, the Redcliffe-Maud Commission) relied on provincial councils to co-ordinate the work of the unitary authorities, to assemble a strategic plan, and to facilitate the joint provision of certain highly specialised services where a unitary authority could not be self-sufficient. Though provincial councils were not discussable under the terms of the White Paper, the AMC nevertheless resolved to 'organise on an area basis consultations designed to evolve a pattern of two-level administration' along the lines of its original evidence to the Commission.[11] As Alderman Marshall pointed out to delegates 'what we do know is that legislation will depend on the next Parliament. What we do not know is what Government will then be in power.' The associations and individual councils had to plan a campaign which included two contrasting sets of tactics, depending on the result of the coming general election. Alternative models of reform could not be ditched, though they could not easily be unveiled in the February 1970 climate.

The Conservative Opposition: a Commitment Emerges

We have already seen that the Conservative Party took no firm line on the Redcliffe-Maud Report during the summer and autumn of 1969. On the other hand, the issue of local government reform did occupy much of the time of shadow minister Mr Peter Walker, and he attended a series of regional conferences with councillors and local party activists. Privately he showed signs of being anxious to introduce legislation should the Conservatives be returned to power — at least that was the impression given to a deputation from Cheshire County Council in August 1969.[12] At that private meeting Walker's concern for the future of county government was also apparent — a not unnatural situation given Conservative strength in the shires.

There was little in the way of a public commitment to reform from the Conservatives until the House of Commons debated the White Paper on 18 February 1970. Parliamentary debates are often described in uncomplimentary terms by academic observers, and the notion of Parliament as being little more than a rubber stamp runs through many texts and appears on many examination papers for discussion. A feature of the process of local government reform was the important role played by parliamentary debates. We shall see in Chapter VI that the process of legislation was a lengthy and tortuous one during which MPs obtained a number of concessions and amendments to the Government's proposals. The importance of the White Paper debate lay in the contribution of Walker and in the varied nature of back-bench opinion which was revealed.

First, back-bench opinion: the Government decided that the motion to be debated should be to 'take note' of the White Paper. This avoided any possibility of a vote at the end of the debate, especially as the Conservatives decided against tabling an amendment (a Liberal amendment rejected the White Paper on several grounds, but was not selected for debate by the Speaker). It allowed members freedom to take up any aspects of the White Paper, and this they duly did. Of the seventeen who spoke only four (all Labour) accepted the proposals, and two of the four expressed doubts about parts of the package. Two other members gave qualified support in terms of the implications for their areas. Eleven spoke against the plan.[13]

A simple division of six for and eleven against would have suggested that the Government had neatly polarised opinion. In fact the polarisation was anything but neat. Four of the eleven appeared to favour the unitary concept, two of the six did not: at the most eight of the seventeen speakers seemed, therefore, to support this crucial notion of the all-purpose authority. The rest favoured two-tier government, but in almost every conceivable shape or form. One supported Derek Senior's report, two wanted strong provincial councils, four expressed a preference for a modified status quo. Party membership meant little in all this — supporters for any particular viewpoint might be from either side of the House. The Government no doubt expected strong criticism. But at the end of the day it must have felt reasonably satisfied — opposition from all sides there was, but on the Labour side there were few signs of it being organised in such a way that it might come to present a united front. At least four of the Labour speakers made blatant 'constituency speeches', criticising the proposals for their particular area, and this was the right time for such an approach as they did not have to follow these criticisms up with an abstention or a vote against the whip.

Peter Walker's speech required close study. Immediate press comment tended to miss the significance of it. This was partly because it inevitably contained a lot of unconstructive criticism, questioning and opposition, and partly because the positive proposals within it were scattered about rather than in one place. A line by line examination of the sort undertaken immediately by the associations and by many council clerks revealed a series of statements which together constituted the clear beginnings of a commitment to an alternative set of proposals.

Like so many later ministerial speeches by Walker on the subject, this one opened with the vision of stronger local government. This became a major selling point in later debates on the Conservative White Paper and the subsequent legislation. In this first major speech comment was restricted to criticism of additional central controls recently imposed or threatened in the housing and education fields. The Government was attacked for claiming in theory to support a policy of increasing council powers while actively reducing them in practice, and Walker stated that this was 'the main division between the Opposition and the Government' (words which were to rebound on him during Conservative Government actions on housing rents and on primary school milk in 1970-2).[14]

On local government areas, Walker made a number of points at separate intervals. Collectively they spelled out a two-tier system with much smaller metropolitan counties. Perhaps because of the intense activities of the Lancashire and Cheshire county councils he chose to illustrate some of his remarks by looking at the north-west: 'I concede the need for the creation of major metropolitan areas which bring a reality to the boundaries of the major conurbations, but beyond that I do not believe that it will be to the benefit of the people concerned to break up authorities such as Cheshire and Lancashire, with their considerable resources.'[15] He went on to advocate a second-tier everywhere and a similar pattern all over the country: 'There are functions in which it is essential to retain some sensible basis of government nearer to the people than is envisaged in the unitary authority.' But neither the local council nor the district committee could perform this role — the White Paper plan for the latter was vague with many unanswered questions: as to the former 'we must ensure that the bottom tier has worthwhile functions to perform and I reject the concept of local councils as envisaged in the White Paper.'

The beginnings of a policy were there. Equally important was a public commitment to action. 'If there is a change of Government we would wish to proceed with a sensible local government reform in the early period of such a new Government' concluded Mr Walker.[16]

Undoubtedly these alternative proposals were very much the work of Mr Walker himself rather than the outcome of lengthy collective discussions by shadow ministers or of the deliberations of a policy group such as had been in action in a number of policy areas during the party's period of opposition. Mr Chataway's concluding speech for the Opposition added nothing at all to the Walker blueprint, nor did the speeches a fortnight later in the House of Lords by Lord Brooke and Earl Jellicoe. Local government reform was Mr Walker's 'baby' and his growing status within the party ensured that it became a priority. Ten days later he repeated his pledges to the party's annual local government conference and received cheers when he once again promised to transfer more decision-making power from Whitehall.[17] In June the election manifesto repeated the policy of introducing 'a sensible reform', a phrase which was retained in the Queen's Speech. It was only when, as Secretary of State, Walker was supported by several junior ministers that responsibility for dealing with local government reform began to be more widely shared. Later Graham Page and Michael Heseltine helped Walker to pilot the legislation through the Commons.

Until the June 1970 General Election consultations continued on the basis of the White Paper. A Circular in March outlined the points on which discussion was possible, but added nothing to the White Paper proposals.[18] Mr Crosland, however, did appear to waver a little on two occasions, and this gave the AMC the impression that perhaps, after all, an alternative pattern of many additional unitary authorities was discussable. In the White Paper debate he stated that 'if a case is made for a different pattern of unitary areas in any particular part of the country, we shall consider that also', though this remark was obscured by an unhelpful intervention from Mr Eric Heffer asking whether this meant that there could be all-purpose authorities in a metropolitan area.[19] A parliamentary question on 3 March received a reply suggesting again that new patterns could be considered, and this was confirmed when the AMC met ministers.[20] On the other hand the statements that no divisions of the proposed unitary authorities could be contemplated also remained firmly on the record in both White Paper and Circular.

How far any alternative proposals like those of the AMC would have got in the course of discussions with Crosland and his civil servants we shall never know. The calling of a General Election towards the end of May nipped the new round of consultations in the bud before they had really got off the ground. Councils and associations had tabled their views but these were destined for dark and dusty pigeon-holes. The Conservatives took office on 19 June 1970. Prime Minister Heath quickly appointed Walker as Minister of Housing and Local Government (by the end of 1970 he had become Secretary of State for the Environment as a result of Heath's major reorganisation of Government Departments. The new Department became responsible for transport and public works as well as for housing, planning, public health, and local government.)

New Minister, New Agenda
Councils, groups and associations, as well as MPs and civil servants, were now faced with an entirely new situation. A feature of the June 1969-June 1970 period had been the attempt by the Labour

Government to keep discussions about a new structure within fairly narrow confines. The other groups of proximate decision-makers had had to keep to the agenda or risk being ruled out of order. What agenda would the new Minister set?

The Conservative manifesto for the General Election had given a first guideline. 'We are convinced of the need for reform of the present structure of local government', it said. Furthermore 'we will bring forward a sensible measure of local government reform which will involve a genuine devolution of power from the central government and will provide for the existence of a two-tier structure.'[21] Full consultations were promised. We saw earlier that Walker had placed considerable emphasis on the concept of stronger local authorities and a relaxation of central controls. From now on this became the main plank of the Government's platform. Almost every major ministerial speech opened with remarks about the intention to boost the powers of councils. The two-tier concept was also a commitment brought forward from the February 1970 White Paper debate. As yet there was no flesh on the bare bones, but the Redcliffe-Maud blueprint of unitary authorities appeared to be no longer discussable. Or did it? Later in June Mr Walker announced that the Commission on the Constitution had been asked for its views on the Redcliffe-Maud Commission's proposed indirectly elected, largely non-executive provincial councils. This seemed to suggest that a two-tier plan of weak provinces and strong 'most-purpose' authorities such as that favoured by the AMC was in fact discussable. The Queen's Speech on 2 July did nothing to clarify the situation. It virtually repeated word for word the phrases contained in the election manifesto.

In his early statements as Minister, then, Walker appeared to refrain deliberately from closing the door on any options. A Circular from the Ministry to all local authorities on 9 July 1970 seemed in part to confirm this interpretation.[22] It made no mention of two-tier systems but merely asked for comments on the Labour Government's proposals (many of which the Ministry had already received). The very short Circular concluded with the statement that 'naturally authorities would be in no way committed by these comments in relation to any fresh structural proposals the Government may put forward for the purpose of further consultations.' Councils and their associations had been pressing the Minister for an early clarification of the position. On 8 July the CCA warned its members of the impending Circular, but stated that it had not been consulted about the detailed contents — it did not even know, for example, whether any reference would be made to the earlier proposals for large metropolitan areas (none was). But it did encourage members to submit their views to the Minister as soon as possible, so that 'as much influence as possible can be brought to bear on the Minister at an early date'. The CCA smelled victory — 'the proposals of the new administration may well be very much in line with the original evidence submitted to the Royal Commission by the Association' — and was anxious to press for a clear Government commitment 'particularly as there will doubtless be a quick response from the county and non-county boroughs, encouraged by the Association of Municipal Corporations'.[23] This was the start of a brief but bitter struggle for supremacy between the associations.

Individual councils were better placed than the more cumbersome national associations to respond quickly to the new political situation. Several, like Lancashire and Cheshire, had for months been preparing contingency plans knowing that an election could result in a change of Government. As a result Lancashire was able to confer with 106 of its 108 district councils as early as 6 July. The concept of a two-tier structure for Lancashire seemed to be generally well received (it must not be forgotten that the county boroughs, which would have been at the core of the proposed unitary authorities in central Lanchashire, were not at the conference). A working party of officers and a steering committee of councillors were appointed to fill in the details.[24] In Cheshire, the county council was able to produce a detailed plan before the end of July. The council was pressing for a two-tier system based on the whole of the existing county and no mention was made of possible losses of territory to Manchester- or Liverpool-based conurbation authorities. Later in 1970 the two county council chairmen got together with Cumberland and privately submitted two alternative schemes to the Minister. These accepted the concept of a Manchester-based county, though with quite narrow boundaries making it completely urbanised.[25]

Nationally the Rural District Councils Association was quickest off the mark. In mid-August it produced a booklet 'The New District Council: A Blueprint for the Future'. As the title suggested, the Association took the view that there was a clear government commitment to a system of district councils (an interpretation which the AMC was to challenge). This was welcomed, predictably, as leading to a more 'democratic' and more 'effective and economical' structure than that proposed by the Royal Commission and endorsed by the Labour Government. But lip-service to the 'proper' objectives of democracy and efficiency could not conceal the Association's natural concern with self-preservation. A geographical area with a district council should normally have a population of 50,000-100,000, it should be made up from existing whole units, and its citizens should live within twenty miles of the offices. But at 'area' (i.e. top-tier) level the Association was much less specific about the geography or about continuity between the old and the new structures. Nor did it spell out some of the difficulties inherent in its proposals for a division of responsibility between area and district in the highways, transportation and planning services.

The concordat between the CCA and the two district councils associations which had developed in the autumn of 1969 was maintained. The three jointly put forward a two-tier scheme similar to that proposed in 1969. The UDCA and the RDCA concern to keep the minimum population of new districts low in order to antagonise as few members as possible was reflected in the use of 50,000 'as a general rule', though even smaller districts were considered feasible in remote areas. The CCA's anxiety was also to avoid a split, and the figure of 500,000 minimum population for top-tier authorities, which the Association had advanced on several previous occasions, was again adopted.

The main feature of this package was its lack of specificity. These associations were able to avoid spelling out awkward details such as exact boundaries, or the precise delimitation of powers, because their immediate goal was to seek a broad commitment from the Government to the principle of a county-district structure. They felt that such a commitment was already almost present following the White Paper debate in February 1970 and the June manifesto, and that it was unnecessary for them to prove that every detail of their two-tier package was workable. Though ministers were saying little during the autumn of 1970, the signs were that this approach by the associations — which avoided acrimonious internal debate on details — would succeed. For example, early in November 1970 Graham Page, Walker's junior minister responsible for local government, was reported as having stated that the coming White Paper, expected around the turn of the year, would map out tentative areas for new counties and the division of responsibilities between them and district authorities (whose areas would be worked out later).[26] This proved to be yet another extremely accurate report by the *Guardian*'s specialists in regional and local government affairs.

The AMC, on the other hand, was in a more difficult situation. There were clear signs that it was on the defensive, and its leaders had to decide how best to seek to persuade the new Government that the boroughs' solution was the most desirable. Would a set of principles suffice, or was it necessary to show that its alternative was capable of detailed application? Prevailing political needs plus the fact that its plan involved a radical departure from the existing structure of local government persuaded AMC leaders that a detailed workable alternative to the county-district plan was necessary.

The AMC stuck to the principles which its members had already approved in 1969, and in November 1970 unveiled a proposal for fourteen provincial councils and 132 most-purpose authorities with a minimum population of 150,000-200,000.[27] As with any two-tier system there were difficulties over the detailed division of powers — the province would, for example, be responsible for 'strategic planning', which was spelled out as 'town and country planning in broad outline; determination of the main highway network; traffic and transportation planning; planning of overspill housing' and one or two other items. As later debates during 1971-2 showed, it was very difficult indeed to translate this kind of phrase into legislative action in such a way as to clarify the powers of each level without incorporating friction and costly clashes of interests: this distinction between plan-making and plan-implementation remains a major source of concern to British public administrators and planners.

But it was the detailed map which took the eye and caused most problems for the AMC. We have already seen that in both 1966 and 1969 its members were often divided in their views about boundaries, particularly in the north-west and north-east. The new AMC map was extremely detailed — it even specified the exact division down to parish and ward level of many existing councils, particularly rural districts, and every borough could see exactly what fate was in store for it should the plan ever be implemented by the Government. In the north-west, Salford found itself still placed with Manchester, and the Bury-Rochdale unit remained (two surprising decisions, as in each case the units could easily be divided to form authorities of well over the AMC's 150,000 minimum). In the north-east, Newcastle found itself a tightly drawn unit, separated from the other parts of the Tyneside conurbation which were to form three further units. The City Council still preferred a Tyneside authority along the lines of the unitary authority proposed by the Redcliffe-Maud Commission, and the council leader stated that 'it is most unfortunate that this report has been published. The views of the AMC do not in any way represent the views of Newcastle Corporation.'[28]

These and other criticisms were vented at the AMC council meeting which adopted the scheme. An amendment was moved to delete the proposed areas from the document, but was lost by a large majority (100 to 14). However, as a concession to the critics it was agreed by AMC leaders that the suggestions for areas would be described as no more than 'illustrative proposals'. The fact that the plan was capable of being translated into action was its strength, asserted Alderman Marshall, still AMC chairman in 1970.[29]

Publication of the AMC plan brought the conflict between the associations to a head. The CCA reacted by describing the plan as 'totally unacceptable' to its members. The most-purpose authorities espoused by the AMC were not large enough to be able 'to exercise effectively and efficiently the main functions of local government', and there were no lower-tier authorities 'needed to preserve local democracy'. The UDCA criticised the lack of 'a responsive local unit of limited size but with a wide range of directly conferred functions exercised as of right'. Though all the four associations agreed to meet to try to find common ground, attempts to obtain a compromise acceptable to all were not successful. Again the situation was reminiscent of that in the 1950s, when in May 1952 the AMC broke off talks with the counties and districts. The AMC and the other three were too far apart in their thinking for there to be any real chance of a joint approach to the issue. While all continued to pay lip-service to the concepts of efficiency and democracy, the inevitable concern with self-interest and self-preservation was the over-riding consideration. Mr Walker was faced with a choice — accept one of the two conflicting schemes emanating from the associations, or produce a two-tier system of his own.

Mr Walker's White Paper[30]
On 16 February 1971, just a year after the Labour Government's White Paper had been published, Mr Walker unveiled his own set of proposals. As most observers had predicted, these were very much based on the principles put forward by the CCA and the two associations of district councils. The concept of unitary authorities was rejected in favour of a two-tier county-district model. This, in turn, had two variations. In six conurbation areas it resembled, in many respects, the metropolitan area-metropolitan district proposals of the Redcliffe-Maud Commission and the Labour Government. Over the rest of the country the top-tier would be based on the long established shire county tradition, with district councils based on existing districts wherever possible.

Though a major plank in the earlier proposals — the unitary concept — had been jettisoned, the new White Paper did adopt other important principles laid down by the commissioners in 1969. First, the general diagnosis of the weaknesses in the existing structure of local government in Walker's White Paper bore a close resemblance to that found in Crosland's and in the Redcliffe-Maud Report. All the usual references were there — to the horseless carriage era of 1888, the out-dated areas, and the confused and confusing division of functions — and the language was pretty strong.* The 'Purpose'

*Strong enough for Mr Raphael Tuck, MP for Watford, to suggest during the Commons debate on the White Paper that 'on reading [it] one would imagine that the first few pages were written by one man and then he died and the rest was written by somebody else with completely different views', *Hansard (Commons)*, vol. 817, cols 1365-6 (19 May 1971).

and 'Objectives of Reform' differed from earlier versions only in the commitment to a two-tier structure and in the great importance attached to the evolution of a new structure through building on the existing system rather than through radically changing areas and authorities.

Second, the Government accepted the view that the right range of population for authorities providing major services was from 250,000 to 1,000,000, though these limits were not to be inflexible. By accepting that both the Commission and the previous Government had got the size of authority about right, the Conservative Government had avoided reopening this issue. Given the complex nature of the size problem (we saw in Chapter II that its solution involved a series of difficult value judgements), it clearly made political sense to translate a judgement into a 'fact'. Those, like the AMC, who sought to argue in favour of a lower limit for major authorities, were ruled out of order.

Third, the concept of conurbation counties was accepted and extended to further areas. To the Commission's three (Merseyside, Greater Manchester, West Midlands) were added three more (West Yorkshire — also part of the Crosland scheme — South Yorkshire, and Tyne and Wear). The Labour Government's South Hampshire plan was dropped in favour of a Hampshire 'shire' county.

Finally, the desirability of merging town and country was also endorsed, and 'the artificial separation of big towns from their surrounding hinterlands for functions whose planning and administration need to embrace both town and country' was criticised.[31] This was an important endorsement because it overthrew a fundamental principle of the existing structure, that towns had a claim to some form of self-government. This was a principle which could be traced back to the Municipal Corporations legislation of 1835 and beyond. Now both major political parties were abandoning it.

These similarities in approach could not, however, conceal the differences. Like so many critics from mid-1969 onwards, the Government attacked the unitary model on grounds of both democracy and efficiency. Concentrating all authority at a single level 'carries the grave penalty that if such areas are to be large enough for some services, they will be too large for others. . . . Above all else, a genuine local democracy implies that decisions should be taken — and should be seen to be taken — as locally as possible.'[32] In the Government's view, some services required large administrative areas but others did not. A county-county district model best fitted this situation. Districts could be quite small, and a minimum desirable population level of 40,000 was put forward (clearly acceptable to the RDCA and UDCA, as the concordat with the

CCA had mentioned a figure of 50,000). At county level the new authorities, it was claimed, 'will in no sense be a continuation of the existing county authorities'.[33] It was true that county boroughs lost their autonomy and therefore changed the physical and social character of many a county, but most of the proposed new counties had boundaries which looked very like those of existing county councils. In the same paragraph as the disclaimer that new and old counties were similar came the statement that 'where possible, existing county boundaries will be retained in order to keep the maximum existing loyalties and to minimise the administrative problems'. So much for the first statement!

In another important sense the geography contradicted the principles. The merger of town and country was real enough in the shires, where county borough and county were to merge at top-tier level, and urban and rural district at second-tier level. But in the case of the metropolitan areas this was incompatible with the continuance of counties adjacent to the conurbation centres like Cheshire, Worcestershire and Northumberland. Here the 'shire county' principle overrode that of the ending of the urban-rural dichotomy. Metropolitan counties were only to include 'areas of continuous development and any adjacent area into which continuous development will extend',[34] a return to the Special Review Area concept which, as we saw in Chapter I, had caused many problems to the 1958 Local Government Commission. As a result those counties adjacent to, and part of, the conurbations retained large amounts of territory which had earlier seemed lost.* Only the West and South Yorkshire metropolitan areas were to include substantial rural areas. This reflected the Yorkshire geography, with large industrial towns like Halifax and Huddersfield separated by a few miles of rural land. It also reflected the local political situation, for there was no future West Riding County Council to which the fringe areas could be attached on grounds of tradition and history.

Walker's determination to retain existing county boundaries 'where possible' was carried to great lengths in some areas. In a number of cases a large county borough fell on the very edge of a county, and as a result there seemed to be good reasons for altering the county boundary. In two cases — Bristol and Teesside — completely new counties centred on these cities were proposed. But in other cases like Plymouth, Brighton and the fast growing Milton Keynes the new geography bore little resemblance to settlement and travel patterns. The Devon-Cornwall boundary was retained, the

---

*For example, Lancashire was to retain the Southport-Ormskirk area, Cheshire the Chester-Winsford-Knutsford area, Worcestershire the Redditch-Kidderminster area, and Staffordshire the Stafford-Lichfield area.

East Sussex-West Sussex boundary would continue to run through the Greater Brighton mini-conurbation, and Milton Keynes was very close to the junction of Bedfordshire, Northamptonshire and Buckinghamshire.

Some other unexpected boundary proposals further suggested that Walker's concern was as much with practical politics as with the principles so firmly enunciated in the White Paper. Sunderland was to be part of Tyneside (later to be named Tyne and Wear as a result) and Coventry part of the West Midlands, whereas Warrington was excluded from both Greater Manchester and Merseyside. In all three cases the councils concerned had expressed a preference for such a solution in the consultations which preceded publication of the White Paper. In the case of Warrington this decision provided some recompense to Cheshire, which stood to lose large areas at each end of the county even under the tightly drawn outer boundaries of the new metropolitan counties to its north.

Though most immediate attention was focused on the proposals for boundaries (which were published in a separate Circular[35] or, in the case of the new districts in the non-metropolitan counties, were to be decided upon later by a new Local Government Boundary Commission), those for functions were at least as important. Here the Government again mirrored the Redcliffe-Maud Commission in seeking to give closely linked services to the same authority, and to create a system under which services could be provided 'effectively and economically'.[36] In the cases of education, housing, and town and country planning the White Paper's proposals were certain to lead to controversy.

The new education authorities were to be the non-metropolitan counties and the metropolitan districts. Nobody could argue about the former, given that the new non-metropolitan districts would be very small, but the dispute about responsibility for education in the conurbations had already been apparent in 1969-70. We saw that the Labour Government disagreed with the Commission, and allocated education to the top-tier in its White Paper. Walker returned to the commissioners' preference. His districts were described as 'substantial... generally compact... sensible and effective units'.[37] But those who had earlier pressed for education to be a metropolitan county function on the grounds that many of the Redcliffe-Maud metropolitan districts were too small and weak could now point to an increase in the number of these districts with a population of less than 250,000. This increase was due partly to the creation of additional metropolitan areas and partly to the narrower outer boundaries. Eleven of the 34 metropolitan districts outlined in detail in Circular 8/71 fell below the target figure, whereas only four of the commissioners' twenty had done so.[38]

Housing was by far the most important of the few functions allocated to all second-tier authorities. Traditionally this was a borough, urban or rural district council responsibility, though in the 1960s many experts had argued that at least some housing powers should reside with county councils. This was acknowledged in the vague proposals that counties be given 'certain reserve powers, e.g. for overspill' and that they should 'deal with those housing problems that transcend the boundaries of the districts'.[39] The interpretation of these phrases was bound to involve lengthy arguments and discussions, particularly as housing and planning were closely linked services and the latter was to be primarily a county responsibility. But the chances of the district councils retaining the vast bulk of their housing powers seemed high, at least in the non-metropolitan areas. Without housing the new districts would have so few important tasks that the new structure would be close to a unitary model, and Mr Walker was unlikely to allow this situation to develop given his commitment to a two-tier structure and his earlier emphasis on the importance of districts as service providers.

As with housing, responsibility for planning was to be divided.[40] Plan-making and 'broad planning policies' had to be a county function. When all was said and done, they were a major reason for establishing physically large top-tier units. But development control (taking decisions on planning applications) should, the Government felt, be a district responsibility, because it 'raises issues of close local interest'. The difficulty was that plan-making and development control cannot easily be separated — a series of decisions on planning applications can often limit the alternatives open to the plan-making authority. In London relations between the GLC and several London Boroughs had been damaged by such disputes. A further problem lay in the large numbers of professional staff that would be required to man several hundred planning departments (by suggesting that districts should have responsibilities in this field the White Paper was, in effect, proposing to double or treble the number of planning authorities). In order to alleviate these difficulties the Government proposed 'a unified staff structure serving both counties and districts',[41] but this in turn raised other problems such as the control of staff, their multiple loyalties and the apportioning of costs. Here again the scene was set for argument and conflict.

Mr Walker and his civil servants had covered a lot of ground in a fairly short period of time. To come up with a blueprint for local government reform in a little under eight months is no mean feat. Walker was apparently determined to build on the reform momentum which had been generated during the 1966-70 period, and to press ahead with legislation in the early years of the new

Conservative Government. We saw earlier that he had chosen to act constructively when in Opposition, whereas he could have opted for a critical negative approach. He was rapidly emerging as a leading member of Prime Minister Edward Heath's Cabinet team, and this was an issue on which a major piece of legislation was politically and administratively feasible as well as one capable of being portrayed as in line with Heath's dispensation to modernise the machinery of government. Heath's own White Paper in autumn 1970 on the structure of central government had apparently been based on the administrative doctrine that streamlining was beneficial and that 'bigger means better'.[42] This had made Walker head of the new giant Department of the Environment. Walker was applying the same doctrine to the structure of local government, though with care.* His choice of a county-district scheme was very much in line with party grass-roots thinking and reflected party strength. Though many large cities were under Conservative control and were thus being led by party members hostile to the new proposals, it was clear that their reign was a temporary phenomenon resulting from the acute unpopularity of the Labour Government in 1967-9: it was the leadership in the shires which represented the permanent core of the Conservative Party.

High priority was attached to this issue. The White Paper promised legislation in 1971-2, which gave civil servants only eight or nine further months in which to finalise the drafting of the Bill. Clearly there was much work to be done. The White Paper was very short (twelve pages compared with the thirty-four of Labour's 1970 White Paper) and contained many proposals which could only be translated into law after lengthy consultations (for example, the exact allocation of functions, and the concept of a unified staffing structure for planning). The boundaries of counties and of metropolitan districts contained in the accompanying Circular were open to comment, though only up to a point. Just as the previous Government had announced that certain decisions were firm and could not be re-opened, so too did Walker make it clear that the consultations on boundaries were limited. The acceptance of 250,000 as a minimum size ('only in special circumstances should a new unit be established with a population below this figure':[43] a slight loophole, but no more than slight); the closure of discussion about the unitary concept ('the Government's proposals for reorganisation are based upon the need for two levels of executive authorities throughout the country, and they are not prepared to

---

*The doctrine was further applied in May when Walker announced that the Government and the associations were to appoint a committee to advise the new councils on 'the best management structure', *Hansard* (*Commons*), vol. 817, cols 1291-2 (19 May 1971).

entertain representations contrary to this view' [44]); the statement that no further metropolitan areas could be considered; and the sacrosanct nature of the boundary of Greater London were all designed to forestall any major debate on boundaries.

Signs of haste in the drafting of the White Paper were also apparent from the large number of issues left on one side for further consultation with no clear Government line being offered. Urban parish councils, borough status for districts, management structures, payment of councillors, length of term of office, electoral systems, and the future of aldermen were all to be discussed with the local authority associations and other interested bodies. 'The timetable proposed is tight and inevitably it will place a considerable load of extra work on members and officers of individual authorities, and on their associations' concluded the White Paper.[45] This point, at least, could not be disputed.

Early Reactions: the Battle-lines Emerge

Inevitably, publication of the new proposals provoked strong comments. 'I weep for Nottingham' (Leader of the City Council); 'I think this is disastrous for local government' (Town Clerk of Blackburn); 'We shall fight these proposals to the last ditch. I am amazed that a Tory minister should, by one stroke of a pen, demote large cities to second-class councils' (Leader of Stoke-on-Trent City Council). Such extreme statements made the headlines, but more quietly a very large number of county and district councils were able to 'heave a sigh of relief' (Clerk of Cheshire). Mr Walker had, like the commissioners and the Labour Government, divided the local government world.

This time, however, the division was different. The commissioners had invented a scheme which was so at variance with the traditional structure that it neatly divided the members of each of the two great associations, of counties and of boroughs. The new Walker proposals returned the associations to the position that they had occupied in the period before 1966, that of outright opposition to one another and a (fairly) united membership. The Walker plan could only be interpreted as a victory for the CCA and the district associations, which represented the smaller town and rural areas, and defeat for the large cities, represented nationally by the AMC.*
How would the AMC react?

A fight to the last ditch would undoubtedly have embarrassed the Government. The co-operation of all the associations during the period of consultations was essential to the timetable. True,

---

*'The Countryside Fights Back — and Wins' was the title of an article in *New Society* by Professor Peter Hall (17 September 1970) predicting the contents of the coming White Paper.

decisions could, if necessary, be imposed. But on many complex issues the expertise of the associations was invaluable if decisions capable of translation into practice were to be made. Civil servants in Whitehall have always relied on the associations to bring to their attention administrative problems on the ground, for the career structure of a civil servant normally precludes him from having any experience of the local implementation of laws and policies by elected councils.

AMC leaders were realistic. Mr Walker was obviously intent on legislation. The other associations, all broadly happy with the new White Paper, were certain to co-operate in the consultative process. The association could gain little or nothing from a policy of non-cooperation, whereas tactical victories could emerge from detailed discussions. For example, the association could press hard for greater powers for the district councils, for a continuation of borough status, and for the borough electoral system (of three-member wards, with one retiring in rotation each year). Having rubbed the noses of the big cities into the ground on the general principles of reform, the Minister was unlikely to take a 'CCA view' on all the subsequent issues. Indeed, he might well bend towards the AMC in an attempt to limit criticism of his partisanship. Furthermore the CCA and the district associations were far from united on the distribution of functions, and on this important issue the AMC would be able to side with the latter against the CCA. Later, in July 1971, it formally joined with the two district associations in putting an alternative plan for the allocation of powers before the Minister. Sir Frank Marshall put these points to members of the AMC at a meeting on 18 February 1971. 'Protest now would be less effective than reasoned argument', he stated, though AMC statements were strongly worded, containing phrases such as 'the substitution of bureaucracy for democracy'.[46] In accordance with Marshall's view, nine days after the publication of the White Paper the AMC Secretary joined with his opposite numbers from the other associations in a meeting with ministry officials to hammer out details of the timetable and the method of consultations.

The Labour Party also had to consider its position. The White Paper rejected many of its own proposals made when in government, but we saw earlier that these proposals by no means represented the united opinion of party members — the 1969 party conference had heard criticism of the Redcliffe-Maud scheme, and the debate on Crosland's White Paper had revealed a divided House of Commons with the division cutting right across party lines. Of course the party would oppose the new plan — this was its constitutional duty. The two questions to be considered were how strongly to oppose, and what (if any) commitments to make about future amendments when the party again returned to power.

Crosland, architect of Labour's White Paper, was shadow minister. His first response was to describe the new plan as 'feeble and dispiriting', and he condemned the muddle and confusion of a two-tier system. In May 1971, in a debate on the White Paper, he further attacked the proposals, largely on the grounds that they gave way to the rural counties at the expense of the cities (where Labour had just regained control of fourteen county boroughs at the local elections).[47] But he was careful to avoid any commitment to repeal or amendment at a later date. All he requested was delay in order to give more time for consultations. Winding up for the Opposition, Mr John Silkin also trod carefully. He called for changes in the proposed division of powers and for the concept of neighbourhood councils in urban areas to be further explored.[48] But there were few signs of a major party conflict during the impending legislative process, and it was already apparent that there was to be a clear contrast with the experience of the reform of London government. There the Labour Party had fought the Bill 'line by line' in a lengthy series of debates in both Commons and Lords during 1962-3, and had made promises to repeal the new law.[49] By the time the party came to power in autumn 1964 the new councils had been elected and repeal would have raised great administrative problems. In addition, Labour had won control of the new Greater London Council and of twenty of the thirty-two new London Boroughs: repeal could have raised political problems as well!

Within the Conservative Party there were few signs of major discontent. In the White Paper debate fourteen government back-benchers spoke.[50] Though several criticised certain aspects of the proposals, all made alternative suggestions which, they claimed, were compatible with Walker's main principles. There were three types of amendment sought by these speakers. Dame Joan Vickers (Plymouth), Mr Bonner Pink (Portsmouth) and Sir Stephen McAdden (Southend) called for the creation of additional county councils in these areas. Sir Tatton Brinton (Kidderminster), Mr Rees-Davies (Thanet), Mr Blaker (Blackpool) and Mr Boardman (Leicester) represented a lobby in support of additional powers being allocated to district councils (either to all districts or to the larger ones). Thirdly, Mr A. Jones (Northants, South), Mr Bell (Buckinghamshire, South), Mr Ramsden (Harrogate), Mr Temple (Chester) and Mr Montgomery (Brierley Hill) expressed concern with the details of boundaries locally. As with the earlier debate on the Labour Government's proposals, the occasion presented a good opportunity for members to make constituency speeches. In the subsequent consultations it was in many cases possible for the Government to incorporate the views expressed in the debate,

though not those where additional counties were being sought.
Though there was some criticism, the chances of a major revolt within the party were non-existent. Mr Walker's package, it must be recalled, had largely developed out of his series of regional meetings with the party's grass-roots. It treated traditional Conservative strongholds favourably. Finally, the Government was avoiding taking the initiative on the boundaries of the proposed non-metropolitan districts. These were certain to be controversial locally, but they were not to be the subject of legislation and draft proposals would not be revealed until the Bill was some way through its parliamentary stages. By setting up a new Local Government Boundary Commission, the Government was putting itself in the happy position of later being able to accept that Commission's proposals and portray them as the result of independent, impartial and expert investigation. Furthermore, no parliamentary debate would be necessary as the proposals would be implemented by statutory instrument. The provision for a permanent Commission was also a valuable tactical weapon during the debates on the Bill's county and Welsh and metropolitan district areas. The Government was in a position to resist amendments by suggesting that, after 1974, the area involved could be properly studied by the Commission. This line was taken by ministers several times, the most notorious occasion being when Mr Gibson-Watt (Minister of State, Welsh Office) agreed that the Rhondda-Pontypridd boundary was 'totally ridiculous . . . an administrative nonsense' but nevertheless refused to alter it.[51]

There were, then, few serious political barriers to reform. And the co-operation of all the major local authority associations made the timetable feasible in administrative terms. By the time the White Paper was published civil servants had worked for nearly eight months on the new proposals and had presumably generated a fair amount of administrative commitment during the course of this work. A strong Local Government Reorganisation section existed in the Department of the Environment with much of the day-to-day responsibility resting on the shoulders of Under-Secretary Clifford Pearce. Those who knew him were aware of his concern for detail and accuracy, and of his great interest in the history and reform of local government. Though other departments like the Home Office, the Department of Education and Science and the Department of Health and Social Security also had a part to play, it was Pearce who was primarily responsible for preparations for the reform of English local government.

Administrative responsibility for local government reform did not, however, lie solely within the Department of the Environment and the other departments mentioned above. The Redcliffe-Maud

Report had been confined to proposals for England; so, too, had the 1970 Labour Government's White Paper. Scotland had had its own Royal Commission whose proposals were the subject of local consultation through the Scottish Office. In the case of Wales the situation was rather different for two reasons. First, we saw in Chapter I that in 1965 Mr James Griffiths decided to consider the question of reform internally within the Welsh Office rather than through the creation of a further Royal Commission, and the Welsh Office had produced its own set of proposals in 1967. Second, the existing local government law related to both England and Wales, and there was a good case for joint reform on grounds of tradition and simplicity, particularly with the advent of a new Conservative Government committed to no particular earlier set of proposals. In 1971 the new Government's proposals for England and for Wales were published as separate documents on the same day, and both were based on similar principles. The Welsh Office became responsible for legislative preparations jointly with the Department of the Environment. In Chapter V the background to this fusion of proposals for the two countries will be traced.

Two Hectic Years

The period June 1969-February 1971 had been, by any standards, hectic. Local authorities and their associations had had to react to three sets of proposals. Civil servants had had to collate and analyse these reactions, and to draft further sets of proposals. They had had to cope with a change of Government and an amalgamation of ministries. Though the issue of local government reform had, for the most part, made only a limited public impact, there were many MPs who had been subjected to considerable local pressure, either continuously or at the time of the 1970 General Election. The fast-moving nature of the debate may have caused problems for the proximate decision-makers; at the same time it allowed the atmosphere of reform, created in 1966 by Crossman, to be sustained.

From February 1971 the content of the debate changed. Walker's commitment to legislation in 1971-2 was firm, and discussion was now restricted to specific details rather than broad principles (except during parts of the parliamentary process when the Opposition could return, with no chance of success, to such principles). But these details were collectively extremely important. A county-district system was claimed by the Conservative Government in its White Paper to have advantages of democracy — with districts being accessible to the public and with councils generally having greater powers than previously — and of efficiency — with major authorities large enough to provide effective services of a specialised nature. Much of the advantage could be lost if boundaries took little account of patterns of settlement and mobility, or if the allocation of functions resulted either in closely linked services being in the hands of separate authorities, or in an awkward division of powers which was likely to be incomprehensible to the public and inoperable without conflict between councils. Finally, how committed was the Government to greater devolution of powers to local authorities? Mr Walker continued to emphasise this point on almost every available occasion, and a review of statutory controls over councils was set in motion soon after publication of the White Paper. There were, though, few signs of major developments. Indeed, the new councils were to lose their personal health services to the new area health authorities, the future of the water and sewage services was under review (with the possibility of these being transferred from local government control as a result), and Government legislation and promised legislation was reducing council freedom of action over the provision of school milk and the level of council house rents.

NOTES

1 Ministry of Local Government and Regional Planning, *Reform of Local Government in England, Cmnd 4276* (HMSO, 1970).
2 *Ibid.*, para. 5.
3 *Ibid.*, para. 10.
4 Department of Health and Social Security, *The Future Structure of the National Health Service* (HMSO, 1970).
5 Cmnd 4276, *op. cit.*, paras 37-9.
6 *Ibid.*, para. 32.
7 *Ibid.*, para. 91.
8 *Huddersfield Daily Examiner*, 11 February 1970.
9 County Councils Association, *Statement of the Association's Preliminary Views* (4 February 1970), and *Memorandum Elaborating the Association's Views* (16 February 1970).
10 *Municipal Review*, Supplement, May 1970, pp. 95-6.
11 *Ibid.*, p. 97.
12 J. M. Lee and B. Wood, *The Scope of Local Initiative: A Study of Cheshire County Council 1961-74* (Martin Robertson, 1974), p. 81.
13 *Hansard (Commons)*, vol. 796, cols 423-546 (18 February 1970).
14 *Ibid.*, col. 447.
15 *Ibid.*, cols. 448-9.
16 *Ibid.*, col. 455.
17 *The Sunday Times*, 1 March 1970.
18 Ministry of Housing and Local Government, *Circular 21/70 — Reform of Local Government in England: Areas and Boundaries* (HMSO, 1970).
19 *Hansard (Commons)*, vol. 796, col. 432 (18 February 1970).
20 *Hansard (Commons)*, vol. 797, col. 256 (3 March 1970).
21 Conservative Party, *A Better Tomorrow* (CPC, 1970).
22 Ministry of Housing and Local Government, *Circular 59/70 — Reform of Local Government in England* (HMSO, 1970).

23 Letter from CCA to Clerks of County Councils dated 8 July 1970.
24 *Guardian*, 7 July 1970.
25 Lee and Wood, *op. cit.*, pp. 74-5.
26 *Guardian*, 10 November 1970. The report was tucked away at the end of an article about the AMC proposals, probably because the author (John Ardill) did not consider it to be particularly newsworthy — he and other observers had, of course, been predicting a two-tier solution for some time.
27 *Local Government Chronicle*, 14 November 1970.
28 *Guardian*, 11 November 1970.
29 *Municipal Review*, Supplement, January 1971, pp. 6-7.
30 Department of the Environment, *Local Government in England: Government Proposals for Reorganisation, Cmnd 4584* (HMSO, 1971).
31 *Ibid.*, para. 6.
32 *Ibid.*, paras 8, 9.
33 *Ibid.*, para. 29.
34 *Ibid.*, para. 32.
35 Department of the Environment, *Circular 8/71 — Local Government Reorganisation in England: Proposed New Areas* (HMSO, 1971).
36 Cmnd 4584, *op. cit.*, para. 7.
37 *Ibid.*, para. 16.
38 Circular 8/71, *op. cit.*, Appendix C.
39 Cmnd 4584, *op. cit.*, para. 23 and Appendix.
40 *Ibid.*, para. 21.
41 *Ibid.*
42 *The Reorganisation of Central Government, Cmnd 4506* (HMSO, 1970).
43 Circular 8/71, *op. cit.*, para. 7.
44 *Ibid.*, para. 6.
45 Cmnd 4584, *op. cit.*, para. 58.
46 *Municipal Review*, Supplement, April 1971, pp. 65-6, 67-8.
47 *Hansard (Commons)*, vol. 817, cols 1292-1309 (19 May 1971).
48 *Ibid.*, cols. 1391-6.
49 G. Rhodes, *The Government of London: The Struggle for Reform* (Weidenfeld & Nicolson, 1970), pp. 127-9, 131-2, Ch. 10.
50 *Hansard (Commons)*, vol. 817, cols 1309-90 (19 May 1971).
51 House of Commons Debates 1971-2, *Official Report of Standing Committee D — Local Government Bill*, (3 vols), cols 2781-3.

Chapter V

WALES

No Royal Commission

Traditionally there was little or no distinction between the structure and organisation of local government in Wales and in England. The major Acts (1888, 1933, 1958) had applied to both countries. The 1945-9 Boundary Commission had studied both. Though the 1958 Act had created a separate Local Government Commission for Wales, its terms of reference were similar to those of the English Commission in General Review Areas. The Welsh commissioners made it clear that they saw their separate existence as no more than 'a recognition by Parliament of Welsh national feeling'. 'We do not believe that the establishment of a separate Commission for Wales is in any way to be regarded as an acceptance by Parliament that the problems of local government in Wales were in essentials different from those of England', they said.[1]

Against this it could, however, be argued that Welsh local government problems were sufficiently different to justify separate consideration, even though the basic structure of counties, county boroughs, districts and parishes was common to both countries. In much of mid- and north Wales the population was sparse, highly scattered and declining (six of the thirteen counties were experiencing falling populations and most of the others were only just holding their own). Communications were frequently difficult both in these areas and in the deeply incised mining and industrial valleys of south Wales. Welsh local authorities were often both extremely small and poor in terms of rateable resources. Montgomeryshire, for example, had only 44,000 inhabitants in 1961 (48,000 in 1931) and a penny rate product of a mere £1,100. As a result 88 per cent of its income came from central government grants. Merthyr Tydfil's rateable value *per capita* was the lowest of any English or Welsh county borough. Finally, Welsh continued to be spoken by large numbers of people (by more than two-thirds of the population in five counties) and there had generally been an upsurge of national consciousness in the 1950s and 1960s.

True to its word, the 1958 Commission had in principle behaved very much like its English counterpart. In its report, published in 1962, it recommended typical county borough extensions in the case of Cardiff, Newport and Swansea, and the demotion of the small (59,000 but declining) Merthyr Tydfil county borough. To eradicate the problem of numerous small counties outside Glamorgan and Monmouthshire it proposed amalgamations reducing the remaining eleven counties to only five. One of the five, Anglesey, would remain unchanged due to its island situation, despite having only 52,000 inhabitants.* However, behind these bare facts lay more detailed proposals about the pattern of boundaries which were far more radical than those found in the reports of the English Commission. Instead of confining itself to the amalgamation of whole counties the Commission had searched for socio-geographic cohesiveness. As a result, Brecon, Merioneth, Cardigan, Denbighshire, Glamorgan and Monmouthshire were to undergo detailed boundary changes. In the case of the latter two the Rhymney Valley boundary was to be moved from the bottom to the top of the hill (80,000 population was involved). South Brecon would be added to Glamorgan, Cardigan and Denbighshire would be divided between two new counties, Merioneth between three.

Merthyr Tydfil and the smaller counties would have almost certainly reacted against the principles of demotion and amalgamation. By opting for non-traditional boundaries in several parts of Wales the commissioners had ensured that opposition to the report would be far more widespread than might otherwise have been the case. This was one reason why the Conservative Minister of Housing and Local Government, Sir Keith Joseph, to whom the report was submitted, seemed to have little appetite for the Welsh plan. There were also two other reasons. First, Joseph was fully occupied in 1962-3 with pushing the highly controversial London reforms through Parliament. Second, he was under great pressure in England from the county lobby which represented areas of Conservative Party strength. This lobby had won a major victory in obtaining a reprieve for Rutland and once Joseph had conceded that case he could not easily go in for wholesale amalgamations across the border. The Welsh county lobby was successful in at least delaying reform not because it represented areas of Conservative Party strength (there are very few of these in the principality), but because it was fighting alongside a similar English movement. After some delay Joseph announced early in 1964 that he did not accept the new county pattern but that the necessary statutory inquiries into the

*One of the five commissioners disassociated himself from the Anglesey recommendation.

county borough extensions would proceed. The Government, he said, would probably produce its own proposals for Wales for discussion in due course.

Joseph's half-promise was not, however, inherited by Crossman. One of Prime Minister Wilson's first moves on succeeding to office in October 1964 was to create a separate Welsh Office with its own Secretary of State (Mr James Griffiths). Crossman and Griffiths inherited two different situations. In England the 1958 Local Government Commission had half finished its work and ministerial decisions on a considerable number of its proposals were awaited. In Wales the in-tray lay virtually empty following the rejection of the 1962 plan, with only the county borough boundary extensions to finalise and the Joseph statement to build upon. The conventional channels of consultation were opened in March 1965, when the Welsh Secretary met leading members of the major associations.[2] He told them that he saw reorganisation as 'both essential and urgent' and suggested the traditional approach of a collective examination of the issue. He planned to establish a working party of senior civil servants and a leading academic, and he hoped that this would be supplemented by an advisory group of association nominees. An assurance was given that participation in this manner would not bind the association to acceptance of the working party's proposals, which might cover functions and finance as well as areas. By opting for conventional consultations with association representatives Griffiths effectively ruled out the possibility of a structure emerging based on new principles. The agenda was rather like that experienced in the 1950s.

Six months later Crossman also came to view the reform issue in England as urgent. However, we saw in Chapter I that several factors led him to opt for an alternative traditional approach, that of appointing an independent advisory commission. In contrast to the Griffiths approach this was given a free hand and was not unduly constrained by local government's vested interests. Presumably there must have been some discussion about whether or not its brief should include Wales. There were at least two good reasons for restricting the Redcliffe-Maud Commission to England. First, the new Welsh Office would be unlikely to want to forego its ability to handle Welsh municipal affairs independently from Crossman's ministry. Second, Griffiths had stressed urgency almost a year earlier, and his working party was well into its stride by February 1966. The Welsh plan was published in July 1967, almost two years in advance of the Redcliffe-Maud Report. Mr Wilson, announcing the Royal Commission, claimed that Wales was excluded as the Government's plans for Welsh reform were 'already at an advanced state of preparation'.[3]

The 1967 White Paper[4]

The Labour Government's proposals, introduced by Mr Cledwyn Hughes who had succeeded Griffiths as Welsh Secretary, built on the 1962 Report. In south Wales the three main county boroughs would be retained, but Merthyr Tydfil would become a district authority. The broad pattern of counties would be as recommended in 1962, except in north Wales. There the Government rejected the three-county scheme and opted for a single county covering the whole area from Anglesey to the Flint-England boundary. In all there would be five counties instead of the seven proposed in 1962. The White Paper also delimited thirty-six district councils as successors to the existing 164 (the 1962 Report had not been concerned with the second-tier pattern), and suggested that a new Welsh Council be appointed.

Though there were to be fewer top-tier councils under the 1967 proposals than had been recommended in 1962, the White Paper was frequently more acceptable to existing authorities because it deliberately amalgamated whole units. Nevertheless it was inevitably attacked from all sides. Traditionalists argued that the county amalgamations went too far. Arguments about a lack of 'democracy' emphasising the value of smallness were much in evidence. It was pointed out that in north Wales the proposed Gwynedd county would consist of five existing counties (Anglesey, Caernarvonshire, Denbighshire, Flint and Merioneth) and would cover 2,500 square miles. Powys and Dyfed in mid- and south-west Wales were only a little smaller.

Radicals, on the other hand, were able to attack three features of the plan. First, the new boundaries almost always represented an amalgamation of whole existing units, which did not necessarily make geographical sense as the 1962 Report had pointed out. Second, the basic principles of the old structure, and in particular the town-country dichotomy in south Wales, were retained at a time when they seemed likely to be abandoned in England. Third, the proposed all-Wales council was to be appointed and largely non-executive.

Nationally, it was the third argument which stole the headlines. The Liberal and Welsh Nationalist Parties were both strong advocates of a Welsh Parliament, as were many members of the Labour Party. Furthermore, there were signs that the two minor parties were in the ascendancy in many parts of Wales (Mr Gwynfor Evans had won a dramatic by-election for the Welsh Nationalists at Carmarthen in July 1966 and his party's candidate had polled extraordinarily well in Rhondda West, normally just about the safest Labour seat in Great Britain, in March 1967). Given this background, the plan came as a disappointment to many.

Why was there no fully blown Welsh council in the White Paper? Largely, it seems, because this was a classic case of an issue which could not be kept separate from other issues. Professor John Mackintosh makes this clear:

> It is no secret that the then Secretary of State for Wales, Cledwyn Hughes, originally proposed an elected Council... but was defeated in the Cabinet, a major opponent being Mr William Ross, the Secretary of State for Scotland, who argued that he could no longer resist some form of elected assembly for Scotland if there were such a body in Wales.[5]

The White Paper acknowledged that several members of the Advisory Group and many outside bodies had advocated an elected Welsh Council, and both the AMC and the RDCA were quick to criticise the indirectly elected alternative (though the CCA seemed reasonably satisfied — presumably it saw a Welsh Council as a threat to the continued existence of county councils). The Government did not portray its decision as being final and for all time. It suggested that further consideration could be given 'in the light of the Royal Commissions' reports [probably the Scottish one in particular] and other developments'.[6] The last phrase proved to be particularly prophetic. The Queen's Speech announcement of the Commission on the Constitution in October 1968 delayed the issue of elected regional assemblies indefinitely.

The reaction of the major associations to the Welsh White Paper reflected the evidence which they had presented to the Redcliffe-Maud Commisson a few months previously, and the attitudes expressed within the Advisory Group. The White Paper reported that three alternative models of reform had been investigated — a single-tier system, a regional or sub-regional system, and a strengthened version of the traditional structure, and that a majority of the advisers had favoured the third approach. These were undoubtedly the CCA and district council association nominees. All three supported the Government's acceptance of this majority view in their early reactions to the White Paper, whereas the AMC preferred a Welsh Council — a fifteen most-purpose authorities model (though once again it was far from united on this point, as several of the smaller Welsh boroughs held views similar to those of the districts). This polarisation of views of the associations is by now more than familiar!

Of critical importance was the proposed timetable. If Welsh reform was to go ahead as a matter or urgency, then a clear statement of intent by the Government was necessary. Given the fact that publication of the Redcliffe-Maud proposals for England was expected within eighteen months or so, the danger that these would provide dissidents with arguments for delay was clear. Unless legislation was at an advanced stage by then, the chances of an early and separate Welsh Act were slim.

If James Griffiths had really hoped for early action (and his use of lengthy traditional consultatory methods makes this seem unlikely), it was apparent that his successor, Cledwyn Hughes, had even less enthusiasm for this issue. The White Paper opened with the statement: 'This White Paper sets out for public discussion....'[7] Though it went on to stress again the 'urgency' of local government reform, a period of public discussion inevitably meant that consultations would fill most or all of the period up to publication of the Redcliffe-Maud Report. Unlike the later English White Papers there was no commitment to legislation in any particular session of Parliament. Indeed, the reform momentum, so apparent in England, was conspicuous by its absence in Wales in the 1960s.

This was particularly worrying for the CCA, which entertained hopes of being able to use 'the recent' Welsh changes as evidence in the coming English debate, assuming that a Welsh Act was based on the 1967 White Paper proposals. In England public debate in 1966-7 appeared to be hostile to an evolutionary approach to reform, yet here was the Labour Government adopting it for Wales. Could the Government debate this approach at length during the passage of a Welsh Act, and then support a more radical reform in England? The CCA naturally felt that it could at least embarrass the Government should this change of commitment be contemplated, though only if a clear commitment to evolution in Wales emerged after the period of public discussion, since the Government could if necessary later argue that the White Paper was really a Green Paper based on the views of informal advisers. The CCA gave four reasons why it favoured rapid implementation of the White Paper. Action on any English proposals might take several years; Wales posed some unique problems; many miniscule district councils were in serious difficulties; the White Paper suggested that if changes were implemented it would be possible to make adjustments later in the light of any English changes.[8]

The AMC, proponents of a more radical approach, countered by questioning whether complex legislation for Wales in advance of the coming English debate was either desirable or feasible, particularly if further changes really were to be contemplated in the light of the Redcliffe-Maud proposals. The association did not accept that the problems in Wales were greater than or different from those found in England.[9] This last question, discussed at the beginning of the chapter, was never decided purely on its merits. Decisions about Welsh reform were influenced as much or more by political circumstances.

For more than a year there was a silence from the Government, and the CCA's hopes for early legislation began to fade. They finally disappeared when Mr George Thomas, the third Secretary of State for Wales to handle the issue in only four years, announced modified proposals in November 1968.[10] The locally much criticised large north Wales county of Gwynedd would be divided to form two counties; Cardiganshire would become one district rather than two; Swansea County Borough ought not to be extended; and the town of Llanberis would transfer to a different district. More important than the details was the fact that Mr Thomas accepted the policy of an evolutionary approach on the grounds that there was 'a sufficient general degree of support to justify my proceeding with further detailed work', but was not prepared to promise early implementation. He emphasised that the necessary further work would 'proceed as rapidly as possible', but went on: 'I cannot at this stage say when it will become possible to produce the legislation.' The 1968-9 session of Parliament was in effect ruled out as there was to be 'further consultation with the local authority associations and others concerned', notably on the allocation of certain functions. The Redcliffe-Maud Report was, of course, confidently expected during that session, and Thomas proposed also to allow councils and their associations to comment further in the light of that report if they so wished.

The Impact of the Redcliffe-Maud Report
For four years the Government had kept separate the two issues of local government reform in Wales and in England. As a result it now found itself faced with conflicting sets of proposals. It could scarcely defend both the Redcliffe-Maud blueprint and the modified 1967 White Paper. Though it had maintained, and for political reasons the CCA had agreed, that Wales had particular problems which justified separate treatment, it became increasingly difficult to argue convincingly that this was the case. Had it opted for an elected Welsh Council then such an argument might have stood up to scrutiny. By adopting the evolutionary approach it could only turn to sparsity of population and the small size of many existing units as factors peculiar to Wales. Even here there were parts of England with not dissimilar characteristics.

Mr. Thomas's decision to endorse the 1967 White Paper seems, in retrospect, to have been a surprising one. By November 1968 the Redcliffe-Maud Commission must have been drafting its report and it is inconceivable that senior civil servants did not have some notion of the outcome of its deliberations. In particular the chances of the Commission underwriting the concept of separate units for town and country had always seemed slight and few witnesses had supported this traditional principle. Yet in Wales the Government was apparently prepared to retain three county boroughs in south Wales. It had also rejected the all-purpose authority. In mid- and north Wales, the White Paper stated, all-purpose authorities would have to cover unacceptably large areas. In south Wales the valley pattern of settlement posed problems, and the all-purpose concept could only be realised at the expense of breaking up the strong Glamorgan and Monmouth counties.[11]

When Mr Wilson presented the Redcliffe-Maud Report to the Commons in June 1969, and announced acceptance of the proposals 'in principle', he appeared to throw open the whole issue of Welsh reform once again.[12] Local authorities in the principality and their associations were invited to comment further on the 1967 plan in the light of the new report, and, if they wished, to suggest that ideas in the report might be included in the Welsh legislation. In October, in the debate on the Queen's Speech, Wilson elaborated on the Government's position. The Secretary of State for Wales, after further consideration of the report and of views expressed upon it, had now decided 'to make a further urgent review of the situation in the geographical counties of Glamorgan and Monmouthshire to see if a satisfactory pattern can be worked out which will avoid the continued division between county boroughs and administrative counties'. An early indication of his conclusions was promised.[13]

For the Labour Government the politics of local government reform in south Wales were particularly difficult to handle. The area has long been a Labour Party stronghold at both county and district council level, as well as in the county boroughs. This remained largely the case even in 1969, a year when the party lost control of all but a few dozen councils in England. Thus there were strong and conflicting pressures on the Secretary of State. The 1967 proposals represented a delicate balance acceptable to most councils because, even though they involved large-scale amalgamations, they were not particularly destructive of the existing pattern of local government. A new and more radical set of proposals was certain to create a storm of controversy.

The March 1970 White Paper on Local Government Reorganisation in Glamorgan and Monmouthshire[14] presented just such a set of proposals. A good deal of emphasis was placed on a socio-geographic analysis which purported to show that the vast bulk of the south Wales population looked towards Cardiff, Newport and Swansea for employment and for the purchase of consumer durables. Other towns such as Merthyr Tydfil, Bridgend and Port Talbot were far less important centres. In the light of this evidence both a two-tier and a unitary system of local government were examined. A metropolitan county solution, it was claimed, was not necessary as the new county would be planning over an area which contained quite separate viable planning units based on the largest towns.[15] Three unitary authorities centred on Cardiff, Newport and Swansea were preferred by the Government. Each was 'a coherent socio-geographic unit' and their populations fell within the limits adopted for England (250,000-1,000,000). Once again the views of councils, associations and the public were requested, though the Government's defeat at the June 1970 election nipped this particular round of consultations in the bud.

Early reactions to the latest plan were, predictably, variable but largely hostile. The district councils associations protested that unitary authority councillors would have to represent large areas and would be out of touch with local needs. They pointed out that there would be a reduction from fifty-three to only three councils in south Wales. In the Commons many Labour MPs were critical, including Mr Foot (Ebbw Vale), Mr Hughes (Newport) and Mr Davies (Merthyr). Conservative, Liberal and Welsh Nationalist spokesmen naturally attempted to capitalise on this division by upholding the values of tight-knit, valley-based communities. Within a fortnight of the new proposals being announced, the *Guardian* reported that dissident Welsh Labour MPs had demanded the withdrawal of the plan and had threatened to vote against it, and a debate in the Welsh Grand Committee on 13 May 1970 seemed to confirm this possibility. But the opportunity for such a vote never came about.

The incoming Conservative Government thus inherited a situation in which it had little to lose. Party strength in Wales was limited to a handful of parliamentary seats. Conservatives controlled few councils, though in 1970 these did include Cardiff following the massive nation-wide electoral swings of the late 1960s. In mid- and north Wales many councils had come to accept a two-tier system along evolutionary lines. Such a scheme had been proposed throughout the 1960s and seemed to most Welshmen to be preferable to a unitary approach. In south Wales there had been far more opposition to the 1970 unitary plan than there had ever been to the earlier two-tier proposals. The controversial concept of a Welsh Council could be left on one side until the Commission on the Constitution reported. A revitalised two-tier system along the lines which Walker appeared to be contemplating for England seemed to be politically feasible: it would upset the county boroughs but most other areas would view it as no worse than the 1967 proposals (on which it would be based).

The fifth blueprint on Welsh local government in ten years was published in February 1971 as a Consultative Document[16] on the same day that Walker unveiled his English White Paper.

The scheme, the responsibility of Welsh Secretary Mr Peter Thomas, envisaged seven new counties and thirty-six district councils. It was remarkably similar to the 1967 plan as modified by George Thomas in 1968. Indeed, half the proposed districts had identical boundaries. There were, however, two main differences. First, the county boroughs would, as in England, become districts. Second, the county of Glamorgan would be divided into two new counties. East Glamorgan would be based on Cardiff and Merthyr Tydfil, West Glamorgan on Swansea, and their boundaries were very close to those proposed by the Labour Government in 1970 for the two unitary authorities.

The general approach to reform in England and Wales was identical — a new structure based on the traditional county-district model. So, too, was much of the phraseology in the two documents. But there were some differences, particularly over the allocation of functions. In England libraries were to be a county responsibility, in Wales the larger district councils might provide libraries. The same applied to consumer protection services, while refuse disposal would remain with the districts in Wales but be at county level in England. Another difference lay in the treatment of parishes and existing boroughs and urban districts. The Welsh document suggested that parishes be restyled 'communities', and that urban districts and boroughs would be able to opt for a community council. The English White Paper was far more cautious about urban parishes and stressed several problems, though it did not entirely rule out the possibility.

Initially senior civil servants and ministers told leading officials of the local authority associations that they were planning separate Bills for England and for Wales. In the event both countries were covered by the one Local Government Bill. The change came about primarily for tactical political reasons. First, it reduced the amount of legislative time which would be required, an important consideration for a new Government with a number of policies which could only be implemented through legislation. Second, it avoided the embarrassing problem of putting the Welsh Bill before the Labour-dominated Welsh Grand Committee: a joint Bill could go to a normal Commons Standing Committee on which there need be only a handful of Welsh members. The costs of this move were the potential embarrassments of having to explain to Parliament why Wales was not considered important enough to warrant separate legislation and why functions were allocated differently in the two countries.

In Chapter VI the translation of the 1971 proposals into legislation is examined in detail. As far as Wales was concerned it will be seen that there were four main features of this process. First, the

Opposition bitterly attacked the absence of separate Welsh legislation, portraying this as an insult to the principality. Second, attempts to embarrass the Government over differences in the allocation of functions were unsuccessful because Ministers were able to resort to procedural tactics in order to avoid any such debates. Third, despite its own record contained in the 1967 White Paper, the Labour Opposition criticised the absence of an elected Welsh Council. Fourth, the controversy about boundaries was intensified in south Wales and in Pembrokeshire (which sought unsuccessfully to retain its county status), though not in mid- and north Wales where counties had come to accept that amalgamations were inevitable after ten years of living with different sets of proposals which all called for such changes. Glamorgan's future became particularly contentious following the Government's decision in November 1971 to further sub-divide the existing county to form three new counties. The third looked very like the City of Cardiff with large boundary extensions and was attacked as a clear case of gerrymandering (Cardiff was just about the only pocket of Conservative Party strength in south Wales). The Government stood firm, however, (see pp.146-7). Under the 1972 Local Government Act there are as a result eight Welsh counties and thirty-seven districts, the extra district resulting from the division of Pembrokeshire into two at the request of all the local authorities in the area.

NOTES

1 Ministry of Housing and Local Government, Local Government Commission for Wales, *Report and Proposals for Wales* (HMSO, 1962), para. 13.
2 *Municipal Review*, Supplement July 1965, pp. 146-7.
3 *Hansard (Commons)*, vol. 724, col. 638 (10 Feb. 1966).
4 Welsh Office, *Local Government in Wales, Cmnd 3340* (HMSO, 1967).
5 J.P. Mackintosh, *The Devolution of Power* (Penguin, 1968).
6 Cmnd 3340, *op. cit.*, para. 57.
7 *Ibid.*, para. 1.
8 County Councils Association, *Memorandum on the White Paper on Local Government in Wales (Cmnd 3340)* (CCA, 1967), para. 3.
9 Association of Municipal Corporations, *Observations on the White Paper 'Local Government in Wales' (Cmnd 3340)* (AMC, 1967), paras 3-6.
10 *Hansard (Commons)*, vol. 773, Written Answers, cols 326-7 (21 Nov. 1968).
11 Cmnd 3340, *op. cit.*, para. 13.
12 *Hansard (Commons)*, vol. 784, col. 1466 (11 June 1969).
13 *Hansard (Commons)*, vol. 790, col. 32 (28 Oct. 1969).
14 Welsh Office, *Local Government Reorganisation in Glamorgan and Monmouthshire, Cmnd 4310* (HMSO, 1970).
15 *Ibid.*, para. 22.
16 Welsh Office, *The Reform of Local Government in Wales* (HMSO, 1971).

Chapter VI

IMPLEMENTATION — (1) THE LEGISLATIVE

PROCESS 1971-2

The Consultative Process
Readers familiar with the London scene will be aware that the working day for many senior executives starts at around 9.30 a.m. It was perhaps symbolic of the need for haste that senior civil servants met with the secretaries of the local authority associations at 9.00 a.m. on 25 February 1971, only nine days after publication of the White Paper, to discuss the coming period of consultation and legislation. Whether or not a light breakfast was provided remains unrecorded in the minutes!

This was a business-like meeting. Department of the Environment Under-Secretary Clifford Pearce had circulated a detailed agenda in advance, and discussion revolved around his proposed timetable and consultative methods. At the same time some areas of concern to the associations also emerged — notably the very short period of time for new non-metropolitan districts to prepare for the vesting day. The draft timetable envisaged elections to the new county and metropolitan district councils in spring 1973, giving them almost a year in which to appoint officers, set up committee and departmental structures, and prepare for the transfer of power on 1 April 1974. This matched exactly the Greater London timetable in 1964-5. However, the boundaries of the other districts would not be contained in the legislation. The Act would create a Local Government Boundary Commission. This Commission's report might not be ready until the end of 1972, and electoral areas would then need to be drafted. Elections in November 1973 had been tentatively suggested in the White Paper,[1] but at the 25 February meeting officials of both the Department and the associations agreed to try to advance the date (they succeeded, and the non-metropolitan district elections took place in June 1973).

Another issue aired at the meeting concerned the work of the proposed Boundary Commission. The White Paper had spoken of 40,000 as a normal minimum population for the new districts,[2] a figure which the association officers felt to be rather small.

The associations representing boroughs and districts were anxious to seek greater powers for the new second-tier councils, but could see that their case would become progressively weaker as districts became smaller. It was agreed that the associations would impress on their members that the figure of 40,000 was not an optimum or a desirable average population, but a minimum only relevant in sparsely populated areas of the country, and reference was made to Walker's statement at a press conference on the White Paper that there might finally be around 300 districts, which implied an average population of 60,000-80,000. Civil servants agreed to emphasise the need for strong districts. They did so in a letter to all local authorities in April, and also in a further circular promised in Circular 8/71 (which had accompanied the White Paper). In July 1971 this circular appeared, following detailed consultations with the associations. It laid down guidelines for the Boundary Commission including the sentence: 'Except in sparsely populated areas the aim should be to define districts with current populations generally within the range of about 75,000-100,000.'[3]

Finally, a rough timetable for discussions on a series of consultative papers to be circulated by the Department was agreed. Pearce envisaged circulating at least seven such papers in March, and a further six in April or May. If the Bill was to be introduced in November 1971 it would be necessary to finalise instructions to Parliamentary Counsel (i.e. the officers responsible for drafting the Bill) by about the end of June. This suggested that the time available for local authority and other interested party reactions to the consultative papers would be counted in weeks rather than months. A corollary of this was that there would be little time for the associations to consult with individual councils or members. A great deal of responsibility lay on the shoulders of the permanent officials of the associations, and on those of the handful of elected members who were able to keep abreast of developments. The large majority of councillors and local government officers had to put their trust in this small group of leaders.

The private and hurried nature of the consultative process caused some resentment and Walker was forced to clarify the situation in his speech during the May 1971 White Paper debate. By then about a dozen consultative papers had been sent to the associations. These had invited comments within periods sometimes as short as two weeks, and all had been stamped 'In Confidence'. Walker assured MPs that this apparent restriction on the debate had not been meant to limit the discussion in any way, and that it represented normal civil service practice during consultations at the pre-legislative stage rather than a directive from any minister.[4] He promised to alter the procedure and announced that the consultative papers were available to anyone interested in receiving them, and the offending phrase was crossed through by hand when copies were circulated after the debate. The Department's attitude was understandable in that it had no desire to be swamped with observations on every consultation paper, but it did not accord with Prime Minister Heath's declared intention of 'open government'.[5] Later, during the Second Reading debate, Walker again referred to the issue of secrecy, claiming that after May 'we have done everything to see that consultation should be as open as possible'. The author's experience suggests that this was not quite the case: in June a letter from the Department enclosing several of the consultation papers ended 'I should make it clear that I hope you will regard this as a personal arrangement and will not advertise it'!

In all there were about twenty-five consultation papers.[6] Some were very short — that on 'Parks, Sport and Recreation' ran to only three paragraphs. Others were fairly uncontroversial — the proposed machinery by which new districts might seek borough status, for example, was generally welcomed. In some cases the Government took a firm line and initiated detailed proposals, in other cases (e.g. the future of aldermen) it sat on the fence and merely asked for opinions.

On many issues the associations were able to reach agreement with the Department, but on three there were disputes which could not be resolved through the normal negotiating processes. First, the system of elections to district councils caused controversy. The AMC naturally favoured the 'borough model' of three-member wards and partial retirement; the RDCA supported single-member wards on the grounds that any other system would create vast wards covering numerous physically separate villages in areas of sparse population (i.e. in rural district council areas). The consultation paper made no firm proposal but eventually the department chose the borough model[7] (only to be forced into concessions during the parliamentary debates). Here the influence of the AMC was apparent, and this was the type of decision which justified its strategy of full cooperation in the consultative process.

Second, there was, predictably, controversy over the detailed allocation of powers. At the consultation stage this was restricted to functions where the White Paper envisaged shared or overlapping powers as there was no need for the Department to issue papers on education, social services and other functions where responsibility was to lie clearly with one level of authority. On housing, the district councils associations supported the Department's proposal that county council 'reserve powers' should be extremely limited. On highways they were less happy, as the paper covering all aspects of transportation reaffirmed the White Paper's plan to place all roads under county control. The paper on town and country planning proposed that all plan-making (structure and local) be a county council responsibility, though the AMC in particular felt that large districts (e.g. those which were based on a county borough) should be able to make their own local plans.

The planning proposals formed a third area of controversy, but one which differed from the first two in that the associations and professional bodies such as the Royal Town Planning Institute were largely united in their condemnation of the proposed 'unified staff structure'. The White Paper had made only brief reference to this concept, which was spelled out more fully in June 1971 in a consultation paper (by now circulated widely — the list of organisations on the Department's address sheet numbered ninety-nine). The Department claimed that the joint employment of planners was 'logical and practical' and 'a way of making the best use of scarce planning staff'. Three methods of operating a unified staff structure were outlined. First, county councils might employ all planners and second some to district councils, with districts represented on the county's planning committee. Second, there might be a joint county-district committee to 'manage the planning organisation'. Third, there could be specially constituted joint planning staff boards for each county area, with the board having powers to precept on the rating authorities. Which, asked the Department, was the best of the three? The weight of opinion against all three and against the whole concept of shared staff (problems of dual loyalties and of elected member control over staff and expenditure were frequently raised) caused the Government to abandon the concept entirely. Of the major interest groups, only the CCA fully supported the concept. It also 'entirely supported' the White Paper proposal that all plan-making, as opposed to development control, be a county responsibility.[8] On both these issues the CCA's opinion was rejected by the Government in its Bill. The district council-AMC lobby was particularly successful over the whole issue of responsibility for town and country planning.

The value to the Government of the consultative process cannot be over-emphasised. Any remaining doubts among observers as to the Government's commitment to legislation were swept away. A good deal of agreement with the associations and other interest groups was reached, which meant that the passage of legislation, already certain to be lengthy and tortuous due to the inevitable complexity of the Bill, would not be unnecessarily hindered by lengthy arguments on issues which were not central to the plan. Areas of dispute were identified, and Government spokesman could be briefed with replies to the arguments which MPs who supported particular associations and groups would be certain to raise in Parliament. Some concessions were made in cases where the Government could expect to be placed under severe pressure in Parliament. Private concessions made at the pre-legislation stage were less embarrassing than those forced from ministers during the passage of a Bill.

Consultations were not restricted to those between the Department and the associations. Simultaneously individual councils were reacting to the county and metropolitan district boundary proposals contained in Circular 8/71.[9] One division of the local government reorganisation section at the Department of the Environment concerned itself solely with boundaries.

For the most part the reactions of individual councils were predictable. Many counties were content to be reprieved, others sought to return even further towards the status quo. Cheshire asked for six districts in Merseyside and Greater Manchester to be added to the county; Buckinghamshire sought to retain Slough; Northamptonshire did not relish losing its southern tip around Brackley to Oxfordshire; Surrey was anxious to retain Gatwick Airport and the neighbouring village of Charlwood. Many districts and boroughs were more concerned with the coming Boundary Commission and the new pattern of non-metropolitan districts than with the Circular, but those in metropolitan areas frequently reiterated the views expressed earlier in response to the Labour Government's plan. There were a few unusual decisions such as letting Southport, at its request, be included in Merseyside. This was presumably made on the grounds that, as part of a metropolitan district, it would retain control of education and the social services (which would be county functions if the town were to stay in the new Lancashire), though the prospect of amalgamation with Bootle to form a 'double-headed' district in order to satisfy the 250,000 population requirement might have offset this argument.

Councils were given until 31 May 1971 to comment on the boundary proposals contained in Circular 8/71, though in several instances this deadline had to be extended. In the May local government elections the Labour Party regained some of the ground it lost in 1968, and political control of more than a dozen large towns changed hands. The new council sometimes wished to disown the comments of its predecessor. Warrington, for example, was no longer happy at the prospect of inclusion in Cheshire. Instead it sought a transfer to either Merseyside or Greater Manchester.

'Sensitive' areas like Warrington were then discussed at a series of meetings in the regions. Junior ministers met senior councillors and officers and were able to test the local temperature. The Government was able to claim that its promise of full consultations on detailed boundaries had been fulfilled. On the other hand a two-hour meeting might be concerned with a dozen or more areas, and critics occasionally complained that the discussions were, in fact, superficial.

The Bill and Second Reading
At the meeting with association secretaries on 25 February, Department of the Environment officials had expressed the hope that the Bill might be published 'as early as possible in the 1971/2 session — say November 1971'. A further measure of the success of the consultative process is in relation to this deadline, which was met with ease. The Bill was presented to Parliament on 4 November.

It was a formidable document, running to some 351 pages and containing 251 clauses and thirty schedules. Its contents were, for the most part, predictable — particularly to those closely involved in consultations during the spring and summer. Despite requests for additional counties from twenty-four boroughs including Luton, Southend, Plymouth ('Tamarside' county) and Stoke-on-Trent (a 'North Staffordshire' county), and for extra metropolitan districts for towns such as Bury and Rochdale (still seeking separation), the Bill created no further major authorities in England, though in Wales there would be a new county of South Glamorgan dominated by Cardiff. There were, however, more than sixty boundary changes, classifiable under three main headings.

First, all six metropolitan counties had been reduced in size, with territory being conceded to the neighbouring counties. The principal towns returned to their traditional counties were Glossop, Skipton and Harrogate, and Ellesmere Port, originally scheduled to be in Greater Manchester (Tameside district), West Yorkshire (Leeds district), and Merseyside (Wirral district) respectively. In addition Durham, Northumberland, Cheshire, Lancashire, Derbyshire, Staffordshire, North Yorkshire and Warwickshire were to benefit from smaller changes (in the case of Derbyshire only a single parish). Around 150,000 people had been transferred from metropolitan to non-metropolitan areas.*

Second, there were exchanges of territory between shire counties, designed, again, to restore areas to their traditional counties. The new counties of Avon and Teesside (later to be renamed Cleveland) were reduced in size, the former losing the Frome area to Somerset, the latter Easington to Durham and a large party of Stokesley RD to North Yorkshire. Brackley was returned to Northamptonshire, Lowestoft to Suffolk, Long Eaton to Derbyshire, Aldershot to Hampshire, and the Ingleton area of the Yorkshire dales to North Yorkshire. Mr Walker put it this way: 'I have endeavoured, to the

*The addition of Southport to Merseyside, discussed earlier, was the only significant alteration involving an enlargement of a metropolitan county. The one other example involved part of a parish near Worksop.

maximum degree possible commensurate with bringing about a sensible measure of reform of local government, to pay respect to the natural loyalty of people towards their counties.'[10]

Finally, three quite large changes were made in exactly the opposite direction, and traditional county boundaries were ignored. The smallest of the three saw the transfer of Sedbergh RDC from Yorkshire to Cumbria. A major proposal was that Colchester and the adjacent north-east Essex area were to be added to Suffolk, leaving a smaller Essex county based more clearly on Chelmsford and Southend, on the grounds that the Colchester-Ipswich area should be treated as one and that most councils in the area had asked for the transfer (a view later to be hotly disputed).[11] Further north, the new Humberside county was extended to take in a substantial part of north Lincolnshire (Grimsby and Scunthorpe). In the White Paper the River Humber had been the boundary. Now the Government claimed to be creating a unit which would be viable after the promised Humber Bridge had been built.[12]

The Bill also named the new counties. Most, of course, were continuations of existing counties, but a few caused problems. Tyneside was not a name to command support in Sunderland and was changed during the parliamentary proceedings to Tyne and Wear. Malvernshire was a compromise for the combined Herefordshire-Worcestershire county, but, again, was unpopular locally and, contrary to the Government's policy of seeking to avoid lengthy names, later became Hereford and Worcester. Cumbria, Humberside and Avon all proved generally acceptable, but Teesside was altered to Cleveland in order to demonstrate that this physically small county was not to be thought of as little more than an extension of the only recently created Teesside county borough.

Electoral arrangements revealed the concession to the AMC discussed above. The 'borough model' was chosen for all district councils, a decision quickly challenged by the RDCA. The abolition of aldermen was generally welcomed, and the procedures of the Local Government Boundary Commission had been agreed with the associations during the consultative process. One set of proposals about the basic structure was, however, certain to provoke further debate: there was no provision for an immediate extension of parish councils to existing urban areas. Many felt that the smaller boroughs and urban districts should be given the chance of obtaining parish-type powers and of retaining their ceremonial functions (as had happened in Salop, Devon and Cornwall under the 1958 Act — towns like Bishop's Castle, Ludlow and South Molton had been created 'rural boroughs'). Mr Walker acknowledged the strength of feeling on this issue and, during the Second Reading debate, announced that he intended to ask the Boundary Commission to review the proposals for urban parishes after the main authorities had become operational in 1974.[13]

The allocation of functions was certain to be contested in Parliament. The Government had made several concessions to the AMC and the district councils associations, and these gave districts responsibility for clean air zones, the maintenance of minor urban roads, municipal public transport undertakings (except in the metropolitan counties), and some local plan-making. But no concessions had been made with regard to libraries (whereas in Wales some districts might be designated library authorities), nor had the claims of large cities like Plymouth, Stoke, Leicester and Nottingham for extra powers over and above those of smaller districts been met. The associations of district councils and the AMC welcomed what changes there had been, though complained that even more powers should have been allocated to the second-tier — a predictable line of approach, as was the CCA's in welcoming the Bill but criticising the involvement of district councils in plan-making and highways. Individual local reactions to the boundary proposals were also predictable. In some cases councils were protesting for the fourth time in twenty-nine months, while in other cases there was victory to be celebrated (Cheshire sent congratulatory telegrams to ministers, flew the county flag, held a champagne lunch for members and senior officers, and gave all staff half the afternoon off!).[14]

Few of the changes made during the post-White Paper consultative process can be said to have been based on the concepts of 'democracy' and of 'efficiency' outlined in Chapter I. With the exception of the new proposals for Sedbergh, Colchester and north Lincolnshire, the changes of area were clear concessions to the county lobby or, in the case of Southport, to a town council under Conservative control. Southport was also interesting because its inclusion in, and Ellesmere Port's exclusion from, Merseyside made Conservative control of that new metropolitan county a very real possibility in an election year favourable to the party. 'Political' objectives appeared to be over-riding those of democracy and efficiency.

The changes in the distribution of functions could also be said to have only limited relation to these two concepts. Walker was quick to point out that the Bill abolished 100 statutory central controls and that he was reviewing a further 300 which no longer appeared necessary. It could be, and was, argued that the notion of responsibility being as local as possible (viewable as advantageous in terms of both democracy and efficiency) justified the decisions to divide responsibility for certain key services like highways and planning. On the other hand, a policy of shared powers results in the creation of additional administrative units and blurs responsibility. The new decisions did not appear to accord with the White Paper's welcome statements that the Government was 'determined ...to ensure that local government is given every opportunity to take initiative and responsibility effectively, speedily and with vigour', and that reorganisation would 'end the difficulties which arise through the present division of responsibility for highways and traffic'.[15] Nor was Walker's statement during the Second Reading debate that this was 'a new, clear-cut system. All the difficulties of one authority being answerable to another will come to an end. Functions will be at one level of local government or another', easy to justify.[16] We shall see that the parliamentary process cast further doubts on the Government's willingness to withstand pressure from those whose motives were, understandably, based on self-interest. Political objectives again transcended the concepts of democracy and efficiency in several instances.

It was apparent during the Second Reading debate that the Government was only standing firm on the major principles of two-tier government. Walker and Graham Page (who was to steer the Bill through the lengthy line-by-line examination in committee) made it clear that detailed boundaries were still open to negotiation, that the proposals for Humberside and the Colchester area (which had aroused a good deal of local hostility) would be re-examined, that urban parishes might still be included in the legislation, and that negotiations on the date of the first elections to new non-metropolitan districts were still taking place. They placed great emphasis on the coming Committee Stage debates in which the details of the Bill would be closely examined.

The Second Reading debate occupied two days and forty-four MPs (eight of whom were ministers or their shadows) spoke. For several reasons it was an unsatisfactory occasion. The atmosphere was for the most part distinctly low key, with the Government offering further consultations and concessions, and with Opposition spokesmen failing to launch a full attack on the Bill — apart from a strongly-argued complaint that Wales should have been treated in a second quite separate Bill — until the penultimate speech on the second day by Mr Denis Howell (who, with Mr John Silkin, was to lead the party at the Committee Stage). The Bill covered so many different topics — broad structure, detailed areas, functions, future changes, transfer of staff and property, elections, financial clauses — that back-bench speakers had to be selective and speeches rarely related to previous speeches. There was also a natural desire on the part of back-benchers to make 'constituency speeches' again, and twenty-seven of the thirty-six restricted their remarks to comments on detailed boundaries in a debate that, in theory, was about the principles of the proposed legislation. Finally, ministers did not attempt to answer the bulk of the points made by back-bench and Opposition spokesmen — they wound up the debate each day with speeches which had for the most part been prepared well in advance.

The debate revealed that both the main parties contained dissident members. Some Labour members, like Mr Jack Dormand (Easington), welcomed the two-tier system, though sometimes with reservations. There were critical Conservatives like Dame Joan Vickers from Plymouth, a city happy to be at the centre of a unitary authority and now violently opposed to inclusion in a mammoth Devon county, and Mr Mark Woodnutt from the Isle of Wight, which was pressing for a continuation of its county status (conceded later by the Government). Just how large the dissident groups within each party were it is impossible to say, as there was only a two-line whip in operation both at the Second Reading and at the subsequent stages of the legislative process. This made extensive 'pairing' possible and in the vote (251-231) only Dame Joan Vickers went into the lobbies against her party. But the Government's majority of twenty was about ten below that of its nominal overall majority in the Commons, an indication that several other back-benchers chose to abstain or absent themselves.

Apart from detailed boundaries, a number of important issues were raised during the debate. Several MPs from both parties pressed for still more powers at the district council level. Most were members from county borough areas where the council was to lose most of its functions under the provisions of the Bill, despite the concessions made to districts during the consultative process. Under the Bill such towns would lose control of education, libraries, social services, consumer protection, fire, refuse disposal, main roads and structure planning. Other members, again from both parties, were concerned about the exact division of planning powers, certain to be contested in committee. Demands for urban parishes were expressed by three speakers (two Conservative, one Labour). Finally, the opposition of the police to a further reorganisation of police areas, and the concern of some educationalists and of the CCA that metropolitan districts were too small to run education were both expressed.

As usual, most of these speeches were based on briefs sent to members by councils, associations and interest groups. Mr Tom Swain (Derbyshire North East), for example, read out a detailed Derbyshire county council case for its retaining several northern areas adjacent to Sheffield. Plymouth, Glamorgan and many other councils had provided briefs for their local members. The local authority associations circulated all MPs; the CCA sent them an eight-page document which 'generally welcomed' the Bill, but which expressed reservations, particularly on the allocation of planning, highways and education functions. It also criticised the decision to abolish the post of alderman, and the creation of a new county of South Glamorgan around Cardiff. This entry into discussion of detailed boundary proposals was unusual as the major associations normally avoided involvement in arguments about individual areas. It indicated the strength of feeling against this proposal, which had been included in the Bill without any prior consultation with councils in the area, and which was viewed by many as an attempt to satisfy Conservative-controlled Cardiff, which had fought hard to retain its independent status, by a Government with little political affinity with the Labour-dominated Glamorgan County Council.

Many interest groups chose to contact only 'friendly' members with their briefs.[17] The National Farmers Union, to give one example, expressed concern at the possibility 'of the legitimate interests of rural areas and of agriculture being absorbed by large and essentially urban dominated local authorities', and specifically called for even tighter outer boundaries of metropolitan counties. The Humberside, Avon and Glamorgan proposals were also criticised, as was the Government's call for non-metropolitan districts of 75,000-100,000 (the NFU preferred the original White Paper statement of 40,000). Finally, the union called for all planning powers to be exercised by county councils, partly to avoid a multiplicity of authorities and policies and partly on the grounds that 'the county can take a more objective and comprehensive view on planning matters and will not be so subject to local pressures.'

Committee Stage
The Second Reading debate had revealed the tactics to be adopted by both Government and Opposition. The Government would be prepared to make concessions on what it regarded as points of detail, and would stand firm only on broad principles. The Opposition would not launch a major assault on the Bill, but would content itself with harassment and with attempting to embarrass the Government. These tactics of delay began with an Early Day Motion signed by over fifty members (all Labour) criticising the Government's decision to send the Bill to a committee for the whole of Committee Stage:

This House regrets ... the Government's intention to send the whole of the Local Government Bill, which affects the constituencies of 448 honourable Members, to a Committee upstairs in view of the precedent of the London Government Act 1963, which affected the constituencies of 99 Honourable Members, when four days were allotted on the floor of the House for the consideration of Clause I and Schedule I which determined the boundaries of individual authorities.[18]

Following the vote to give the Bill a Second Reading, a further division took place on this motion. At 252-229 the vote was, not surprisingly, virtually identical.*

With many concessions on boundaries and on functions being sought, Committee Stage could pose problems for the Government. Its majority on the committee would be one, two or three depending on whether total membership was 15, 30 or 45. In theory it would not be difficult for a handful of Conservative back-benchers, acting as a united group, to force changes upon the Government.

Two decisions made the lives of ministers a little easier than might have been the case. First, a committee of forty-five gave the Government a majority of three, thus preventing a back-bencher from causing difficulties when acting alone. Second, the Commons Selection Committee appointed as Conservative members a large number of back-benchers who came from areas of the country where there was broad satisfaction with the boundary provisions of the Bill. Only one of the eighteen Conservative back-bench members of Standing Committee D came from a constituency where feelings about boundaries ran high (Mr Anthony Fell from Great Yarmouth), but Fell's speech in the Second Reading debate had made it clear that the future of only nine parishes was at stake and a compromise was easily obtained in committee. Aggrieved areas like the large seaside towns (Blackpool, Bournemouth, Plymouth), the small counties (Isle of Wight, Westmorland), and divided counties (Glamorgan, Somerset) were not represented, on the Government side at any rate. In contrast Kent, Dorset and Wiltshire, with county boundaries either untouched or enlarged, each had two MPs on the committee. Members from constituencies in Northamptonshire, Staffordshire, Bolton, Cardiff, Exeter and Sheffield were also unlikely to be under intense local pressure about boundaries.[19]

Despite this judicious selection of the membership, Comittee Stage still proved to be a lengthy process. From 25 November 1971

*The tactic of delay was aimed at other even more controversial legislation due to be passed in the 1971-2 session. This included the Housing Finance, Sound Broadcasting, and European Communities Bills, on all of which feelings ran high.

to 20 March 1972 the committee met on fifty-one occasions, making a total of 150½ hours of debate. At first there were three meetings each week, but this was increased to four after Christmas, and to six in March. The original target of Royal Assent in July 1972 laid down in Pearce's timetable of February 1971 had no chance of being met by the time the Bill was returned to the full House for the Report and Third Reading and for transferral to the House of Lords.

There were two main reasons for the length of the committee's proceedings. First, the Labour Party had every intention of making the Government fight for its legislation, though without offering root-and-branch opposition. Proceedings began, for example, with a six-hour debate on the first amendment, designed to replace the proposed new areas with those recommended by the Redcliffe-Maud Commission.[20] This was a major debate of principle, the sort which, in theory, should have taken place on Second Reading. Many of the speeches were lengthy and repetitive, and only one Government back-bencher spoke (for a mere eight minutes). The Government comfortably won the division by 23-17, with one Labour member abstaining and two others absent unpaired (an indication that the Opposition was less than united and that its own proposed legislation would have been difficult to carry). Delaying tactics continued, and on occasion it seemed as if a Government 'guillotine' motion might prove necessary. However, from time to time unofficial timetables were agreed privately between the two front benches. These took the form of targets to be met each day and they were adhered to with precision. This could mean both long and short sittings on occasion. On 3 February 1972 the afternoon session lasted for only twenty-eight minutes instead of the normal two and a half hours because progress on the clauses about elections had been rapid. A fortnight later a seven-hour sitting included a bitter debate of more than an hour on an unexpected Government amendment allowing the new councils to choose between district and private audit.

Coupled with this tactic was the concern with the contents of the Bill of close to one hundred interest groups, several hundred individual local authorities and numerous local *ad hoc* organisations. Members received a mass of briefs from these bodies.* Labour members took the view that all expressions of concern with the Bill should be aired and answered by the Government (a decision which led them to propose many amendments which the party as a whole would never have supported), and much of the

*Whose efficiency was variable. Even the UDCA, one of the better organised, circulated a brief on the clause relating to public health functions almost a week after the debate had taken place!

proceedings consisted of ministerial replies to amendments proposed by individual members without the support of their full party group. Conservative back-benchers also spoke on behalf of interest groups, and the threat to the Government came more from its own members than from the Opposition. Interest groups naturally sought support from the Government side of the committee, and the CCA and National Association of Parish Councils, for example, had a valuable ally in the form of Mr Charles Morrison (Conservative, Devizes). He regularly tabled their proposed amendments, and spoke no less than eighty-nine times. Only three front-benchers and Mr John Roper (Labour, Farnworth) contributed more frequently. In all, some 1,852 amendments were tabled, 1,300 of them by the Opposition and back-bench members.

For the most part the debates were conducted in a fairly quiet manner (in contrast to proceedings in the adjacent committee room, where the Housing Finance Bill was under scrutiny). There were only twenty-five divisions, not all of which were forced by the Opposition front-bench. For example, Mr Maddan, Conservative member for Hove, insisted on a vote on his amendment to move East Grinstead from West Sussex back into East Sussex. He lost by 17-4.[21] Ten divisions concerned areas and boundaries, and the debates on the Bill's geography occupied twenty-two of the fifty-one sittings, reflecting concern outside Parliament with the geographical details. Only twice was the Government's majority threatened. First, an amendment to exclude the police from further reorganisation was lost only on the chairman's casting vote after Messrs Fox and Montgomery had voted with the Opposition.[22] Second, Fox moved an amendment by which the right to stand for election would be extended to those aged 18-21. Seventeen members spoke in a two-hour debate during which the Government suggested that the issue be referred to the Speaker's Conference.[23] Five Government back-benchers, including Fox, were satisfied with this reply but two (Miss Fookes, Mr Reed) were not. They voted with the Opposition and the Government scraped home by two votes only because by accident three Labour members were absent unpaired. Two of them were front-bench spokesmen and the Labour Whip was not at all pleased with their behaviour.

In recent years academic observers of the parliamentary process have paid more attention to Select and Specialist Committees of the Commons than to its Standing (legislative) Committees. On occasion the impression has been given that these latter play a limited role and it is only recently that Professor J.A.G. Griffith has redressed the balance with his detailed study of the passage of legislation.[24] Stuart Walkland's *The Legislative Process in Great Britain*, for example, devotes less than a dozen pages to committee stage, and these are in a chapter entitled 'Government *Control* [sic] of the Stages of Parliamentary Scrutiny and Criticism'.[25] It is true that there are examples of legislation where the Government does stand firm and uses its majority to repel all or most amendments, but the Local Government Bill is equally typical of a mass of legislation where some modification is acceptable to the Government provided that key principles are retained. Only a handful of Bills each session are fought on the basis of inflexibility and constant three-line whips.

Looking at the Commons Committee Stage of the Local Government Bill it is possible to discern five major justifications for the investment of up to 150 hours' time by forty-five MPs on detailed discussions. The first is that it provided the opportunity for the Government to amend its own proposals. In this Bill no fewer than 547 Government amendments and new clauses were approved by the Committee, or rather more than one and a half per page. Basically these changes came about for two rather different reasons. One was that the draftsmen made mistakes. Quite frequently Bills are drafted in a hurry, and, particularly when they amend or repeal scores of older Acts of Parliament, it is easy to overlook points of detail. Thus no fewer than 121 of the Government amendments altered Schedule 30, the list of earlier Acts repealed by the new legislation. There is, of course, no particular reason why a formal committee of members is needed to oversee this process of amendment. The second type of Government-sponsored change was the more important — this is where the Government had 'second thoughts'.

Though some amendments owed their presence to a reappraisal within the administration, for the most part such reappraisals were the result of successful lobbying by interest groups. Sometimes the Government itself tabled amendments reflecting the outcome of negotiations with groups — as was the case with Clause 177 dealing with town planning. Here the Government clarified and slightly strengthened the role of the county council in plan-making. District council plans were now to be certified by the county, and not all districts would be allowed to make plans. Simultaneously, as a *quid pro quo* to the districts for this loss of powers, the role of district councils over development control was strengthened by a reduction of the list of reserved 'county matters' in Schedule 16.[26] The town planning clauses were extremely controversial and the Government was continually faced with two conflicting alliances of local authority and professional associations. The CCA, the Royal Town Planning Institute and the Town and Country Planning Association attacked the Bill and favoured amendments designed to strengthen the role of the county. The AMC, UDCA and RDCA were on the defensive. They were satisfied with the concessions which they had gained during the pre-legislation consultations and continued to issue joint statements broadly in support of the Bill. Several interesting ministerial speeches reflected this delicate political situation.

The second justification for Committee Stage was that the Government could be forced to alter its detailed proposals because of the adverse reactions of members of extra-parliamentary interest groups represented in debates by friendly MPs. If such groups had been unable to obtain a change of heart from the Government during the consultative process, they turned to members — normally to Government back-benchers as a first priority and then to the Opposition. More than fifty different interest groups 'briefed' MPs about parts of the Local Government Bill, and doubtless all had first tried to persuade the Minister to table his own amendments.

Members of Parliament were here expressing the hopes and fears of such groups. The impression was given to the casual observer or reader of Hansard that the Minister had given way because of the strength of feeling expressed in committee. This was, of course, only part of the truth. Frequently no more than a handful of members had spoken. What had happened was that the Government was prepared to use this process as a method of accepting representations in cases when it did not feel willing to acknowledge overtly private pressure by tabling its own amendments. Take the case of the new local authority boundaries. Nine changes were made in committee — but in no case was it possible to conclude that this was due solely to the oratorical performance of members. Indeed, in agreeing to move Skelmersdale from Merseyside back into Lancashire, the Minister openly said:[27] 'I pay tribute to those who presented the case for Skelmersdale [at a meeting with him]...because it was obvious that the arguments put forward this morning by the Hon. Members for Widnes and Farnworth were deeply felt locally.'* It was indeed rare for a Minister to be seen to change his mind as a result of the debate: if he conceded an amendment he normally arrived armed with a brief from his civil servants which outlined the reasons for the concession (and fifty-two amendments moved by the Opposition front-bench or by back-benchers were passed in committee).

More common than outright concession was agreement by a Minister to 'look again' at a matter. The Government frequently took this line — and this resulted in numerous Government-

---

*This was a good example of a Labour member's amendment which did little to assist the party. It made Merseyside even more marginal in electoral terms as Skelmersdale was a solid Labour town. When making the concession Mr Heseltine was smiling and, it being 21 December, he described himself as 'a sort of Father Christmas benefactor' (*Standing Committee D*, col. 569).

sponsored amendments being made later at Report Stage and in the House of Lords. An interesting case related to Teesside. In the Bill the proposed new county of Teesside embraced the Whitby area as well as the Teesside and Hartlepool county boroughs. Whitby and the villages of Whitby and Stokesley rural districts fought strongly to be transferred to North Yorkshire, but acceptance of their case would have left the new county dominated by Teesside county borough to such an extent that Luton, Plymouth and several other large towns would have been able to claim that their cases for being made into additional counties were no different from the Teesside situation. This led Page to suggest that Teesside and Durham might amalgamate but, in the end, he accepted the new county, renamed Cleveland and without the Whitby area. Teesside county borough had agreed to its division into several districts and had suggested the name Cleveland in order to avoid the 'domination' argument.[28] There were two other important examples — first, the plan for urban parish councils. In committee the Minister agreed, at the end of a long debate in which the contents of the Bill were criticised by two Government back-benchers, to seek a solution to the desires of many small boroughs and urban districts to remain in existence as parishes.[29] On Report he unveiled his plan, which was passed without debate. The Local Government Boundary Commission was asked to judge, before 1974, which borough and urban district councils should remain in being as parish councils (many with town council status and town mayors rather than just as a parish council with a chairman). Second, the Government produced changes in the electoral system at Report Stage, as a concession to the RDCA and UDCA. The Bill proposed three-member wards for districts. The RDCA pointed out that this would entail the creation of massive geographical wards covering several villages in sparsely populated districts, and the Minister agreed in committee to reconsider the plan. Under his revised proposals, single-member wards became possible in non-metropolitan districts though not in metropolitan ones. The new district councils would be able to choose their electoral system.[30]

A Bill is a dry legal document, and it is often uncertain from the wording alone just how the Government proposes to supervise the implementation of its provisions. How would it handle disputes between authorities where functions were shared? What would be its attitude to proposals from the Local Government Boundary Commission? Those who would be actually operating the new system locally were anxious to receive answers from ministers to this type of question. Committee Stage was a place for eliciting such information, and this was a third, and arguably the most important, role of the committee (for, though such information can be elicited at all the legislative stages, it is in committee that time is most available).

Many examples of important Government statements of intent could be quoted. The controversial planning clause was discussed at length and during the course of the debate the Minister made it quite clear that he would issue regulations and circulars to try to clarify the question of which districts should be allowed to make Local Plans. Under the Bill the presumption was that all districts were local plan-making authorities. This was criticised heavily by certain professional bodies as well as the CCA on the grounds that small districts would not have sufficient staff and that the shortage of professional town planners would be exacerbated if they were spread between hundreds of authorities. The Minister clarified the situation by stating quite clearly that, although 'the Government view is that we should presume that the local plans are a function of the districts', in the case of a dispute he would *not* find in favour of districts lacking either 'the resources or staff to prepare even a simple local plan'.[31] Under the Act counties must draw up a 'development plan scheme' in consultation with district councils. The scheme outlines a programme of Local Plans and assigns responsibility for their production between county and district. It was at this stage that disputes were expected to arise.

A second illustration of this point concerned the status of proposals emanating from the Local Government Boundary Commission. Under the Bill the Minister could either implement, reject or modify these, and members pressed for clarification. Government intentions were made clear — 'if the Commission is to have any credibility it is essential that we have a convention that the Secretary of State accepts the Commission's proposals, unless there is an exceptional reason which he is prepared to justify to the House for refusing to proceed on these proposals.'[32] Third, the Government made many references to clause 100, which became known as the 'agency clause'. This allowed an authority to use another authority 'for the discharge of any of their functions', though not in the case of education, police and social services. Amendments designed to increase the powers of district councils at the expense of counties were resisted partly on the grounds that counties could use districts as agents for the administration of several important services such as libraries, highways and consumer protection. Just how this clause would work in practice was unclear and the Government promised to issue guidance on agency arrangements at a later date.[33]* These examples were typical of many cases where the Government indicated its view of how the Bill would work in practice. Although such statements in Parliament

*See pp. 170-3 for further details of this important clause.

have no legal standing (unlike the situation in some other countries) they are normally treated by Governments as morally binding.*

Service on a Standing Committee like this one also added to the education of members — a fourth justification for Committee Stage. It added immensely to their knowledge of local government, and few came to the committee with considerable expertise on the subject, (as was evidenced when Mr Heseltine, the junior minister, declared at an early meeting of the committee [col. 342] that parish councils were not elected). It gave back-benchers an opportunity to have a reasoned debate with Ministers on a face-to-face basis (debates in the full House are conducted in a glare of publicity and, except in Committee of the Whole House, a member normally speaks only once to a motion). Ministers also had to master the subject and answer the debate (constant straight reading from the brief was not popular!), and future Ministers like Mr John Silkin or Mr Keith Speed obtained a greater understanding of the sort of mastery of the subject that is needed in order to be successful. Whether it was worth spending all this time in committee just for the sake of 'education' is certainly questionable, but this was only one of several functions of the committee and it does deserve consideration.

Finally, Committee Stage could be a place for full-dress debates and for major statements of policy by the Opposition as well as by the Government. Though for the most part there was a bi-partisan approach, several major debates in Committee were conducted in a highly political atmosphere. We saw earlier that a debate on the Opposition's proposals for unitary authorities *à la* Redcliffe-Maud to replace the Government's proposed two-tier system took over six hours. Later, despite its own record when in office, Labour attacked at length the Government's failure to propose an elected Welsh Council (and pledged a future Labour Government to legislate on this), and sought to move education from the metropolitan district to the metropolitan county. Briefly, but bitterly, the Opposition criticised the Government's plan (unveiled without prior consultation) to allow the new local authorities to use private auditors as an alternative to the district auditor if they so wished. Less briefly (four members spoke for at least forty-five minutes each in a debate which took six hours), the three-way division of Glamorgan was strenuously contested, though the resultant vote was inevitably lost.

In Glamorgan debate[34] was particularly interesting because it

*In Chapter I we saw that Crossman felt obliged to accept the Government statements about the outer limits of Special Review Areas made during the committee stage of the 1957-8 Local Government Bill, despite the fact that they had been made by a Conservative Minister.

provided a rare example of the Government determined to resist pressure however weak its case. Labour speakers claimed that the Government had made false statements about the amount of support in the area for a three-county system, and an analysis of the letters and briefs sent to MPs suggests that they were correct. They pointed out that the new mid-Glamorgan county would be extremely poor and referred to the CCA's criticism of the plan, the only case where the Association had concerned itself with boundaries. One Conservative (Mr Roberts, Cardiff North) supported the Cardiff-based county largely on grounds of community of interest, but the Minister's defence (cols 2701-14) was less than persuasive and led Mr George Thomas to complain that he had 'never heard such a hopeless, insulting pretence at a reply as the Minister of State gave us tonight'. In a final statement the Minister relied largely on the fact that there had been a good deal of criticism of the original two-county plan, but he chose not to compare this to the hostility to the new proposals which appeared to be supported only by Cardiff and by one or two local organisations in the city. A massive 'Save Glamorgan from the Carve Up' campaign sponsored by the county council and featuring a broken daffodil motif, the efforts of a 'Two Not Three' committee and opposition from every council in Glamorgan which wrote to MPs did not succeed. A coachload of Welshmen attended the debate and went home extremely dissatisfied.

Members and Committee Stage: A Survey
Members' attitudes to Committee Stage were tested through the issue of a written questionnaire, completed by twenty-five of the forty-five. All but one commended the extensive Notes of Guidance issued by the Government to all members on the Committee. These notes ran to around 1,000 typescript pages, and they explained the background to and consequences of each clause. The advantage was that this avoided lengthy explanatory speeches from ministers. All but two MPs thought the size of the forty-five member Committee was 'about right', and all but three felt able to speak as much as they wished (two of the three were members of the Government unable to participate freely — a whip and Mr Walker's parliamentary private secretary). No member complained of an overdose of party politics during the debates, and one (Labour) felt that more would have been desirable.

Members (in each case about 80 per cent of respondents) viewed the process as being valuable in three main ways. It educated them and their colleagues, it made the Government explain in some detail the provisions of the Bill, and it improved the wording of the legislation (no MP replied that Committee Stage was 'not valuable'). Fourteen of the twenty-five singled out the debates about the allocation of functions as being particularly important, though seven chose those about provincial councils and five mentioned cases of individual boundaries (several mentioned more than one topic). The two-tier principle, urban parish councils, and clauses on qualifications for election (where two important issues arose: that of reducing the age of eligibility for election to eighteen, and the proposed continuance of the rule that local government officers should not be eligible for election to their employing authority) were also mentioned by two or more members. Ten thought that areas had received too much discussion, and six that clauses on functions had suffered from a lack of debate. The evidence supports this view. First, more than 40 per cent of the time was spent on areas, less than 25 per cent on functions. Second, with the creation of a permanent Boundary Commission, the new areas were flexible and would be more easily adaptable in future than the allocation of functions, which would normally require amending legislation.

A series of questions related to the activities of individuals, councils and pressure groups seeking to alter the Bill. Almost all respondents found their contacts with such bodies helpful, and a majority admitted that more material was received than they had expected. All but three members had direct personal (as opposed to written) contact with individual councils in their constituency, as one would have expected. Four had similar contacts with other councils — Gatwick, Plymouth, Southampton and Herefordshire were specifically mentioned. The associations of local authorities were in regular personal contact (the CCA and AMC had officials present at virtually every sitting of the committee), while individual MPs also referred to the Library Association, Justices Clerks Society, Police Federation, Magistrates Association, Town and Country Planning Association and individual amenity societies (by name) as having sought to influence the debates through interviews as well as written briefs.

Four criticisms were made of the written briefs by eight or more MPs: that these briefs were sometimes too long, too late (seventeen mentioned this), overstated, or that they did not contain a draft amendment which could easily be tabled. The CCA and the AMC were most frequently mentioned as 'impressive', as one would expect in view of their efficient organisations and reservoir of expertise built up over the post-1969 period during the debates on the Redcliffe-Maud Report. Small authorities were commonly classed as 'unimpressive'.

Finally, MPs were asked 'could Parliament in any way change its procedure in order to make the consideration of a Bill such as this more effective?'. Eleven were completely satisfied, while ten offered positive ideas, some of which related to the Opposition's criticisms of the absence of a separate Bill for Wales or of a Committee of the Whole House on at least the geographical clauses. Of the suggestions which appeared not to be motivated by party considerations, two were particularly interesting. One member felt that there could have been more statistical information and a greater use of visual aids to explain parts of the Bill (the 1,000 pages of explanatory notes had themselves been an unusual form of briefing by the Government*), another that it would have been helpful to hear and cross-examine witnesses (as happens with Private Bills). There would seem to be some merit in both these ideas, though the latter would have been extremely time-consuming had every issue been considered in this way.

From Committee to Royal Assent
Statistically the rest of the legislative process (Report and Third Reading in the Commons, plus all stages in the Lords) was also impressive. To the 599 Committee Stage amendments were added a further 654 on Report (of which nineteen were moved by the Opposition or back-benchers) and 633 in the Lords. Thus in all no fewer than 1,886 amendments were made to the original Bill, a figure which must be one of the largest ever recorded.† Progress remained slow: seven days — totalling seventy and a half hours of Commons Report Stage, eight days and fifty hours in Committee in the Lords, and a further three days and seventeen hours on Report Stage there. Finally, the Commons spent a further two days discussing and accepting all but one of the amendments made in the upper House. In order to complete the Bill's passage the Lords had to sit through most of September and, unusually, sat until the small hours on one occasion. The Royal Assent was finally given on 26 October 1972.

But length and content must be clearly distinguished. Much of the post-Committee Stage debate was repetitive, and it was in Committee that the main areas of dispute were isolated. An amendment withdrawn in Committee, as most non-Government ones were, could often be reintroduced and redebated at Report Stage. In the Lords it could again be discussed twice. Thus some detailed boundary amendments came up on four separate

---

*In the House of Lords the Government was thanked for these and the hope was expressed that this innovation would become common practice, *Hansard* (*Lords*), vol. 335, col. 1528 (22 Sept. 1972).

†The total includes some double counting, as in a very few cases a second amendment reversed a first one (e.g. on refuse disposal, see below).

occasions, while two or three debates on an issue were commonplace.

The main difference between Commons and Lords lay in the strength of the various lobbies. In the Commons the AMC and district councils associations were well represented. The Government had to react to pressures on it to increase the powers of second-tier councils. It gave little away, though at Report Stage it was defeated by four votes (190-186) when an amendment transferring responsibility for refuse disposal from counties to districts was proposed by Mr Arthur Jones, a Conservative back-bencher. Three Conservatives supported him in the debate, and one or two more in the lobbies.[35] The Government easily managed to reverse this amendment in the Lords, and when the Commons debated the Lords' amendment the dissident Conservatives accepted defeat, though they once again spoke in favour of uniting refuse collection and disposal at district level. The Government also conceded to pressures for the creation of two additional metropolitan districts through the division of Bury-Rochdale and of St Helens-Huyton.

When under pressure about the allocation of functions, the Government relied on a standard defence: that it interpreted the Bill as being flexible over levels of responsibility due to the presence of the 'agency clause'. In the Notes for the Guidance of Members, clause 100 had been portrayed as 'a new code which gives the local authorities greater freedom over their internal organisation and the way they discharge their functions' (partly a reference to the general ability, included in it, to delegate powers to officers for the first time). The subsection allowing a council to use another council was described in low-key language: 'It might be right for one council to make the policy and decide on the expenditure and get another authority to act as its agent for the execution of the job. The Government want to leave the authorities themselves to decide what is the right sort of arrangement in the particular case and in the light of local circumstances.'

In committee there was no real debate on the clause. Because it preceded those on the allocation of particular functions its significance was not fully apparent to members at the time. Later Page and Heseltine constantly referred to clause 100 when answering amendments designed to increase district council powers over refuse disposal, transportation, food and drugs, and libraries. Under pressure, Heseltine agreed that the Government would 'issue guidance within the powers of Clause 100 concerning the way in which these agency arrangements would work'.[36] On Report MPs from all parties spoke in support of the district council lobby and sought to alter the clause by allowing a right of appeal to the

Minister by aggrieved councils. Eventually Mr Walker conceded and agreed to arbitrate on disputes between councils arising prior to 1 April 1974.[37] It had also become apparent that an 'agent' would have more responsibility than that suggested in the original Notes for the Guidance of Members — for example, to choose between minor highway improvement projects up to an agreed total sum.

In the Lords, the Government's task was slightly different. There the county and rural interests were particularly well represented and there was pressure on the Government to increase the powers of counties as well as to draw metropolitan boundaries even more tightly. Against Government advice the Lords removed Wilmslow and Poynton from Greater Manchester and returned them to Cheshire at the last possible moment — in the case of Poynton by a single vote.[38] The Government also conceded the case for a separate Isle of Wight county despite the island's population of only about 100,000. By leaving this concession until Report Stage in the Lords the Government ensured that there was no time for the campaigners for separate Pembrokeshire, Herefordshire and Anglesey counties to launch a further assault on the Bill using the Isle of Wight decision as a precedent. It was also made quite clear that geographical circumstances made this a special case and that it should not be viewed as a breach in the 250,000 population guideline.[39]

A new clause on 'agency', giving statutory force to the ministerial arbitration procedures promised by Walker in the Commons, ran into criticism by CCA spokesmen who quoted at length from a critical brief: 'A number of my colleagues on the County Councils Association would like to see this clause eliminated' declared Viscount Gage.[40] However, after a seventy-five-minute debate the new clause was accepted without a vote, possibly because it had been so firmly promised by Walker. Later, on Report Stage, Gage and his colleagues again sought concessions, this time by proposing that appeals against agency arrangements be made before the end of 1973. Their concern was that a district might at the last minute, say in February or March 1974, decide to appeal against a county council proposal and that such action would make a smooth transition on 1 April 1974 more difficult to achieve. The Minister agreed but preferred to leave the timetable to a circular of guidance worked out by the department in consultation with the associations. Through this method of approach, said Lord Aberdare, 'we shall get our flexibility, and we shall not put ourselves in the position of having to make any last-minute decisions.'[41] In the event, as we shall see in Chapter VII, he was being over-optimistic.

The agency clause was one of several relating to the distribution of functions on which the county lobby put pressure on the Government in the Lords. Three and a half hours were spent on attempts to increase county powers in relation to historic buildings preservation and to conservation areas. The CCA had sought concurrent powers in the Commons Committee and the Government had agreed to reconsider the matter. No consultations had taken place by Report Stage, and after a long debate in the Lords Committee the Government, under pressure, again agreed to reconsider the position. But the delay had forced the CCA and other interested bodies to focus their argument more narrowly. On Report the issue became one of ensuring that districts only acted after obtaining adequate specialist advice, and of making provisions for the retention of strong county teams. The Minister promised to use powers to make districts obtain advice, and early regulations and other forms of guidance would be issued.[42]

The town and county planning clauses caused less trouble in the Lords than might perhaps have been expected. These were the provisions which 'have caused the Association the greatest concern', said CCA Secretary Alistair Hetherington in a letter to members at the end of the Commons Committee Stage.[43] The CCA had sought seven changes to the original Bill. In Committee two had been fully met by Government amendments. The first made counties solely responsible (the Bill had made this a joint county-county district responsibility) for 'development plan schemes' under which decisions were made as to the timing of and responsibility (district or county) for local plans, and the second ensured that districts notified counties of the contents of all planning applications. Government amendments at Report Stage in the Commons, following promises made in Committee by Ministers, satisfied a third CCA ambition. County council 'certification' that a local plan complied with the county structure plan was now necessary before a local plan could be published by a district council. County reserve powers over planning applications (i.e. a list of types of application which could not be decided by district councils) were also clarified, and the CCA felt reasonably satisfied with the outcome. Of the remaining three CCA objectives, two (relating to the locus of decision as to whether or not a planning application was a 'county matter', and to whether a county could 'brief' a district before the district commenced work on a local plan) had been largely met by Government amendments and promises of guidance through circulars. The seventh objective, to avoid a presumption that local plans were to be drawn up by districts, had been sought unsuccessfully in the Commons where a statement making this very presumption was on record as we saw earlier. In the Lords this was the only issue raised by members sympathetic to the CCA, but Viscount Colville of Culross (for the Government) stuck firmly to the line taken by Graham Page in the Commons.[44] The CCA had achieved many of its objectives, but remained unhappy about local plan-making. It saw the change from the White Paper proposal for this to be a county function as no more than a concession to the 'county borough lobby', probably an accurate assessment.

Though the Government lost four divisions in the Lords (all on areas: Lymington, Rothwell, Wilmslow, Poynton) and finally conceded the case for a separate Isle of Wight county, the upper House forced few other major concessions from ministers. It also spent a long time on the Bill — fifty hours in Committee, seventeen and a half on Report — and added a further 633 amendments to the 1,253 made in the Commons.* It mirrored the Commons in spending 40 per cent of the time on detailed areas and 25 per cent on the allocation of functions, which suggests that not only MPs make 'constituency speeches'. The issues raised were also similar, for interest groups frequently had sympathetic members in both Houses. The staff organisations like NALGO pressed the Government on the rule that no officer is eligible for election to his employing authority, producing new amendments at each stage in response to ministerial statements at the preceding stage. It persuaded the Government to recognise and acknowledge the problem that over 2,000,000 officers, the vast majority of whom were 'field workers' rather than advisers to the council, were debarred under this rule. No concessions were made in the Bill, but the Government was persuaded to set up an inquiry, and it did so in October 1973 by appointing another Committee under the chairmanship of Lord Redcliffe-Maud. This reported in 1974 in favour of retaining the law so much criticised by the trades unions.[45] The incoming Labour Government, however, was to some extent committed to a relaxation of this rule and it referred the issue to another new formal commission, set up to review Standards of Conduct in Public Life following the Poulson cases.

The Police Federation continued its campaign to avoid a further set of amalgamations, though without success. The National Parks lobby sought, also unsuccessfully, to avoid county council control of the parks committees. The Campaign to Save Education in the

*All but one of the 633 were accepted by the Commons after a further seventeen hours of debate (the disagreement related to a Lords amendment preventing a council from advertising its conference and tourist facilities abroad). One third of the seventeen hours was spent on areas, with close votes approving the Lords decisions about Wilmslow and Poynton (the Government majority falling to eleven and twelve).

Conurbations produced an excellent pamphlet by George Taylor (former Chief Education Officer, City of Leeds) criticising the small size and limited resources of many of the northern metropolitan districts.[46] He suggested that such districts would be unable to provide a first-class education service whereas the large, rich, southern county councils were advantageously placed. The Campaign's case for the transfer of responsibility for education to the metropolitan county was supported by the CCA (and had, in 1970, been proposed by the Labour Government), but was resisted by the Government. The CCA and the other main local authority associations were also opposed to a new clause, proposed by the Opposition and accepted by the Government at short notice and with minimal consultation on the very last day of the Commons Committee Stage, which allowed the press and public access to all local authority committee meetings. The Society of Justices Clerks and the Magistrates Association sought changes in the composition of magistrates courts committees. In all these and several other cases no major concessions were achieved, though frequently the Government agreed to reconsider the consequences of the legislation and to issue guidance in the light of the debates, as well as to undertake the conventional consultations which precede such guidance. It became increasingly clear that implementation of the Act was to be a complex process, entailing a mass of consultations and a steady shower of circulars.

The Value of the Legislative Process
The success of the parliamentary process may be judged in both general and specific terms. Generally it was an example of accountable government. For 300 hours ministers participated in debates about the proposed legislation. Their role was to defend, explain and, if necessary, propose or agree to the amendment of the Government's plan for local government reform. As we have seen, there were numerous issues where ministerial statements interpreted the proposals clearly for the first time, where ministers agreed to concede points, and where the Government stood firm. The Bill was, in fact, a curious mixture of clauses of varying importance in terms of its main principles, and the debates reflected this unevenness.

Of course, not all Bills are so open to change as was this one. In the same session of Parliament the other major pieces of Government legislation were conducted largely through highly partisan debates in which ministers were reluctant to make concessions. The European Communities Bill was entirely unamended, and alterations to the Finance, Housing Finance, Housing Finance (Scotland), and Sound Broadcasting Bills were far less numerous and easy to obtain than was the case with the Local Government Bill.[47] Indeed, more than 1,800 amendments must surely constitute something of a record.

In general terms, then this was a good illustration of a legislative partnership between Government and Parliament, corresponding to some extent with nineteenth- and early twentieth-century notions of 'parliamentary government'.[48] Though this was Government-sponsored legislation, a large proportion of it was not to be defended to the last ditch. This was because of the nature of the legislation. First, it directly affected the interests of every English and Welsh MP and constituency. Second, it consisted of many detailed proposals behind which there could not be any particular political philosophy beyond that of a concern for representative local government which is common to the philosophy of all major political parties in this country. To take an extreme case, it is hard to think in terms of a political clash over Dr Marshall's successful amendment that in the list of 'offensive trades' the phrase 'rag *and* bone dealer' be replaced by 'rag *or* bone dealer', described by Mr Page as the 'Steptoe and Son' amendment![49]

A clear distinction must, however, be made between the general success of the legislative process and an assessment of the specific value of this considerable investment of time and effort. Was the Local Government Act 1972 an improvement on the Bill of 1971?

Here there are a variety of opinions to be obtained from our groups of proximate decision-makers. Concessions such as the agreement to issue advice and to arbitrate on disputes between councils about the use of the 'agency' clause added to the work of civil servants during the period of supervision of implementation. There were several such examples and a spate of circulars had to be drafted and processed. It is unlikely that civil servants viewed the alterations to the Bill in an entirely favourable light. Ministers were likely to have broadly similar views, though were comforted by the thought that they had achieved their broad aim of reforming local government without too much intra-party blood-letting. The Opposition could look back on successfully proposing more than fifty changes and forcing the Government to bring in others — notably it had been influential over public access to council committee meetings, the abolition of aldermen in London, and the early creation of urban parish councils.

Individual councils had frequently tasted success. Skelmersdale, Poynton, Bury, Wilmslow, Great Ayton (whose residents sent friendly MPs a Christmas card of thanks in 1972!) and the Isle of Wight were examples of boundary alterations pressed successfully by the respective local authorities. Other attemps had failed — those of Plymouth, Lincolnshire and Glamorgan, for example.

Council views on the value of the legislative process inevitably varied according to the treatment afforded to them.

Pressure groups and local authority associations also had varied reactions. The unions representing local government staff had received two important rebuffs during the passage of the Bill. First, they had failed to persuade the Government to redraw the line between eligibility and ineligibility for election. Second, they had unsuccessfully contested a new clause added during the Commons Committee Stage which was designed to restrict councils in the award of pay rises shortly before an amalgamation. In London several councils had upgraded staff before they handed over powers to the new authorities, and the Government was anxious to prevent wholesale pay awards unless there was a good case — under the new clause the Local Authority Conditions of Service Advisory Board had to approve changes in remuneration or conditions of employment.[50] On pages 153-4 several other examples of largely unsuccessful attempts to amend the Bill by pressure group activity were cited.

All the major local authority associations could point to a mixture of success and failure. The CCA had, in its view, improved the clauses relating to planning and resisted the proposals for further reductions in county responsibilities, though not in the case of highways and traffic management. The AMC had, along with the district associations, fought hard in this field. Education remained a metropolitan district council function, and the pressures for greater powers at district level had eventually forced the Government to place great emphasis on the 'agency' clause and to agree to arbitration between counties and districts. The RDCA was further satisfied with the important concession on district council electoral systems. All the associations viewed the Act very much as they had viewed the Bill — the CCA and districts 'welcomed' it, the AMC viewed it as disastrous. Victories and defeats were sometimes important, but not sufficiently important to alter these broad attitudes radically.

To judge the value of the legislative process by doing no more than taking the opinions of interested groups of proximate decision-makers would be to accept their values and attitudes without question. Our concern has been to review the progress of local government reform in the context of the overall objectives of effective and convenient local government, of efficiency and democracy. In terms of these concepts, was the Act superior to the Bill?

Though we attempted to define and refine the meanings to be attached to these concepts in Chapter I our efforts then do not allow us now to offer conclusions acceptable to all. Some would argue that both the geographical changes, mostly consisting of a return to traditional boundaries, and the functional amendments, the bulk of which blurred responsibility by increasing the possibilities of sharing the provision of services through adding to the role of district councils, made the new structure more 'democratic' than that outlined in the Bill. Their grounds would be, first, that it is desirable to build on people's existing loyalties when seeking areas to which people will feel attached and, second, that the enhancement of district councils means the provision of services at the level of government nearest to the public and, therefore, most accessible, most easily identified, and best known.

An alternative line of argument is almost diametrically opposed to this. Here the stress is on other meanings of democracy and efficiency, particularly on those which relate to service delivery and municipal accountability. The 1972 Local Government Act can be criticised on four grounds. First, the amended boundaries frequently placed emphasis on tradition at the expense of functional requirements. The exclusion of towns and villages on the edge of metropolitan areas makes co-operation between new metropolitan and non-metropolitan counties essential if town and country planning and highways and transportation services are to develop effectively. Yet there is no guarantee that such co-operation will be forthcoming: indeed, past history suggests that there is every chance of conflict, not just because councils are 'bloody-minded', but also because they are often legitimately representing very different interests and pursuing quite different objectives from one another.

Second, responsibility for several important functions (planning, highways, cleansing) is statutorily shared between county and district. Others (parks, museums, car parking, baths) are concurrent, with powers given to both county and district. Others (libraries, consumer protection) could be administered through 'agency' arrangements. This makes it exceedingly difficult for the public to understand the new system and to be able to identify the locus of decision. Sharing, concurrent powers and 'agency' were all contained in the Bill, but were all extended during its passage, either by clear amendment or by Government statements of interpretation. Mr Walker's declaration at Second Reading that this was 'a new, clear-cut system' does not stand up to close examination.

Third, changes in the Act increased the number of new councils falling below the desired level of 250,000 population. We must be a little more cautious here in that we saw in Chapter II that there is no clear proof of the validity of this as a minimum figure. It was, however, accepted by both Labour and Conservative Governments and so became one of the principles behind the proposed new structure. Amendments creating additional major authorities in Bury-Rochdale, St Helens-Huyton and the Isle of Wight all ran contrary to this principle by creating smaller units. But the doubt about the validity of 250,000 and the geographical good sense of these changes (with the possible exception of the division of the St Helens-Huyton district) means that criticism here should be muted.

Finally, we also looked at democracy and efficiency in terms of the overall role of local government, the breadth of responsibility and the relationship with central government. Once again the evidence is two-sided. Several detailed amendments abolished central controls, for example over local authority land acquisition (clauses 119-20 of the Bill, 120-1 of the Act). The Government resisted demands for the addition of Medical Officers of Health and Chief Public Health Inspectors to the list of mandatory council appointments,[51] and for the attendance allowance payable to councillors to be fixed centrally.[52] In the House of Lords the amount of money which a council may spend on projects not otherwise authorised by statute (frequently known as the 'Free Penny') was raised from a maximum of a halfpenny in the pound rate to a twopenny rate, through a successful back-bench amendment.[53] But these developments have to be set against one major blow, the decision by the Government, announced during the passage of the Bill, that it accepted the recommendations of the Central Advisory Water Committee (which had reported in 1971) and intended to proceed with the creation of new Regional Water Authorities.[54] Local authorities would be longer be responsible for the provision of water and sewage services. When we add to this the earlier decision to remove the personal health services and the new legislation reducing local authority freedom in the setting of council house rents we can see that there was no reason to be optimistic about the prospects of the 1972 Local Government Act heralding an era of more powerful, more autonomous local government.

To sum up, the legislative process was undoubtedly a good example of Government-initiated legislation passed by Parliament only after close scrutiny and (for the most part) dispassionate debate. Few would argue with this assessment. The improvement of the contents of the legislation is, however, more debatable. Here one's assessment depends on the values one holds. The traditionalist and localist saw much to please him. The functionalist and advocate of accountable local government was much less happy. In both cases the evidence was, in any case, patchy and variable. It was not possible to discern a clear thread of principle running right through the 1,800 amendments and dozens of ministerial statements of intent and interpretation. Nor was it possible at the end of twelve months' parliamentary debate to pass a final judgement on the legislative output. Much activity was still necessary before the Act could be implemented.

NOTES

1 Department of the Environment, *Local Government in England: Government Proposals for Reorganisation, Cmnd 4584* (HMSO, 1971), para. 56.
2 *Ibid.,* para. 34.
3 Department of the Environment, *Circular 58/71 — Local Government Reorganisation: Areas and Names* (HMSO, 1971), Annex, para. 2.
4 *Hansard (Commons),* vol. 817, col. 1284 (19 May 1971).
5 *The Reorganisation of Central Government, Cmnd 4506* (HMSO, 1970), para. 3.
6 They were not 'published' but parts were reproduced in *Municipal Review,* Supplements 1971-2. The associations' comments appear in the minutes of the various associations for the period 1971-2.
7 *Local Government Bill 1971,* sec. 8.
8 CCA, *Local Government Reorganisation in England and Wales: Memorandum on Allocation of Functions and Participation by District Councils in County Council Functions* (CCA, 1971), para. 13.
9 Department of the Environment, *Circular 8/71 — Local Government Reorganisation in England: Proposed New Areas* (HMSO, 1971), Appendix A.
10 *Hansard (Commons),* vol. 826, col. 235 (16 Nov. 1971).
11 *Ibid.,* col. 236.
12 *Ibid.,* cols 235-6.
13 *Ibid.,* col. 241.
14 J. M. Lee and B. Wood, *The Scope of Local Initiative: A Study of Cheshire County Council 1961-74* (Martin Robertson, 1974), p. 82.
15 Cmnd 4584, *op. cit.,* paras 5, 19.
16 *Hansard (Commons),* vol. 826, col. 249 (16 Nov. 1971).
17 I am indebted to Mr John Roper MP for making available to me material sent to him during the passage of the Local Government Act 1972. In all, it filled two large suitcases.
18 *House of Commons Order Paper,* 11 Nov. 1971, col. 414. A similar attempt to obtain a Committee of the Whole House on the Sound Broadcasting Bill also failed.
19 For a more detailed analysis of membership see B. Wood, 'Politics of Reform', *New Society,* 9 Dec. 1971, p. 1148.
20 House of Commons Debates 1971-2, *Official Report of Standing Committee D — Local Government Bill,* (3 vols), cols. 6-125.
21 *Ibid.,* cols 1030-6.
22 *Ibid.,* cols 2274-2304.
23 *Ibid.,* cols 1401-38.
24 J.A.G. Griffith, *Parliamentary Scrutiny of Government Bills* (Allen & Unwin, 1974).
25 S. Walkland, *The Legislative Process in Great |Britain* (Allen & Unwin, 1968), pp. 72-83.
26 Standing Committee D, *op. cit.,* cols 1878-2000.
27 *Ibid.,* col. 571.
28 *Ibid.,* cols 913-45; Teesside CB, *Case for a Cleveland County* (1972).

29 Standing Committee D, *op. cit.,* cols 335-42.
30 *Hansard (Commons),* vol. 841, cols 70-106 (17 July 1972).
31 Standing Committee D, *op. cit.,* cols 1922-4.
32 *Ibid.,* col. 1204.
33 *Ibid.,* col. 2129. This statement was made during a debate on traffic management. The clauses on the allocation of functions were discussed after clause 100 had been approved, and the full importance of that clause had not been apparent at the time.
34 *Ibid.,* cols 2641-2748.
35 *Hansard (Commons),* vol. 841, cols 717-52 (19 July 1972).
36 See note 33.
37 *Hansard (Commons),* vol. 841, cols 249-51 (17 July 1972). Section 110 of the 1972 Local Government Act, added to the Bill in the Lords, laid down the procedures.
38 *Hansard (Lords),* vol. 335, cols 1580-1602 (16 Oct. 1972).
39 *Ibid.,* vol. 335, cols 1680-4 (17 Oct. 1972).
40 *Ibid.,* vol. 335, col. 768 (18 Sept. 1972).
41 *Ibid.,* vol. 335, cols 1778-81 (17 Oct. 1972).
42 *Ibid.,* vol. 335, cols 1851-90 (18 Oct. 1972).
43 Letter from CCA to Clerks of County Councils, dated 9 March 1972.
44 *Hansard (Lords),* vol. 335, cols 946-52 (19 Sept. 1972).
45 *Report of the Committee on Local Government Rules of Conduct, Cmnd 5636* (HMSO, 1974), para. 123.
46 G. Taylor, *The Threat to Northern Education* (Campaign to Save Education in the Conurbations, 247 Hills Road, Cambridge, 1971).
47 Burton and Drewry, *op. cit.,* pp. 149-63.
48 Walkland, *op. cit.,* pp. 14-17.
49 Standing Committee D, *op. cit.,* cols 1831-2.
50 *Local Government Act 1972,* sec. 261.
51 *Hansard (Commons),* vol. 841, cols 279-86 (17 July 1972). The list was much shorter than under the old legislation and a relaxation of central controls over the internal organisation of local authorities was very apparent in the Bill. Soon after 1974 this relaxation became apparent to a wider audience when Somerset County Council hit the headlines by deciding to sack their Chief Executive. Before 1974 he would have been able to appeal to the Minister under the 1933 Local Government Act, but the 1972 Act abolished this right. See N. McVicar, 'The Gaffney Affair', *Public Administration Bulletin,* June 1975, pp. 34-8.
52 *Hansard (Commons),* vol. 841, cols 328-334. Main debate: Standing Committee D, *op. cit.,* cols 1711-46.
53 *Hansard (Lords),* vol. 335, cols 814-26 (18 Sept. 1972).
54 Department of the Environment, *Circular 92/71 — Reorganisation of Water and Sewage Services: Government Proposals and Arrangements for Consultation* (HMSO, 1971).

Chapter VII

IMPLEMENTATION — (2) PREPARING FOR THE APPOINTED DAY

Constitutional Issues
By the end of the legislative process in October 1972 many features of the new structure of local government were clear. There were to be two levels of authority independent from one another and with their own range of responsibilities. Several functions had been clearly allocated by Parliament to either the county or the district. The boundaries of counties and of Welsh and metropolitan districts were defined in detail (though they could be altered at a later date following a review by the new Boundary Commission). Other important features, however, still required clarification. The boundaries of English non-metropolitan districts had not been delimited, nor had any electoral areas. Parish status in urban areas had yet to be finalised. The precise allocation of functions was to be the subject of negotiation between counties and districts and, under the provisions of the agency clauses, arbitration by the ministry was possible.

The centre of decision on all these issues lay in Whitehall, town and county halls, and the Local Government Boundary Commission. Personal ministerial involvement had reached a new height during the legislative process, as had the influence of Members of Parliament. While ministers continued to be concerned, by 1973 they had new worries such as the steering through Parliament of the Water Bill under which water and sewage services were to be reorganised, or the disputes over the implementation of the 1972 Housing Finance Act. A mass of Circulars, Administrative Memoranda, Notes for Guidance and Statutory Instruments poured out of Whitehall — so many that the Department of the Environment produced a Circular which merely listed other Circulars and similar documents! The local authority associations continued to be heavily involved through the conventional channels of consultation. Locally, officers and members had the difficult task of preparing for amalgamations which had frequently been bitterly contested.

Two sets of issues required resolution during the transitional period. First there were decisions to be taken about areas, electoral arrangements and the allocation of functions. These were central to reorganisation, and the boundary between parliamentary involvement and extra-parliamentary responsibility for decisions was not easy to draw. The Act, for example, had outlined district boundaries and allocated urban parish status in Wales but not in England. It had clearly allocated responsibility for some services, but not for others. Such issues may be described as 'constitutional' and an analysis of this aspect of the transition is the concern of this chapter. In addition there was a second group of problems which may be described as 'administrative' or 'technical'. Arrangements had to be made for the transfer of property, loan debt, local bye-laws and, not least important, staff from old authorities to new. Decisions here were frequently the cause of much concern locally, and a close analysis of this process has recently been undertaken by Professor Richards.[1] This second group of decisions is not discussed in this book. They are not central to a study of the policy process whereby the reform of local government was achieved whereas the constitutional issues shaped important parts of the new structure.

The New Areas
We saw in Chapter VI that Parliament had devoted around 40 per cent of the 300 hours of debate on the Local Government Bill to a consideration of the detailed boundaries of county and metropolitan district councils. Despite this mammoth investment of time, much remained to be done after the Bill became law. Decisions on the boundaries of the English (non-metropolitan) county districts and on urban parish council status in England were required in the short term. The Local Government Boundary Commission for England was to advise on both issues, and, in the longer term, it would embark on a succession of reviews of the new boundaries (as would a sister Commission for Wales). Ministers had used the permanent existence of the two Commissions as a long stop when criticised over detailed boundary proposals during the passage of the Bill,[2] and the Commissions had a considerable agenda to keep them busy after 1 April 1974.[3]

The first task of the English Boundary Commission was to recommend a pattern of county district boundaries. This involved a long process of gathering evidence, seeking further comments on draft proposals, and drawing up a substantial report which was published in November 1972. Legally the Commission did not exist until the Act received the Royal Assent in October 1972, but it had been set up as a non-statutory advisory body immediately after the

Second Reading in November 1971. While Parliament debated the Bill in 1971-2, the Commission was simultaneously discussing the geography of the districts and many local councillors were more concerned with this process than with events at Westminster.

The Commission was given guidelines by the Government. These had been published along with a request for evidence from local authorities in July 1971.[4] The general population range was to be 75,000-100,000, though 40,000 was the normal minimum figure. Whole existing areas should be amalgamated wherever possible, the 'general objectives' of reform contained in the White Paper of February 1971 should be taken into account, and the identity of large towns was to be maintained. These guidelines had been drafted by Department officials and discussed in detail with the local authority associations, though there were only two differences between the proposals of the consultation paper[5] and the contents of the July 1971 Circular. One change emphasised the need to consider the future population of New Towns or towns undergoing 'rapid expansion' under the Town Development Act (a concession to the ambitions of several such towns to avoid a merger with neighbouring district councils). Another, a concession to the CCA, charged the Commission with a duty to consider the effective operation of *all* local government services and not just district council services (as the draft had proposed). Several counties used this as a justification of proposals for districts at the top end of the population range, on the grounds that this would enable them to decentralise effectively major county services to sub-areas coterminous with a single district council.[6]

The Commission-Designate's draft proposals,[7] published in April 1972, received a mixed reception. The accompanying text of less than five pages did not include a detailed discussion of each provisional decision, but merely reiterated the guidelines and laid down procedures for consultation. The need for 'a substantial measure of agreement among the local authorities concerned' was stressed if the Commission was to make amendments to its draft, and the detailed proposals revealed that the Commission had worked closely to the guidelines relating to population, the identity of towns and the amalgamation of whole areas. Of the 274 proposed new districts 113 fell within the 75,000-100,000 range. There were none under 40,000. No town had been dissected (though, later, Teesside County Council was divided into three districts), and only thirty-five existing authorities had been divided by the Commission.

Nationally the AMC, UDCA and RDCA viewed the draft proposals as giving 'overwhelming support' to their parliamentary campaign for the allocation of additional powers to districts.

164   *The Process of Local Government Reform 1966-74*

Predictably, district council hostility locally frequently related to the alleged 'largeness' of many of the proposed units. The usual phrases of criticism (such as 'undemocratic' and 'a take-over') once more dominated local papers and the identification of democracy with physical size was again apparent. Up and down the country public campaigns against the proposals were common. In some places these ran alongside campaigns against the county areas being discussed in Parliament, and amendments to the Bill could affect the Commission's work. Towns in the Rossendale Valley in Lancashire, for example, had a stronger case for a separate district when Whitworth was removed from Greater Manchester as this bolstered the Rossendale population by nearly 10,000, bringing it up to almost 75,000. Under pressure, the Commission conceded the case for eighteen additional districts and recommended in its final report that 296 be created.* Despite the statement in its draft proposals that any alternative pattern should only contain districts 'within (or close to) the preferred population range (75,000-100,000)', no fewer than fourteen of the concessions led to the establishment of districts with a population of under 40,000, and thirty-five *additional* districts of under 75,000 were finally created, making a total of 111 of the 296 falling below the 75,000 target for minimum size.[8] The conflict between 'local wishes' and 'the prospects for the efficient performance of local government services' was acknowledged, but the Commission claimed that the additional small districts were all cases 'of exceptional treatment to meet special circumstances'.[9] Sparsity of population was cited as the main factor, though it seems fair to assume that the receipt of over 28,000 written representations was another![10]

This was a double victory for many rural areas. We saw in Chapter VI that a concession had been made by the Government allowing for the continuation of single-member wards so that the tradition of a district councillor representing a single village could in many areas be retained. Now in several cases the Boundary Commission had modified its first proposals. The combined result was that representation could continue to be based on rural geography, though this did not necessarily guarantee a more 'viable system of local democracy' than might otherwise have been the case (under the old structure, RDC election returns regularly indicated an average of 75 per cent of seats in which a candidate was returned unopposed). Nor was the 'effective' provision of services necessarily guaranteed. The smaller district councils have limited

---

*The draft proposals did not cover Teesside/Cleveland as there seemed some doubt about the future of this new county. The Government withdrew the proposal in Commons Committee pending discussions with local authorities in the area, but reinstated it on Report. Hence the 'missing' four districts (296 minus 274 = 22).

resources and may not be able to attract good staff. Furthermore, they must frequently form part of a complex sub-area arrangement for the provision of county services. The extremely diverse size of districts also means that 'agency' arrangements have to vary from district to district within many a county, thus creating additional difficulties of public and county councillor intelligibility. Obviously the pattern of district councils has to take account of physical and demographic features, but it can be argued that perhaps too much emphasis was placed on these. The secretaries of the local authority associations, it will be recalled, had requested that emphasis be placed on the figure of 75,000 rather than 40,000, and their request was initially met by the Minister.[11] The Commission paid heed and lip-service to it, but ended by creating a pattern in which nearly 40 per cent of the new districts fell below the 75,000 target.

Urban Parishes
The establishment of urban parish councils posed fewer problems for the Commission. In Wales former parishes, boroughs and urban districts were styled 'Communities' and all except the six largest towns were able to resolve to establish a Community Council covering the whole area of the old authority. By 1974 thirteen Welsh borough and urban district councils had decided against such a move, but ninety-one urban community councils were in existence (covering ninety old areas, as one urban district was divided between two new authorities).[12] Under the Act, these areas are to be reviewed by the Welsh Boundary Commission as its first task.

The English Commission laid down guidelines for the creation of urban parishes.[13] These had emerged from consultations between the Department of the Environment and the associations and from ministerial statements during the passage of the Bill. A 'successor parish', as the urban parishes were officially styled, was to represent 'a clearly distinguishable community'. The maximum population would normally be 20,000, and anything larger would be 'the exception rather than the rule'. If the town concerned contained more than one-fifth of the population of the entire district within which it fell then 'it would not normally qualify', though, as with the 20,000 maximum, 'no rigid limit is suggested.' The process of decision was fairly straightforward. Existing urban authorities were invited to propose that they be constituted a parish, and the Commission agreed unless the guidelines were clearly breached. The first list published by the Commission contained just over 260 towns but led others to have second thoughts. Eventually exactly 300 urban parishes were established in

England. Twenty-four are in metropolitan areas.[14]

The case for urban parish councils had been pressed by the Association for Neighbourhood Councils. The aim of the Association had been the creation of representative bodies covering a genuine community, and the Association had hoped to persuade the Government to pass legislation enabling such councils to be set up in *parts of* a town. In this respect the campaign has so far been unsuccessful as the first urban parishes are restricted to small towns and to the whole area of the town based on pre-1974 council boundaries, regardless of the quality of these boundaries. Sometimes the new council will be an effective body representing a tight-knit community. In other cases the decision to opt for a council was probably taken by borough or urban district councillors primarily seeking to retain a role in the new system. The Association is continuing to press for further legislation and a consultation paper in 1974 from the new Labour Government appeared to favour such a development, which is possible in Scotland under the Scottish local government reforms.[15]

Of immediate concern is the confusion resulting from the 1972 Act's provisions. First, parishes may choose 'Town' status and, as a result, have a 'Town Mayor'. No official statistics are available as the Department does not have to be notified of such decisions, but it appears that at least 300 parish councils (including several which were previously parishes in rural districts) have opted for town status.[16] Frequently this means that there are now two local Mayors — for the town and for the district, as more than 160 metropolitan and non-metropolitan district councils were awarded charters and borough status. Second, five 'towns' have been awarded City status and thus have a 'City Mayor'. Thirdly, in forty-nine former boroughs where there is no parish or town council and where the new district council does not have borough status there are to be 'Charter Trustees'. These number at least three and are made up of district councillors representing that area. They elect one of their number to be Town or City Mayor. One criterion of a democratic system discussed in Chapter I was that it was intelligible to the public. By seeking to retain as much of the ceremonial as possible, the Government reduced criticism of the new system from those whose interest is focused on tradition and the 'dignified parts' of local government, but at the cost of creating appendages to the new structure which confuse and which blur the public's vision of lines of communication and responsibility.

Electoral Arrangements

The concession to rural interests during the passage of the 1972 Act broke up the initial Government proposals for a simple pattern of an election each year on the first Thursday in May in all areas. This pattern is retained in the metropolitan areas but will vary elsewhere depending on decisions taken by the new district councils. All have a general election in 1976 and from then onwards will choose whether to have regular general elections or the election of one-third of the council each year. In either case the wards can return any number of councillors and the metropolitan district pattern of three-member wards need not apply.

Of more concern to this chapter are the arrangements which had to be made for the first elections, held in April, May and June 1973. Because so little time was available, administrative feasibility in the drawing up of wards was a paramount consideration with the result that in many areas arrangements were temporary. Electors faced the prospect of exercising their choice in 1973 in quite different wards and electoral divisions from those which would apply later, when more permanent arrangements could be worked out. The advantage was that the new structure could be brought into operation with the minimum of delay. The cost was that the identification of an elector and of a councillor with his ward will take that much longer to establish. In addition, frequent changes of ward boundaries only add to the general confusion which exists in the minds of the public about the structure of local government.

In one important respect the electoral arrangements in 1973 were superior to those in London in 1964. There the initiative on warding rested with the old authorities acting through Joint Committees. The Home Office, the responsible department, reacted to proposals coming from local authorities and appointed commissioners to hear objections to these proposals and to make recommendations. Two difficulties arose. First, the pattern of wards varied not only from London Borough to London Borough, but also within an individual Borough (only seven of the thirty-two adopted wards each returning a similar number of councillors). Second, inevitably there were disputes, often between the political parties, yet the time constraint gave the commissioner insufficient scope to formulate his own compromise proposals adequately. Frequently he had to accept one of the schemes proposed by a council or an opposition group, even though all the schemes before him had weaknesses.[17]

This unsatisfactory experience caused the Government to take the initiative in 1972. The problem stems from the imprecision and potential incompatibility of the statutory warding criteria (the ratio of electors to councillors to be 'as nearly as may be' the same in every ward, but account is to be taken of likely population changes in the next five years, and the importance of local ties and of easily identifiable boundaries),[18] which allow for a variety of self-evident disputes. Instead of allowing such disputes to develop locally, the Government proposed that it should prepare draft electoral schemes for the counties and Welsh and metropolitan districts. These were to be the subject of 'informal consultations' and a 'small independent advisory committee' would vet the outcome of these consultations. For the non-metropolitan districts this vetting would be undertaken by the Boundary Commission.[19] It was made quite clear in the 1972 Act that 'as soon as is practicable after the first election' the Boundary Commissions for England and Wales would review the warding systems with a view to creating a more permanent set of arrangements.[20] In London there had been no such provisions for a review.

The contrast between the experience in London and the 1972 Act procedures illustrates the concern of the civil servant with administrative feasibility and with the avoidance of what, to him, constitute unnecessary arbitration procedures. The London experience was not one which Home Office officials wished to repeat! By taking the initiative in 1971 the Home Office retained firm control of the situation. Draft electoral schemes were published from late 1971 onwards, and consultations took place alongside discussions on the Bill in Parliament and on district council boundaries in the Boundary Commission. Thus leading local politicians and senior council officers sometimes had to handle three important reorganisation issues simultaneously, and there were several instances where the Home Office had to amend draft schemes later in 1972 due to legislative changes (Wilmslow, Bury, Isle of Wight and others). The 1971-2 arrangements worked smoothly and, in the short term, were an administrative success. The price to pay was a set of elections, based normally on existing wards or their amalgamation, which often were hardly fair to either candidate or voter. Several victors faced the near-certainty that 'their' ward would disappear before they were due to seek re-election. This meant a further round of local party selection committees, and the selection of candidates had often been a painful experience in 1972-3 with over 10,000 fewer council seats and the abolition of aldermen. Voters would find it necessary to learn a new warding system before the second election to many new authorities. Furthermore, the temporary arrangements often resulted in highly variable wards in terms of population size (in Cheshire the 1973 county election was fought in electoral divisions where the councillor-elector ratio varied from one to under 6,000 to one to over 16,000), and there were instances where the notion of single-member wards for county elections did not apply (e.g. in Wigan, Warrington and Chester). Here the public would even have to understand a new basic system before 1977, the date of the second county elections. The initial schemes in many metropolitan districts seemed less likely to require early radical change, but those in most county districts and many counties were particularly unsatisfactory due to the merging of urban and rural areas which had had very different electoral traditions.

Shared Functions
Government concessions and statements of intent in Parliament over the allocation of functions had ensured that a good deal of administrative preparation and central guidance would be necessary if the transition to the new system was to be a smooth operation. Advice to councils on the interpretation of provisions for shared and concurrent responsibilities was needed; so, too, was a set of guidelines for the implementation of the 'agency' clause. To illustrate the broad picture, attention will be focused on two areas — town and county planning, and agency arrangements.

The 1972 Act divided responsibility for town and country planning somewhat imprecisely. A good deal depended on county-district agreements about local plan-making, and about county attitudes to the issuing of policy statements designed to create a framework for development control decisions. The main Departmental Circular began by correctly stating that 'the effective discharge of planning functions . . . . depends on constructive working arrangements between authorities. . . .'[21] The objectives were to give both tiers 'an opportunity to play a part in the development and implementation of planning policies' — counties through strategic guidelines, districts through their responsibility for the detailed application of these strategies. Effectiveness would be tested by 'the extent to which the public receive[s] the planning service it is entitled to expect', though it is by no means clear just what standard of service is to be expected, and planning is a function where it is notoriously difficult to lay down desirable standards.

Partly because of this last problem, and partly because of the inevitable disagreement between the local authority associations, the Circular was restricted to broad general statements. Possibilities such as shared staff, joint committees and consortia were mentioned but not underwritten by the Department. 'Clear arrangements' and 'a constructive relationship' were re-emphasised at several points. It was important to avoid 'unnecessary misunderstanding or conflict',[22] a tacit acceptance that conflict was, on occasion, to be both a necessary and an inevitable outcome of the two-tier, shared-function structure.

The Circular illustrated the dilemma in which the Government found itself. Pressures placed upon it at the pre-legislative and legislative stages had left it in the difficult position of referee in a match where conflict was on occasion inevitable. The objectives of county and district could not but be in conflict, for each represents a different 'public interest'. County highways, industrial and commercial development or mineral workings strategies, for example, are highly likely to be unacceptable to particular sub-areas. If both county and district were to be given formal status as planning authorities in their own right, then all that the Government could hope to do was to emphasise the desirability of authorities maintaining close informal and formal links so that the area of dispute was minimised. In this way it was hoped that functional effectiveness would be maximised. The costs of the legislative provision were two-fold: first, functional effectiveness was limited through built-in conflict and the sharing of scarce personnel, and, second, levels of responsibility were blurred in such a way as to make accountability (of officers to councillors and of councillors to the public) and intelligibility of the system difficult to achieve.

At several places in Chapter VI we noted that the 'agency' clause provided the Government with an important escape route when under parliamentary pressure over its proposed allocation of functions. The result was that the clause became of sufficient stature to cause the Government to introduce arbitration procedures and to promise guidance on the possible usage of agency. The Departmental tactics were clear: it was important to minimise the number of requests for arbitration. Unlike the Circular on planning co-operation, more detailed guidelines and firm indications of governmental attitudes were necessary if this objective was to be realised.

The time-scale was also important. For the new authorities the 'shadow year' of 1973-4 was one in which they had to create management structures and appoint staff.* Unless the allocation of responsibilities was known in detail, such decisions could not be made with confidence. Officers in those services shared between county and district would also be disadvantaged if, when seeking posts, levels of responsibility were unclear. It will be recalled that attempts in the Lords to set a deadline to requests for ministerial decisions on disputed agency matters had failed, but there had been a promise to comply with the spirit of the amendment.[23] Accordingly, after rapid consultations with the associations, a major thirteen-page Circular was published in December 1972, within two months of the Act reaching the statute book.[24]

*The 'shadow year' refers to the period up to 1 April 1974 during which the old authorities continued to run the services while the new ones prepared to take responsibility.

The meat of the Circular lay in the five Annexes which dealt in some detail with highways, planning, refuse disposal, consumer protection and libraries. On libraries, for example, the importance of 'a strong county library service' was emphasised, and it was clear that agency should be restricted to 'the larger urban non-metropolitan districts' (i.e. former county boroughs and similar-sized towns). However, even here it was felt that professional staff should only be 'attached' to the districts and should all be county council employees.[25] For highways, traffic and road safety agency opportunities were more apparent, partly because existing boroughs and urban districts (though not rural districts) had duties in this field and therefore had engineering staff: 'There will be particular scope for agency arrangements between the county council and those districts with a substantial urban content.' In mixed urban-rural areas the clause could still be applicable as 'the exercise of functions by a district council in part only of their area may be an appropriate solution' (one which was sometimes termed the 'polo mint' approach). Such phrases related to road construction and improvement, and to road safety education.[26]

The bulk of the introductory material in the Circular consisted of a mixture of general statements about reform and of paragraphs reflecting the contrasting attitudes of the local authority associations. The CCA had ensured that it was made quite clear that 'agency arrangements cannot alter the allocation of functions laid down by the Act and must not derogate from the ability of each authority to comply with its overall responsibilities.' On the other hand, 'the greatest measure of initiative' compatible with overall policy and strategies should be given to the agent, and 'the need for flexibility in applying the guidelines' ensured that the former county boroughs would press for additional responsibilities over and above those offered to other districts by a county.[27]

It soon became clear that the aspirations of departmental officials were pipe-dreams. Neither the deadline for ministerial decisions (early November 1973), nor the call for 'few' applications to be submitted for arbitration were to prove feasible. Scarcely a county avoided some dispute about agency, and more than 200 applications for a ministerial directive were provisionally filed, though a large number were later withdrawn. The Circular plus a series of ministerial speeches indicating a natural reluctance to issue directives had failed to dissuade dissatisfied authorities.

The withdrawal of a number of provisional applications followed early Government decisions, of which only the first set met the November deadline. These related to the highways function in Leicestershire, and provided little comfort for district councils.

On an important issue of principle (whether Blaby DC should be entitled to agency powers or not) Mr Geoffrey Rippon (who had succeeded Walker as Secretary of State for the Environment) accepted the view of Leicestershire County Council that the district lacked a body of suitably qualified staff. This was a reflection of Blaby's former status as a rural district which had had no highways powers and no engineer. On several more detailed matters concerning land acquisition and traffic regulation orders Mr Rippon declined to issue a directive, again a decision favourable to the county council.[28] But shortly afterwards a second set of decisions carefully restored the balance between county and district and clarified the issue of principle. Humberside and Warwickshire were ordered to offer highways agency to several districts containing former boroughs and urban districts which had, of course, had engineering departments.[29]

In two places the Circular on agency stressed the need to seek 'the convenient and efficient operation' of services. 'The objective should be to improve the effectiveness and democratic discharge of local government functions',[30] yet the outcome scarcely matched these by now familiar phrases. It is true that the use of agency was at first sight compatible with the White Paper's principle that 'a genuine local democracy implies that decisions should be taken — and should be seen to be taken — as locally as possible'.[31] But a closer examination of the consequences of the emphasis paid to agency arrangements reveals a more disquieting situation. First, early opportunities arose for conflict between counties and districts. Circular 131/72 was one of many documents and speeches stressing the need for co-operation if the two-tier system was to be effective, yet from the outset relations between county and district councillors and, at least as important, between their officers, were certain to be strained. All this happened before the new authorities became fully operational on 1 April 1974: they were plunged into conflict within weeks of their election in spring 1973. Second, however carefully framed, the agency agreements are subject to varying interpretations and future disputes about them are quite likely. Furthermore, those agreements which were the result of a ministerial directive may, under the 1972 Act, be reopened in 1979 (as may some others, depending on the locally agreed terms), so this friction between councils could prove to be a continuing feature of the new structure. Third, the variety of agreements both between and, perhaps more importantly, within a county council area add to the complexity of the reformed structure. It is not only the public who are affected: undoubtedly many councillors find it difficult to be certain of the exact allocation of responsibilities under agency arrangements. This confusion appears to be a sound recipe for delay, friction, 'passing the buck' and officer-level decision-making, particularly in the case of highways, town and country planning and consumer protection.

When tension between bodies is creative, then it is of value. The conflicts between counties and districts which arose over the allocation of functions cannot be placed in this category. They were centred on means rather than on ends and represented a power struggle waged by groups seeking to enhance the status of their authority. The impact of decisions on the public and the quality of council services was not central to disputes about agency and power sharing. Little, if any, overall thought was given to the need to create comprehensible, accountable systems of local government. Nor was it ever demonstrated that the sort of agency arrangements with which the country ended up were likely to add to council efficiency. The original clause in the Bill had not, it seems, been drafted with wholesale usage in mind. The Notes of Guidance issued to MPs in 1971 had stressed flexibility and 'the right sort of arrangement in the particular case and in the light of local circumstances', and had criticised delegation arrangements made under the former acts as 'too formal and legalistic'.[32] The outcome has been a set of agency agreements which are often quite formal and which are based on national guidelines as much as on local circumstances. Once the Government had conceded the case for an 'arbitration clause' this was probably inevitable, and the main Circular emphasised the need for agreements 'recorded in adequate detail for the avoidance of later doubt or dispute'[33] when offering guidance on what could and could not form the basis of agency arrangements.

Other shared functions and the two-tier system in general had and have implications for the effectiveness of local authorities. There must inevitably be some duplication both of administration and of information collection and dissemination. The 1972 Act requires district planning authorities to notify both counties and parishes of all planning applications. The county structure plan relies on information from two levels of authority. Co-operation in England between districts as refuse collection authorities and counties responsible for refuse disposal is of crucial importance. The same can be said of the highways function. Governments can and did stress this in Circulars and through speeches, but legal provisions cannot create an effective working relationship if the will is not there locally.

NOTES

1. P. G. Richards, *The Local Government Act 1972: Problems of Implementation* (Allen & Unwin, 1975).
2. This long stop was on one occasion used in three cases (Whitworth, the Tyne and Wear-Durham boundary and the Leeds-North Yorkshire boundary) within three and a half hours in the House of Lords. See *Hansard* (*Lords*), vol. 334, cols 1174, 1244, 1261 (9 August 1972).
3. Local Government Boundary Commission for England, *Report No. 6* (HMSO, 1973) presented the future programme of work.
4. Department of the Environment, *Circular 58/71 — Local Government Reorganisation: Areas and Names* (HMSO, 1971).
5. *Local Government Reorganisation in England: The New District Pattern* (27 May 1971 — not published).
6. In Cheshire the county council used this argument while Winsford, an expanding town, made use of the other change. See J. M. Lee and B. Wood, *The Scope of Local Initiative: A Study of Cheshire County Council 1961-74* (Martin Robertson, 1974), pp. 164-74.
7. Local Government Boundary Commission for England — Designate, *Memorandum on Draft Proposals for New Districts in the English Non-Metropolitan Counties Proposed in the Local Government Bill* (HMSO, 1972).
8. Department of the Environment, *Local Government Boundary Commission for England Report No. 1, Cmnd 5148* (HMSO, 1972), para. 32.
9. *Ibid.*, paras 35, 40.
10. *Ibid.*, paras 40, 70.
11. See above, pp.128-9.
12. Department of the Environment, *Local Government in England and Wales: A Guide to the New System* (HMSO, 1974), Table 4 (g).
13. Department of the Environment, *Local Government Boundary Commission Report No. 3* (HMSO, 1973), para. 3.
14. Guide to the New System, *op. cit.*, Table 4 (a). The additional creations were recommended in the Commission's Reports Nos 5 and 8.
15. The consultation paper is reproduced in an Association pamphlet which describes the activities of five non-statutory neighbourhood councils: Bob Dixey, *A Guide to Neighbourhood Councils* (ANC, 48 Parker Way, Halstead, Essex, 1975).
16. *Municipal Year Book 1975* lists 293.
17. B. W. Gower, 'The Method of Division of the London Boroughs into Wards: Three Case-Studies' (BA Dissertation, University of Manchester, 1970).
18. *Local Government Act 1972*, sched. II.
19. Home Office, *Consultation Paper on Electoral Arrangements in England and Wales*, 31 March 1971 (not published).
20. Local Government Act 1972, scheds 9, 10.
21. Department of the Environment, *Circular 74/73 — Local Government Act 1972 Town and Country Planning: Co-operation Between Authorities* (HMSO, 1973), para. 1.
22. *Ibid.*, para. 8.
23. See above, p. 151.
24. Department of the Environment, *Circular 131/72 — Local Government Act 1972, Sections 101 and 110. Arrangements for the Discharge of Functions ('Agency Arrangements')* (HMSO, 1972).
25. *Ibid.*, Annex 5.
26. *Ibid.*, Annex 1.
27. *Ibid.*, paras 11, 7, 9.

28 *Municipal Review*, December 1973, p. 380.
29 *Municipal Review*, March 1974, p. 458.
30 Circular 131/72, *op. cit.*, paras 13, 11.
31 Department of the Environment, *Local Government in England: Government Proposals for Reorganisation, Cmnd 4584* (HMSO, 1971), para. 8.
32 Department of the Environment, *Local Government Bill: Notes on Clauses for Members of Standing Committee D* (not published), pp. 100/2, 100/3.
33 Circular 131/72, *op. cit.*, para. 20.

Chapter VIII

THE PROCESS OF REFORM 1966-74

Why Handle a 'Hot Potato'?
'It is axiomatic that anyone who speaks on local government reform who does not have to wants his head examining. Any Government embarking on local government reform are likely to make more enemies than friends, both within their own party and on the opposite side of Parliament.'[1] With these words Mr Harold Wilson, leader of the Opposition, opened his single contribution to the 1971-2 parliamentary debates on the Local Government Bill. He was reflecting a common view among politicians that the reform issue was 'a political hot potato', to be handled with extreme caution. Why, then, did successive Governments in the 1966-74 period decide to tackle the problem of reorganising local government?

There were both long- and short-term factors, and the two happened to coincide at this particular time. Long-term reasons for reform revolved around the generally accepted weaknesses of the former structure of local government — its geography, its complicated division of powers, the existence of as many as 1,400 separate councils, many of which were very small, and the high degree of public disinterest. Several of these had become increasingly apparent with the development of sophisticated specialist services which taxed the abilities of the smaller authorities to the limit, with the steady deterioration of relations between county boroughs and counties due to boundary disputes, and with the growth of the concept of planning which seemed to require areas more in line with socio-geographic trends.[2] But these were not newly perceived weaknesses. They had long been recognised and diagnosed by a succession of commissions from 1945, and by academic observers from 1918 and earlier. The institutions of local government had been a nineteenth-century invention. By the middle of the twentieth century they were in need of an overhaul, as every post-war government had recognised. The difficulty facing government was tactical: how should it proceed in the face of strong local opposition to radical change? Until 1966 Governments had proceeded delicately, through consensus and weak commissions (except in the case of London).

Suddenly in 1964-6 the situation changed. The juxtaposition of new short-term factors with the long-term factors created a set of conditions favourable to radical reform. First, there was the election of a Labour Government in 1964, with a broad commitment to administrative reform. The 1945 Labour Government had inherited a Boundary Commission barely into its stride, and had allowed the Commission to continue as, at that time, administrative reform was not a major item in the Government's programme. In 1964 the inheritance consisted of an ailing Commission with few results to show for five years' continuous activity, a very different situation from that of 1945. Second, there was the appointment of Mr Crossman as Minister of Housing and Local Government. Mr Crossman was a politician of theory and of vision, an academic or intellectual member of the Government though not always an astute political tactician.* In his own mind, at any rate, Mr Crossman was a man of action. Finally, conditions within his ministry were favourable. Dame Evelyn Sharp was a powerful and experienced civil servant known to support reform in principle. Senior civil servants could hardly have enjoyed the experience of the 1958 Commission, and were handling increasingly awkward recommendations from it. In many instances delaying tactics were in evidence — for example, the request for far wider Special Review Areas in the north-west took seventeen months to resolve. Mr Crossman quickly found that the scope for government action was severely limited under the 1958 legislation. He also discovered that incremental amending legislation would be opposed by some, at least, of the powerful local authority associations to whom the 1958 Act had represented something of a concordat between them and the Government.

In these circumstances a Government initiative was possible. The cost would be hostility from councils which had spent a great deal of time and energy under the 1958 procedures and which had emerged from that process reasonably satisfied; hostility from several of the associations who had found that these procedures did little harm to the bodies they represented (the AMC, in particular, had observed a series of decisions favourable to county boroughs); and hostility from some MPs on all sides of the House. Local public opinion could also be expected to react against change, and this was an important consideration at a time when the Government had an overall majority of fewer than ten seats,

*As was very apparent in 1969 when he announced a 25 per cent increase in certain National Health prescription charges a few days before the local elections.

as a further General Election at a favourable moment was clearly in Mr Wilson's mind.

For all these reasons it was politically prudent to establish a further advisory committee, though this time one which was relatively unshackled by restrictive terms of reference. Hence the decision to proceed through Royal Commission rather than through publishing Government-initiated proposals. The cost was delay and the possibility of unacceptable recommendations, though we saw that a judicious choice of membership and the creation of a continuing atmosphere favourable to reform could, and did, reduce the latter possibility. With hindsight delay was crucial — it gave the initiative to the incoming Conservative Government in 1970. Even in 1966 it seemed unlikely that reform could precede the next General Election. The Royal Commission approach was a gamble which could only work if Labour were returned to power once again. In retrospect perhaps it was 'a failure to govern',[3] but this did not seem to be the case in 1966. The Commission was a strong one and had been requested to move quickly by Mr Crossman — 'I would say that the Royal Commission can do its work in not much more than two years. Then the legislation will immediately follow, I hope.'[4] A request by the Commission for evidence to be submitted within three months, and the nature of this evidence, both indicate that the impression of major reform at an early date was present in 1966, and this atmosphere remained throughout the Commission's lifetime.

By 1969, when the Commission finally reported (a year later than Mr Crossman had hoped), the short-term factors conducive to reform were slightly different. The Government commitment to administrative reform remained, and had been very apparent following publication of the Fulton Report in 1968 when several major recommendations had been accepted. There were, however, doubts as to the determination of Mr Anthony Greenwood to undertake responsibility for a major reforming Bill — his interest in the issue had seemed limited. These doubts were soon resolved when, in a reshuffle, he was replaced by Mr Anthony Crosland — like Crossman an apparent radical and a 'man of action'. In addition, Prime Minister Wilson made it clear that the Government intended to act quickly when he presented the report to the Commons. Finally, there were new short-term reasons for proceeding with reform and for producing a definite Government line. First, opposition to reform within the Labour Party would be reduced at the coming General Election if the manifesto included a detailed statement of intent. Secondly, unpalatable changes to parliamentary constituency boundaries could be delayed if council areas were shortly to be altered. There might have been a further factor had the Commission's proposals clearly favoured the Labour Party in their local electoral consequences, but the evidence here was unclear.

Was the Labour Government as committed to the (modified) Commission's proposals as its February 1970 White Paper suggested? Or was this a phoney atmosphere of reform? Undoubtedly it would not have been easy to secure the passage of a Bill implementing the unitary concept. On the other hand, a compromise by which additional unitary authorities were created might well have satisfied the AMC and several Labour-controlled town councils. It could have been justified on the grounds that, following the Kilbrandon Report and unless that Report was very much opposed to such a move, strong regional assemblies were contemplated. But more important than such speculation about what might have happened is that, at the time, more and more people were convinced that a new Labour Government would indeed proceed with a reform Bill. The momentum towards reform was maintained in 1969-70.

At this point the story could so easily have ended. With the advent of a Conservative Government in June 1970 the long-term reasons for reform remained, but there was a new set of short-term factors. These could have led to the quiet abandonment of the notion of major reform through a policy of consultation and compromise. The associations could have been approached in an attempt to seek a consensus. The clock could have been turned back nearly twenty years.

How can the Conservative initiative be explained? What were the new short-term factors favourable to reform? First, there was the appointment of Mr Peter Walker, the man who, as shadow minister, had been handling the issue in the 1969-70 period. Mr Walker was an ambitious politician who was close to Mr Heath, the Prime Minister, who in 1970 had campaigned on a platform of modernising government. Like Crossman and Crosland, Walker was unlikely to allow the issue to die slowly. Three major issues faced his new giant Department — housing, pollution and local government reform. He was anxious to take action on all three. Pollution was, at the time, a fashionable topic on which legislation would be popular but complex. Immediate tangible returns would be limited. Conservative proposals for housing were certain to be highly controversial. In normal circumstances so, too, were plans for local government reform, though here legislation would achieve immediate visible effects. But 1970-1 was not 'normal' — Mr Walker inherited a situation where the need for reform appeared to have been broadly accepted by the vast majority of proximate decision-makers. Furthermore, the public debate about the Commission's proposals had revealed the possibility of creating an alternative based on the two-tier concept which was likely to be particularly acceptable to large parts of the Conservative Party. Those critical of local amalgamations of any description might be prepared to accept this in preference to the Redcliffe-Maud/Labour Government unitary authority blueprint — it was the lesser of two evils. Mr Walker could go down in the history books as the architect of the great municipal reforms of the twentieth century, a point not to be ignored in the case of an ambitious young politician. Reform was also compatible with the Conservative Government's oft-stated target of increasing efficiency. Walker was anxious to ensure that the new councils would be organised on the basis of modern management methods, but he could not incorporate this in his Bill. Instead he persuaded the associations to support the appointment of the Bains Committee. He was 'anxious to see that the new authorities receive the best possible advice' on management structures, he told the Commons.[5] Later, in a Foreword to the Bains Report, he stated: 'I look upon this Report as being one of the most important and vital aspects of local government reform.'[6] For the third time in five years long- and short-term factors coincided. All three occasions were crucial — had any one of them not occurred it can be argued that local government would not have been reformed. The process of reform was continuous, with each stage building on the momentum gathered previously.

Policy-making
This study of the process of local government reform has revealed a number of points of more general applicability to the policy-making process in Britain. Though every issue is unique in its detailed content and history, all are typical in that public policy changes ultimately reflect government commitments and attitudes and depend upon actions by ministers, civil servants and, sometimes, Parliament. Local government reform was a classic example of the advisory committee-positive governmental reaction-legislation process which apparently approximates to a system of bounded rationality ('bounded' largely because of restriction at the investigatory stage through the terms of reference given to the investigators). It was typical in that it involved a variety of interest groups and much use of conventional channels of consultation. Untypically it placed a very large number of politicans under conflicting pressures due to a division of loyalties. MPs are not merely members of a parliamentary party — they are also locally selected representatives of individual communities. In the particular issue of local government reform there were inevitably many communities in dispute with the Government, and

many MPs in an uncomfortable position as intermediaries. In this situation there had to be concessions. Fortunately these were frequently possible without seriously endangering the overall reform programme, though, as we saw in Chapters VI and VII, concessions could often weaken the contents of the final policy.

Like many issues, that of changing the structure of local government emerged from problems associated with past policies. Rarely is a problem tackled following strategic or theoretical thinking, largely because politicians, civil servants and interest groups have little or no time or inclination to undertake such thinking. Problems arise because decisions have to be taken in circumstances where answers are increasingly difficult to find. It is significant that Mr Crossman in 1964 inherited a large batch of recommendations from the Local Government Commission which had been awaiting attention for many months — his predecessor had found himself unable to adjudicate on complicated disputes between Commission and councils. In clearing his in-tray Mr Crossman soon discovered the reasons for this inheritance. He identified a problem and publicly proclaimed its existence.

Mr Crossman's contribution to the process of reform lay in his presentation of the problem. He tackled the issue head-on in his major speech to the AMC in September 1965. Instead of suggesting that the difficulty lay in the restrictive 1958 Act procedures, he boldly announced that the whole structure of local government was faulty and out-dated. This was a major reversal of official attitudes — the 1958 Act had been firmly based on the premise that there was nothing radically wrong with the status quo, and that only marginal changes were necessary. Mr Crossman's radical interpretation of the problem represented an important breakthrough and forced local government's powerful vested interests to reconsider their traditional approaches.

The issue, then, arose out of the increasing inability of existing policies to cope with changing circumstances, a common enough feature of British government. The new circumstances were the result partly of technical problems and partly of political developments following the 1964 General Election. The issue identified, the Government's response was the traditional one of seeking outside aid rather than formulating its own policies. This method of proceeding can pose problems at a later date, but can equally have great advantages, both tactical and strategic. Difficulties can arise through delay while a commission sits — such delay can, on occasion, aggravate the issue or cause it to be interpreted rather differently (as happened in the case of local government in the post-1958 period when attitudes hardened and structural weaknesses became increasingly apparent). Other difficulties are associated with the resultant advice, which may prove to be politically unacceptable. Governments can find themselves in the embarrassing position of seeking to avoid implementation without wishing to launch a frontal assault on the findings of a body of experts appointed by government. Finally, by appointing a commission the Government loses control of the timetable. Though deadlines are often set — two years in the case of the Redcliffe-Maud Commissions — they are rarely met. A Government which sets up a commission during its first year or two of office can be fairly sure that the report will arrive shortly before a General Election is due, at a difficult time for implementation to be feasible should the issue be controversial. This, of course, was just what happened to the Redcliffe-Maud Report. On the other hand, the appointment of a commission at a later stage in the life of a Government frequently results in the publication of a report after the next election, when that Government may well be no longer in office. One suspects that in some instances this is precisely why a commission is appointed — the *Guardian*'s charge that the Commission on the Constitution was 'a recipe for delay' will be recalled.[7]

There are also advantages to offset these difficulties. First, a Government can cite a report as evidence in support of new policies and can, to an extent, ride along 'on the coat-tails' of a commission. Tactically it can share or even largely avoid direct responsibility for controversial actions. Strategically it can implement policies which would never have been politically feasible had they been initiated internally. Such might have been the case with local government reform had the Labour Government won the 1970 election. The contrasting example of Wales suggests that the radical unitary concept would not have emerged from internal deliberations. Second, following publication of the report the Government can set the parameters of the debate. It can narrow the scope of the issue during the conventional consultative process by declaring that certain recommendations are non-debatable as they are firmly accepted by government. This was a crucial aspect of the policy process discussed in this book. At various stages both Labour and Conservative Governments declared themselves to be totally wedded to certain geographical proposals — for example, the Labour White Paper declared that the creation of additional metropolitan areas and the division of unitary areas could not be contemplated.[8] The scope for constructive opposition through the submission of an alternative blueprint was immediately reduced.

Perhaps the most important example of tactics designed to stifle debate lay in the acceptance by governments of both parties of the

Commission's recommendation that a population of 250,000 was necessary if an authority was to be an effective provider of major services such as education. The Commission's line of reasoning was discussed in Chapter II, when it was very apparent that this recommendation represented a judgement based on uncertain evidence. It was a critical part of the report. If the 250,000 figure was disputable all sorts of new possibilities arose — the AMC plan for double the number of unitary authorities immediately became discussable, for example. Governments foreclosed debate about such possibilities by, in effect, translating a value into a fact: the AMC could not discuss a lower figure with the ministry, nor could the CCA press for its preferred 500,000.[9]

A further restriction on the public debate lay in the Commission's interpretation of attitudes to reform. This was typical of the ability of governments to stress, and perhaps exaggerate, one part of the expert advice to further its own ends. Given that legislation was the aim, it was important to create the impression that there was no alternative to, and no serious opposition to, some kind of reform. The constant theme of government spokesman in the 1969-72 period was that responsible opinion favoured reform. A statement by the Commission[10] that there was 'widespread agreement among witnesses on the need to change the present local government system' was seized upon. This was a fair statement, though in fact a large number of local authorities had proposed changes along traditional lines (e.g. boundary extensions) rather than reforms based on new principles. Less accurate was the Labour Government's translation: 'The great mass of evidence to the Redcliffe-Maud Commission showed that an overwhelming body of opinion, both inside and outside local government, believed that *fundamental* [author's italics] structural changes were required.'[11] Such statements, however, served the purpose of maintaining the momentum towards reform and helped to ensure that the debate was restricted to disputes about the type of reform; at no stage was a serious anti-reform lobby in evidence.

Rarely is a problem totally discrete or self-contained: its boundaries overlap with those of other issues. The process of local government reform illustrated three contrasting categories of overlapping. First, there are occasions on which, for tactical reasons, Governments claim that decisions cannot be taken in isolation as they have ramifications elsewhere. During the passage of the Bill an attempt was made to lower the age at which a person may stand for election to a local authority from twenty-one to eighteen, in line with the earlier decision to extend the franchise to that group of people. Under strong pressure the Government resisted the amendment on the grounds that the issue could not be separated from the question of eligibility for election to Parliament, and that this was a matter for a Speaker's Conference rather than for the Standing Committee on the Local Government Bill.[12] The amendment was moved by a Conservative (Mr Fox, Shipley) and supported by several colleagues. Fox accepted the Minister's 'wider issues' argument and voted with the Government. Miss Fookes (Merton and Morden) and Mr Reed (Bolton East) defied the whip, but the Government won the division by 21-19 due to Fox's abandonment of his amendment and to the unexpected absence of three Labour members. The issue was discussed four times in all during the passage of the Bill, but this was the major debate. In the House of Lords the Government won a division comfortably (101-46) using the same argument.

Though there was obviously much sense in the Government's argument about the issue of eligibility for election, this was essentially a use of the concept of overlapping boundaries for tactical reasons. The second example is one where there could be no dispute about the indiscrete nature of the issue. The establishment of the Commission on the Constitution in 1969 made it nonsensical to take decisions about a regional tier of local government in advance of decisions on that report (which was not published until 1973). This posed problems for the proponents of new structures which included a regional tier. Mr Senior had to propose two alternative regional models. The AMC's preference for many additional small unitary authorities was dependent upon the existence of regional councils. The Opposition initiated a lengthy debate in Committee, but in the circumstances could only describe its proposal for provincial councils as 'a probing amendment'.[13] The reform of local government was effected without more than minimal thought being given to the possibility of later incorporating changes at the regional level following the Kilbrandon Report. Similarly the issue of local government finance was never properly debated. Both omissions were favourable to the Government, giving its predisposition to reorganise local government along traditional lines.

A third example of overlapping issues was handled in quite the reverse way and again illustrates the tactical skill of the Government. It was not easy to see why refuse disposal and library functions should be allocated to one type of authority in England (the county) and another (the district) in Wales. Observers waited in vain for an explanation, because parliamentary procedure made it impossible to discuss both countries in a single debate. English ministers merely stated that they could not answer for their Welsh Office colleagues, and vice versa. Critics had to be satisfied with statements such as 'the Government do not accept the proposition that the allocation of functions in Wales must be exactly the same as that in England' (Mr Gibson-Watt, Minister of State, Welsh Office). When this was challenged as breaking the traditional constitutional principle of local government legislation covering both England and Wales the Committee Chairman ruled the discussion as out of order: 'The proper place to explore this was on Second Reading.'[14]

Policy outputs are the result of numerous decisions of a detailed nature, particularly when the issue is a complex one. By convention Governments consult widely and seek a degree of consensus, provided that such consensus is compatible with its overall objectives. Often it is difficult to keep these clearly in mind when discussing details, particularly when the objectives are not precisely defined and are a mixture of theoretical concepts (democracy and efficiency) and political and institutional considerations (including the desirability of seeking common ground with potential opponents). The Local Government Act 1972 is littered with decisions which would seem to conflict with the original theoretical objectives: those discussed in Chapters VI and VII relating to the complicated division of responsibility between counties and districts for services such as highways and town and country planning provide a particularly good illustration. Though such decisions could be defended, the case relied on an extremely narrow interpretation of the concepts of democracy and efficiency and it was apparent that political expediency was a more important factor. Indeed, it is sometimes difficult to see exactly where the Government did stand firm during the consultative and legislative processes. Exceptions to the 250,000 population size were allowed, the 'whole built-up area' concept of the metropolitan counties was breached, the 'clear-cut' division of powers disappeared, and there was little in the way of a move towards the promised 'stronger' local authorities. The combination of powerful local government vested interests and a Conservative Government pursuing a policy which attempted to build on the existing organisation of local authorities ensured that when tradition and change were in conflict, the former was frequently considered the more important. Working alongside a Labour Government these vested interests might well have been less influential. But, equally, some concessions to them are highly likely to have taken place (and, indeed, had begun to do so with the 1970 White Paper proposals for district committees of unitary authorities).

Concessions are an integral part of the policy-making process, and the timeing of these concessions can be very important. Many were made in the period between the publication of the White Paper and the introduction of the Bill, following extensive discussions with the associations based on a series of Government consultation papers. These were largely on self-contained issues where a degree of consensus between the Government and the local authority associations proved to be possible and where a divergence from the White Paper proposals would not be cited as evidence in favour of further changes (for example, the case of the unified staff structure for planning). Though during this pre-legislative period the boundaries of the metropolitan counties were reduced, the Government deliberately declined to create any additional counties or metropolitan districts. Until the later stages of the parliamentary process in mid-1972, it stood firm on the issues of a separate Isle of Wight county, a new metropolitan district through the division of Bury-Rochdale, and a further reduction of Greater Manchester in the Wilmslow area. By then similar campaigns for separate Herefordshire and Pembrokeshire counties, for the division of other double-headed districts, and for county boundary changes in areas like Gatwick and Weston-super-Mare had largely run out of steam. In addition, the Government could claim that it was forced into the Isle of Wight and Bury-Rochdale concessions in Parliament because they were supported by particularly strong evidence which made them unique, or, in the case of Wilmslow, because the Lords amendment came too late to be rescinded (this was not strictly true). Political capital can be made out of parliamentary proceedings: the Bury-Rochdale division was used to create a great deal of favourable publicity for Mr Fidler, the Bury and Radcliffe Conservative MP who held a marginal seat. The issue was skilfully coupled with a successful amendment to separate Huyton from St Helens, a division which enabled Mr Harold Wilson, Huyton's MP, to increase his own popularity within the constituency, though at the cost of splitting the Liverpool Labour Party.

But the legislative process was more important than this. On the particular issue of local government reform most MPs had something to contribute, and many suffered from divided loyalties. As many as 222 spoke during the Common's debates on the Bill — almost half of the provincial English and Welsh MPs. Many obtained geographical concessions and returned home in triumph (Mr Gordon Oakes, MP for Widnes, was made a Freeman of Hale). Others concentrated their attentions on the functional clauses, and their pressure helped persuade the Government to widen its proposals for use of the agency clause. The Government was walking on a tightrope, with members sympathetic to counties and to districts attempting to pull it in two directions at once. There was only a limited amount of party politics in all this — the main lobbies were represented on both sides and back-bench members felt free on occasion to make their own assessment as to which topics represented 'principles' and which 'details'.

Boundary concessions were possible because an issue of principle to a local community was frequently a matter of detail to the Government. From the Second Reading debate it was quite clear that amendments would be made on this basis, and the Government stood firm only when change could have serious consequences. The outer boundaries of Cleveland and Avon were good examples: here too many concessions to the ancient counties would leave these new ones as little more than Teesside and Bristol with some extensions. It was on the allocation of functions that the distinction between detail and principle was less easy to make. The two objectives of 'a clear-cut division' and 'building on the old structure' were quite incompatible given that the old structure was particularly complicated in the way powers were allocated. Both the Government and its opponents switched their support from one of these principles to the other whenever it was convenient to do so. Thus at one moment the district lobby argued that refuse disposal should be amalgamated with refuse collection to avoid confused levels of responsibility, and at the next moment it suggested that highways should be divided because old district councils were in close touch with local needs and had performed the service successfully in the past.

The Objectives of Reform

During the course of this study it has become quite apparent that to measure the new structure of local government against the original theoretical objectives of democracy and efficiency alone is not possible. Or, rather, it is possible but no two people would agree on the outcome of the analysis. We saw in Chapter I that democracy and efficiency are concepts capable of varied definition. Dominant during the reform process was the view that the two were incompatible — democracy implied small areas and authorities, efficiency demanded large ones. With the failure of local government to increase its range of functions (water, sewage disposal and personal health were actually removed from it), and the refusal of central government to reduce its strategic controls over council activities, the theoretical debate about democracy and efficiency appears to have had little impact on the final policy outputs. In particular, the arguments linking the two concepts through their concern with the services provided by councils were largely ignored.

Much greater impact was caused by the concept of tradition and of building on known foundations. The reception accorded to the Redcliffe-Maud Report was an important part of the policy process. It revealed, not surprisingly, criticism from the majority of local authorities and their associations. Though the unitary concept had been present in county boroughs since 1888, its extension to rural areas appeared to be something quite new. Inevitably it was looked upon with disfavour by many in the local authority world who were naturally concerned with self-interest. It was easy to attack the consequences in terms of representation and accessibility as well as on the grounds that some of the largest and strongest of existing county authorities would be cut into small pieces. The Redcliffe-Maud Commission had neatly divided both the AMC and the CCA but both were, on balance, somewhat hostile. Those who supported the plan never got a pro-Report lobby off the ground.

The absence of such a lobby was extremely important. Without it the impression was given that few saw merit in the plan as it stood. Perhaps a commission should stay in being for several months after publication of its report in order to lead the public debate? Though commissioners addressed many meetings their activities were uncoordinated, and they lacked the support of a secretariat able to develop relations with the press through such devices as the issuing of prepared speeches. At many of these meetings it was the hostility to the Report which made the news, particularly when critics relied on emotive turns of phrase. Amid the mass of pamphlets, press clippings and other reports it is not easy to find a full-blooded defence of the Redcliffe-Maud blueprint.

Mr Senior's memorandum of dissent entered the debate at this point, not because of its overall content (which few read, no doubt), but because it appeared to be based on an alternative, two-tier concept. The debate about the relative merits of one- and two-tier local government was a familiar one which had been incapable of resolution in the 1950s. The Senior Plan offered critics of the unitary approach a handle on which to hang their criticism. Probably none of them would have been anxious for as few as 148 second-tier authorities, nor would they favour the policy of ignoring traditional boundaries, but that did not matter. The important thing was that one commissioner, and the geographer at that, saw a need for much smaller areas than those proposed by the majority.

Suddenly only the Labour Government and a fairly small number of individual local authorities were supporting the unitary concept. Even the AMC, for years the leading advocate of county borough government, had moved to support for a two-tier system, albeit a very different one from that proposed by the CCA and the district associations, and hinted at by Mr Walker. The February 1970 White Paper represented a brave attempt to keep the public debate as narrow as possible, but a General Election was due within the year and few expected the Labour Government to win again. Within that year came the Conservative plan, based on the more traditional two-tier concept and threatening the independence of powerful county borough councils.

As well as the theoretical objectives of democracy and efficiency there were also institutional objectives. The Government wishes to give the impression of governing. Councils and their associations are concerned to preserve what they conceive as the ideals which they represent. Civil servants seek administratively feasible lines of approach to the problem. Public opinion, or anticipated public opinion, can moderate a Government in its thinking. Policy-making was the search for an acceptable solution, capable of implementation without major embarrassments for the Government. The interaction of the theoretical and the institutional objectives with a Conservative Government in power led to the emergence of proposals far less radical than those of the Commission (which had been little concerned with the institutional objectives).

The impression must not, however, be given that the Conservative Government merely went along with the tide. It was fortunate in inheriting a situation in which there had been a good deal of hostility expressed against the unitary approach. But it had no need to act so speedily, and the fact that it did so is not simply a reflection of the choice of Mr Walker as Minister. There were clear party political advantages to be gained from a two-tier reform. First, traditional party strongholds would welcome the emphasis on county government. Second, many large cities with long records of Labour control would lose their independence and be subordinate to the new county councils, a large number of which would stay under Conservative control. Third, the Labour Party would be 'dished', for no Government would be likely to undertake a further major reform until the end of the century. Finally, when local government boundaries are being altered it is always an advantage to be in government as there are some decisions where the technical or geographical balance of advantage is unclear and where electoral prospects can tip the balance. For example, the transfer of Prestwich from Salford to Bury dramatically decreased the chances of Labour control in Bury. The addition of Wilmslow and Poynton made it extremely difficult for Labour to win Cheshire. The removal of Skelmersdale and Ellesmere Port-Runcorn-Widnes from Merseyside made that new county extremely marginal. Several of these decisions will subsequently have consequences at a parliamentary constituency level.

Though it may seem, in theory, to be unfortunate that local government reform is inextricably linked with party politics, this is not the case. Without the stimulus of marginal party advantage, and without the close ties between national and local parties, there might never have been reform. Those hostile to the 1974 changes might welcome this, but they should realise that a lack of government interest in local government (even if much of this interest is for party political reasons) could quickly spell the death of our municipal institutions. The structure was reformed precisely because of political ties between local and central governments. The existence of 'acceptable' objectives like democracy and efficiency was little more than a convenience. Government interest in these concepts was limited to support for the standard diagnosis of the ills of local government as undemocratic and inefficient. Reform was based on a mixture of theoretical, institutional and political objectives. The need for governmental leadership and parliamentary decision ensured that any concern for theory was frequently subordinated to tactical considerations.

NOTES

1 *Hansard* (*Commons*), vol. 840, col. 899 (6 July 1972).
2 J. Brand, *Local Government Reform in England* (Croom Helm, 1974) uses as his major thesis this point about the importance of planning.
3 A. P. Herbert, *Anything But Action?* (Herbert Paper 5) (Barrie & Rockliff, 1960).
4 *Hansard* (*Commons*), vol. 724, col. 645 (10 Feb. 1966).
5 *Ibid.*, vol. 817, cols 1291-2 (19 May 1971).
6 Department of the Environment, *The New Local Authorities: Management and Structure* (HMSO, 1972), p. vi.
7 See above, p. 53.
8 Ministry of Local Government and Regional Planning, *Reform of Local Government in England, Cmnd 4276* (HMSO, 1970), paras 36, 39.
9 See H. A. Simon, *Administrative Behaviour* (New York, The Free Press, 1957), Ch. 3 for the difficult distinction between fact and value.
10 Royal Commission on Local Government in England 1966-9.
11 Cmnd 4276, *op. cit.*, para. 5.
12 House of Commons Debates 1971-2, *Official Report of Standing Committee D — Local Government Bill* (3 vols), cols 1401-38.
13 *Ibid.*, cols 125-222.
14 *Ibid.*, cols 1823, 1825.

A COMPARISON OF THE VARIOUS REFORM PROPOSALS 1969-72*

1. *Areas*

	Redcliffe-Maud Report Majority Proposals (Cmnd 4040, 1969)	Labour Government White Paper (Cmnd 4276, 1970)	Conservative Government White Paper (Cmnd 4584, 1971)	Local Government Bill (1971)	Local Government Act (1972) Plus Later Orders
METROPOLITAN AREAS AND DISTRICTS: NUMBER	3 (20 Districts).	5 (28 Districts).	6 (34 Districts).	6 (34 Districts).	6 (36 Districts).
AUTHORITIES OUTSIDE THE METROPOLITAN AREAS: NUMBER	58 Unitary Authorities.	51 Unitary Authorities.	38 Counties + Districts (normally with at least 40,000 pop.). A Boundary Commission to recommend District areas.	38 Counties + Districts as in Cmnd 4584. (Main changes in county areas: Humberside; N.E. Essex: Harrogate.) (Wales: 8 Counties + 37 Districts.)	39 Counties + 296 Districts (Isle of Wight a county). (Wales: 8 Counties + 37 Districts.)
PROVINCIAL COUNCILS	8 Indirectly elected.	Wait until Crowther Report.	Wait until Crowther Report.	Wait until Crowther Report.	No provisions. (Wait until Crowther/Kilbrandon Report.)
PARISH OR LOCAL COUNCILS	In unitary areas present authorities become local councils. In metropolitan areas only if they so desire.	As Cmnd 4040 but with the possibility of large towns being divided into several local councils.	Present Parish Councils to continue. Urban areas left for further discussion.	Present PCs to continue. Urban PCs possible some time after 1974. (Wales - present PCs to continue as Community Councils. All except 6 largest towns able to have a Community Council. Boundary Commission to review areas soon after 1974.)	Present PCs to continue. 300 MBs and UDCs become urban parishes (nearly all under 20,000 pop.), including several in metropolitan areas. (Wales: as Bill.)

*In Tables 1, 3 and 4 the first three columns refer to England, excluding London. The last two columns (Bill and Act) also include Wales.

2. Areas: North-West

	Redcliffe-Maud Report Majority Proposals (Cmnd 4040, 1969)	Labour Government White Paper (Cmnd 4276, 1970)	Conservative Government White Paper (Cmnd 4584, 1971)	Local Government Bill (1971)	Local Government Act (1972) Plus Later Orders
TOP-TIER IN METROPOLITAN AREAS	2 (SELNEC to include 90 existing authorities; Merseyside 31.)	As Cmnd 4040.	As Cmnd 4040 but smaller. (SELNEC 78; Merseyside 25.)	As Cmnd 4040 but even smaller. (Greater Manchester 71; Merseyside 23.)	Smaller still. (Greater Manchester 68; Merseyside 22.)
SECOND-TIER IN METROPOLITAN AREAS	SELNEC - 9. (Wigan; Bolton; Bury-Rochdale; Warrington; Manchester-Salford; Altrincham; Oldham; Ashton; Stockport.) *Merseyside* - 4 (Southport; Liverpool-Bootle; St Helens; Chester-Wirral.)	As Cmnd 4040.	SELNEC - 9. (Wigan; Bolton; Bury-Rochdale; Salford-Manchester; Stretford-Altrincham; Oldham; Ashton; Stockport.) *Merseyside* - 4 (Bootle; Liverpool; St Helens; Wirral.)	*Greater Manchester* - 9 (As in Cmnd 4584 with minor changes.) *Merseyside* - 4 (As in Cmnd 4584 with minor changes. Biggest change is that 'Bootle' becomes 'Bootle-Southport'.)	*GMCC* - 10. (Bury and Rochdale separated.) *MCC* - 5 (St Helens and Huyton separated.)
TOP-TIER ELSEWHERE	6 Unitary Authorities. (Cumberland; Furness; Fylde; Preston; Blackburn; Burnley.) Also South Cheshire to go with Stoke.)	As Cmnd 4040.	3 Counties. (Cumberland-Westmorland; Lancashire; Cheshire.)	3 Counties as in Cmnd 4584. (Minor changes to boundaries; 'Cumbria' named.	As Bill. Minor changes by reducing metropolitan areas (Poynton, Wilmslow, Whitworth, Skelmersdale).
SECOND-TIER ELSEWHERE	None.	None.	To be decided after Boundary Commission review.	To be decided after Boundary Commission review.	Cumbria - 6. Lancashire - 14. Cheshire - 8.

3. Functions

	Redcliffe-Maud Report Majority Proposals (Cmnd 4040, 1969)	Labour Government White Paper (Cmnd 4276, 1970).	Conservative Government White Paper (Cmnd 4584, 1971)	Local Government Bill (1971)	Local Government Act (1972) Plus Later Orders
METROPOLITAN COUNTY FUNCTIONS	Planning and Transportation; Housing policy; Police; Fire; Water; Sewage and Refuse Disposal.	As Cmnd 4040 except: (1) County to do Education. (2) County to be Rating Authority.	As Cmnd 4040 except: (1) Districts to do some Development Control. (2) County to have minimal Housing Powers. (County not to be Education or Rating Authority.)	Cmnd 4584 plus further powers for districts: (1) Local Plan-making (2) Clean Air etc. (3) Maintenance of unclassified urban roads.	Police; Fire; Consumer Protection; Most Roads; Structure Planning; Passenger Transport; Refuse Disposal; Reserve Housing Powers; plus 'agency' (see below).
NON-METROPOLITAN COUNTY FUNCTIONS	Unitary authorities would be all-purpose.	Unitary authorities would be all-purpose.	As Metropolitan Counties above plus: (1) Education. (2) Libraries. (3) Social Services.	As Metropolitan Counties above plus: (1) Education. (2) Libraries. (3) Social Services but minus (4) Public Transport undertakings. (Wales - all districts do refuse disposal, some may run libraries.)	As Bill with minor amendments. In all areas 'agency' clause allows power sharing (not in the case of Education, Police, Social Services). (Wales - as Bill with minor amendments.)
LOCAL COUNCIL FUNCTIONS	Minor local powers plus possibility of some involvement in running of major services.	Local powers only. (Idea of District Committees of Unitary Authorities for major services floated.)	Present parishes to continue with their powers.	Present parishes to continue with their powers.	As present parishes plus: (1) Right to receive and comment on planning applications. (2) Powers to spend more without permission from above.

4. *Elections*

	Redcliffe-Maud Report Majority Proposals (Cmnd 4040, 1969)	Labour Government White Paper (Cmnd 4276, 1970)	Conservative Government White Paper (Cmnd 4584, 1971)	Local Government Bill (1971)	Local Government Act (1972) Plus Later Orders
ALDERMEN AND COUNCILLORS	Abolish aldermen. Maximum of 75 councillors.	Abolish aldermen. Consult on number of councillors.	Consult on aldermen. No mention of number of councillors.	Abolish aldermen. No provisions on council size.	Aldermen abolished. Most County Councils have under 100 members, most Districts under 80, though no maxima in Act.
PAYMENT OF COUNCILLORS	Uncertain. Possibly pay senior members.	Against. Better expenses favoured.	Considering payment. Better expenses favoured.	A flat-rate taxable Attendance Allowance introduced.	Attendance Allowance.
ELECTIONS	General election with single-member wards. Election date and length of term of office – further study needed.	No proposals. Further consultations to take place.	No proposals. Further consultations to take place.	Counties – general election in single-member divisions. Districts – partial election (1/3 each time) in 3-member wards. All councillors to serve 4 years.	CCs - general election in single-member divisions. MDs - partial election in 3-member wards. CDs – either partial or general, ward size variable. All councillors - 4-year terms of office.

INDEX OF PERSONS AND PLACES

Aberdare, Lord 151
Aldershot 94, 133
Allen, Sir Douglas 70
Anglesey 118, 120, 151
Avon 133, 134, 138, 187
Aylesbury 66

Basingstoke 94
Bath 66
Bedford 79
Bedfordshire 66, 107
Bell, Ronald (MP) 112
Birch, Professor A. H. 24
Birkenhead 66
Birmingham 48
Bishops Castle 134
Blaby 172
Blackburn 21, 66, 110
Blackpool 21, 56, 139
Blaker, Peter (MP) 112
Boardman, Tom (MP) 112
Bolton 56, 139
Bolton, J. E. 40
Bootle 48, 132
Bournemouth 139
Boynton, J. K. 83, 85
Brackley 132, 133
Bradford 66, 73, 76
Brecon 118
Bridgend 124
Brighton 66, 106
Brinton, Sir Tatton (MP) 112
Bristol 48, 76, 106, 187
Brooke, Lord 98
Brown, George (MP) 41, 52
Buckinghamshire 66, 107, 132
Burnley 21
Bury 24, 66, 76, 103, 133, 155, 158, 168, 186, 189

Caernarvonshire 120
Callaghan, James (MP) 48
Cardiff 118, 124, 125, 126, 127, 133, 138, 139, 147
Cardigan 118, 123
Carlisle 67

Carmarthen 53, 120
Chataway, Christopher (MP) 98
Chelmsford 134
Cheshire 17, 42, 76, 77, 78, 83, 96, 98, 101, 106, 106n, 107, 110, 132, 133, 135, 151, 168, 189
Chester 66, 77, 81, 106n, 168
Chesterfield 66
Christchurch 94
Cleveland 133, 134, 144, 164n, 187
Colchester 134, 135
Colville of Culross, Viscount 153
Congleton 76
Cornwall 106, 134
Coventry 39, 41, 107
Crawley 56
Crewe 77
Crosland, Anthony (MP) 72, 75, 86, 99, 104, 112, 178, 179
Crossman, Richard (MP) 15-20, 27, 38-9, 41, 43n, 44, 46, 59, 71, 76, 114, 119, 146, 177-8, 179, 181
Cuckfield 76
Cumberland 76, 101
Cumbria 134

Davies, S. O. (MP) 125
Denbighshire 118, 120
Derby 48
Derbyshire 42, 48, 76, 133, 137
Devon 85, 106, 134
Devons, Professor E. 18
Donnison, Professor D. 31
Dormand, Jack (MP) 137
Dorset 76, 139
Durham 133, 144
Dyfed 120

Easington 133
Eastbourne 66
East Glamorgan 126
East Grinstead 141
East Sussex 66, 107, 141
Ellesmere Port 133, 135, 189
Essex 134
Evans, Gwynfor (MP) 120

196 The Process of Local Government Reform 1966-74

Exeter 85, 139

Faversham 74n
Feather, Victor 40, 41
Fell, Anthony (MP) 139
Fidler, Michael (MP) 186
Flint 120
Fookes, Janet (MP) 141, 184
Foot, Michael (MP) 125
Fox, J. M. (MP) 125
Frome 133

Gage, Viscount 151
Gateshead 18, 76
Gatwick 132, 148, 186
Gibson-Watt, D. (MP) 113, 185
Glamorgan 118, 124, 126, 127, 137, 138, 139, 146-7, 155
Glossop 113
Gosnell, H. F. 31
Great Ayton 83, 155
Great Yarmouth 139
Greater Manchester 17, 76, 77, 105, 107, 132, 133, 151, 164, 186
Greenwood, Anthony (MP) 18, 71, 75, 88, 178
Griffith, Professor J. A. G. 141
Griffiths, James (MP) 20, 114, 119, 120, 122
Grimsby 134
Gwynedd 120, 123

Halifax 76, 106
Hale 186
Hall, Professor P. 110n
Hamilton 53
Hampshire 78, 87, 94, 105, 133
Hanser, C. J. 31
Harrogate 133
Hartlepool 144
Hastings 66
Heath, Edward (MP) 71, 99, 109, 130, 179
Heffer, Eric (MP) 99
Herbert, A. P. 31, 32
Hereford and Worcester 134
Herefordshire 148, 151, 186
Hertfordshire 66
Heseltine, Michael (MP) 99, 143n, 146, 150
Hetherington, A. C. 152
High Wycombe 66
Hill, Sir Francis 40, 41, 43, 66, 88
Huddersfield 76, 94, 106
Hughes, Cledwyn (MP) 120, 121, 122

Hughes, R. J. (MP) 125
Humberside 134, 136, 138, 172
Huyton 158, 186

Ingleton 133
Ipswich 134
Isle of Wight 137, 139, 151, 153, 186

Jellicoe, Earl 98
Jenkins, Peter 71, 72
Jenkins, Roy (MP) 48
Jones, Arthur (MP) 112, 150
Joseph, Sir Keith (MP) 118, 119

Keith-Lucas, Professor B. 164
Kent 66, 139
Kidderminster 66, 106n
Knutsford 106n

Lancashire 17, 21, 56, 66, 73, 77, 78, 79, 87, 94, 98, 101, 106n, 132, 133, 143
Leeds 66, 73, 74, 76, 133, 154
Leicester 135
Leicestershire 16, 76, 171
Lichfield 106n
Lincoln 40
Lincolnshire 134, 135, 155
Littleborough 24
Liverpool 48, 66
Llanberis 123
Long Eaton 133
Longland, Sir Jack 41, 43, 66, 87
Lowestoft 133
Ludlow 134
Luton 133, 144
Lymington 94, 153

McAdden, Sir Stephen (MP) 112
Mackintosh, Professor John 121
Maddan, Martin (MP) 141
Malvernshire 134
Manchester 42, 48, 64, 76, 86, 101, 103
Marshall, Dr A. H. 39, 41
Marshall, Dr E. (MP) 155
Marshall, Sir Frank 74, 95, 96, 103, 111
Maud, Sir John, *see* Redcliffe-Maud, Lord
Medway 66
Merionethshire 118, 120
Merseyside 17, 66, 77, 105, 107, 132, 133, 133n, 135, 143, 143n, 189
Merthyr Tydfil 117, 118, 120, 124, 126
Mid Glamorgan 147
Milnrow 24

Index of Persons 197

Milton Keynes 106
Moate, Roger 74, 74-5n
Monmouthshire 118, 124
Montgomery, Fergus (MP) 112, 141
Montgomeryshire 117
Morrison, Charles (MP) 141
Morton, Jane 83
Mursell, Sir Peter 41, 43, 65

Newcastle-upon-Tyne 18, 41, 76
Newport 118, 124
Norfolk 76
Northamptonshire 107, 132, 133
Northumberland 66, 106, 133
Northwich 76
North Yorkshire 133, 144
Nottingham 110, 135
Nottinghamshire 66, 76

Oakes, Gordon (MP) 186
Ormskirk 106n
Oxfordshire 132

Page, Graham (MP) 99, 102, 136, 144, 150, 153, 155
Pearce, Clifford 113, 128, 129
Pembrokeshire 127, 151, 186
Pink, Bonner (MP) 112
Plymouth 76, 106, 112, 133, 135, 139, 144, 148, 155
Pontypridd 113
Portsmouth 79
Port Talbot 124
Powys 120
Poynton 83, 151, 153, 153n, 155, 189
Preston 21, 66, 81, 87
Prestwich 189

Radcliffe 24
Ramsden, J. E. (MP) 112
Redcliffe-Maud, Lord 20, 38, 40, 153
Redditch 66, 106n
Reed, Laurence (MP) 141, 184
Rees-Davies, W. R. (MP) 112
Rhodes, Gerald 87n
Rhondda 113, 120
Rhymney Valley 118
Richards, Professor P. G. 162
Rippon, Geoffrey (MP) 172
Roberts, Michael (MP) 147
Rochdale 24, 66, 76, 103, 133, 158, 186
Roper, John (MP) 141
Ross, William (MP) 121
Rossendale 164
Rotherham 48

Rothwell 153
Runcorn 189
Rutland 16, 118

St Helens 17, 158, 186
Salisbury 66
Salford 48, 76, 86, 103, 189
Salop 76, 134
Scunthorpe 134
Sedbergh 134, 135
Senior, Derek 42, 43, 55, 84, 188
Sharp, Dame Eyelyn (Baroness) 19, 40, 83, 177
Sharpe, L. J. 44, 45
Sheffield 48, 73, 137, 139
Shonfield, Andrew 32, 33
Silkin, John (MP) 112, 146
Skeffington, Arthur (MP) 72, 77
Skelmersdale 143, 143n, 155, 189
Skipton 133
Slough 132
Smith, T. Dan 41
Somerset 133, 139
South Glamorgan 127, 133, 138
South Hampshire 73, 84, 92, 94, 105
South Molton 134
South Shields 18, 76
South Yorkshire 105, 106
Southampton 76, 79, 148
Southend 66, 133, 134
Southport 66, 106n, 132, 133n, 135
Speed, Keith (MP) 146
Stafford 66, 77, 81, 106n
Staffordshire 77, 106n, 133, 139
Steed, Michael 72
Stoke 77, 110, 133, 135
Stokesley 133, 144
Suffolk 133
Sunderland 107, 134
Surrey 66, 79, 132
Swain, Thomas (MP) 137
Swansea 118, 123, 125, 126
Swindon 66

Tameside 133
Tamworth 66
Taylor, George 154
Teesside 73, 106, 133, 134, 144, 163, 164n, 187
Temple, J. M. (MP) 112
Thomas, George (MP) 123, 126, 147
Thomas, Peter (MP) 126
Tuck, Raphael (MP) 104n
Tyne and Wear 105, 107, 134
Tynemouth 18, 76

Tyneside 17, 18, 73, 76, 86, 103, 107, 134

Vickers, Dame Joan (MP) 112, 137

Walker, Peter (MP) 26, 74-5, 92, 96, 97, 98-9, 100, 104, 106-112 *passim*, 113, 115, 125, 129-30, 134-6, 151, 157, 172, 179-80, 188, 189
Walkland, Stuart 141
Wallis, Reginald 42, 43, 55, 66, 88
Warrington 17, 107, 132, 168
Warwickshire 133, 172
West Glamorgan 126
West Midlands 16, 18, 35, 66, 67, 73, 105
West Sussex 41, 56, 76, 107, 141
West Yorkshire 45, 73, 84, 92, 94, 105, 106, 133
Westmorland 139
Weston-super-Mare 186
Whale, John 92n

Wheare, Sir K. 31
Whitby 144
Whitworth 164
Widnes 189
Wigan 17, 168
Wilmslow 151, 153, 153n, 155, 168, 186, 189
Wilson, Harold (MP) 16, 53, 71, 72, 75, 119, 124, 176, 178, 186
Winsford 106n
Wirral 133
Wiltshire 66, 76, 139
Wolverhampton 66
Woodcock, George 40
Woodnutt, Mark (MP) 137
Worcester 81
Worcestershire 106, 106n, 134
Worksop 133n
Worthing 56

Yorkshire, West Riding 66, 77, 78, 87, 94

SUBJECT INDEX

administrative modernisation, policy of: Labour Government 16, 60, 69-70, 71-2, 177, 178; Conservative Government 109, 179, 180
agency arrangements 28, 161, 165, 169, 170-3; and reform objectives 157, 165, 172-3; Circular 131/72 170-1, 172, 173; local disputes 171-2; parliamentary debates 145, 150-2, 155, 156, 170
aldermen 110, 130, 134, 138, 155, Appendix
ambulances, responsibility for 47, 47n
apathy, *see* interest
areas, *see* boundaries
Association for Neighbourhood Councils 166
Association of Chief Education Officers 22, 82
Association of Education Committees (AEC) 34, 58
Association of Men of Kent and Kentish Men 33n
Association of Municipal Corporations (AMC) 19, 21-2, 41, 74, 100, 101, 163, 177, 181, 183; evidence to RCLGE 21-2, 35; reactions to RCLGE Report 54, 75, 78, 79-81, 84, 188; 1970 plan 99, 102-4, 184; reactions to 1970 White Paper 95-6, 179; reactions to 1971 White Paper 105, 110-11, 129, 130, 131; reactions to Welsh proposals 121, 122; passage of 1972 Act 135, 142-3, 148, 150, 156
associations of local authorities 15, 21, 28, 43n, 54, 97, 109n, 113, 114, 128, 133, 169, 177, 179, 180; evidence to RCLGE 32, 34-5, 37-8, 39, 92; reactions to RGLGE report 60, 75, 84, 86, 87, 92, 188; and 1972 Act 154, 156; and reform objectives 24, 37-8, 189; consulted 20, 77-8, 88, 110-11, 119, 123, 128-30, 161, 163, 165, 170, 185-6; functions of 21, 28, 86, 138, 188; *see also* under names of individual associations

audit procedures 140, 146
Aylesbury and District Vigilante Committee 33n

Bains Committee (1971-2) 38, 109n, 180; *see also* management structures
borough status 110, 111, 130, 166
boundaries: RCLGE and 39, 65-7, 75-7, 79, 85, 86; 1958 Act procedures 16-19, 46; 1970 White Paper 93-4; 1971 White Paper 98, 104-7, 109-10, 113, 132; Boundary Commission (1972) 161, 162-6; disputes between associations 21, 103-4, 110-11; link with politics 72, 86, 113, 178-9, 186, 189; passage of 1972 Act 128, 133-4, 135-9 *passim*, 141, 143, 145, 146-7, 148, 151, 153, 155, 157, 162, 186; PTAs 49, 49n; Wales 118, 120, 123, 124-5, 126, 127
Boundary Commission, *see* Local Government Boundary Commission
Buchanan Report (1962) 49n

Campaign to Save Education in the Conurbations 87, 153-4
Central Advisory Water Committee 158
central-local relations 16, 16n, 20, 70, 158, 187; and democracy debate 26, 88-9, 98-100 *passim*, 114-15, 135, 158, 187
Charter Trustees 166
children service, *see* social services
Circulars 70, 71, 99, 100, 129, 151, 152, 154, 155, 161, 163, 169-70, 173; 8/71 107, 129, 132; 131/72 170-2, 173
city regions 21, 33, 42-3, 67-9, 188
city status 166
civil servants 17-18, 28, 111, 113-4, 123, 128, 177; and RCLGE 56-9 *passim*, 69-71, 87, 88, 94; attitudes 20-1, 28-9, 155, 168, 181, 189
civil service 16, 23, 129; Fulton Report 70, 178
cleansing, *see* refuse

Commission on the Constitution (1969-73) 53, 65, 73, 74, 81, 92, 100, 121, 125, 179, 182, 184
committees, press and public admission to 25, 154, 155
community councils, *see* parishes
comprehensive schools issue 16n
concurrent powers 157, 169
Conservative Government 16, 17, 24, 26, 55, 77, 87, 92, 100, 109n, 118-19, 179-80, 182, 183-5, 189; 1971 White Paper 25, 98-9, 104-10, 110n, 125-6, 128-9, 134, 136, 153, 163, 172, 185, Appendix; reactions to White Paper 110-14, 128-31; 1971 Bill contents 26, 133-5, Appendix
Conservative Party 86, 88, 95, 96, 98-9, 112-13, 118, 125; attitude to RCLGE Report 73, 74-5, 92, 96; attitude to 1970 White Paper 96, 97-9
consultative documents (1971) 129-32
consumer protection 56, 64, 126, 137, 145, 157, 171, 173
conurbations 16-18, 35, 36, 45, 48-9; *see also* metropolitan areas
Council for the Preservation of Rural England 81-2
councillors 27; allowances 93, 110, 158; number of 23-4, 93, 168; minimum age 141, 183-4; term of office 110, Appendix
counties (pre-1974) 16, 18, 21, 29, 33, 48, 49, 59, 76, 78-9, 106, 117-18, 120, 176
county boroughs 19, 21, 33, 48, 49, 56, 59, 79, 101, 106, 131, 171, 176; and 1958 Act 16, 18, 19, 177; and RCLGE Report 76-7, 80; and 1971 Bill 137, 153; Welsh proposals 117-19, 120, 123, 124, 126
County Councils Association 18, 21-2, 41, 54, 103-4, 156, 163, 171, 183, 188; evidence to RCLGE 22, 34-5, 38, 101; reactions to RCLGE Report 78-9, 81, 188; reactions to 1970 White Paper 92, 94; reactions to 1971 White Paper 110, 111, 131; reactions to Welsh proposals 121, 122, 123; 1970 plan 100-1, 102; passage of 1972 Act 135, 137, 138, 141, 142, 145, 147, 148, 151-3, 154

decentralisation 52n, 69, 78, 79, 84-5, 163, 165; and efficiency debate 25-6

delegation 56; problems of 46, 47
democracy 20, 29, 35, 101, 104, 120, 187-9, 190; general definitions 22-5, 27, 37-8, 87-9; RCLGE and 23, 24, 35, 36, 37-8, 58-9, 63, 65, 87; and reactions to RCLGE Report 78, 81, 84-5, 88-9, 91, 187-8; 1970 White Paper and 93, 94; 1971 White Paper and 25, 105, 114-15, 172; 1972 Act and 24, 28, 135-6, 156-8, 164, 166, 170, 172, 185
Department of Economic Affairs 41, 52-3, 70
Department of Education and Science 16n, 58, 94, 113
Department of Health and Social Security 47, 47n, 57, 113
Department of the Environment 92, 99, 109, 113-14, 128-32, 133, 161, 165, 169-70, 172; *see also* Ministry of Housing; Ministry of Transport
Departmental Committee on the Procedure of Royal Commissions (1910) 35n, 43
district auditor, *see* audit
districts: pre-1974 21, 29, 32, 56, 75-7, 132; *see also* non-county boroughs, rural districts, urban districts; Senior plan 73-4; proposed 1971 104-6, 107, 113, 128; non-metropolitan 142, 144, 161, 162-5, 168, 169-73; *see also* metropolitan districts

education 33, 46, 52, 56, 65, 76, 130, 132, Appendix; RCLGE proposals 64, 66, 67; reactions to RCLGE Report 71, 73, 76, 78, 79, 80, 82; 1970 White Paper 84, 86-7, 92, 94; 1971 White Paper, Bill 107, 137, 145, 146, 153-4, 156; size of LEA 42, 56-8, 66-7, 82, 86-7, 94, 107, 153-4, 183
efficiency 22-3, 29, 101, 104, 180, 187-90; general definitions 23, 25-7, 169, 173; RCLGE and 23, 36, 63-4, 87; and reactions to RCLGE Report 87-8, 88-9, 91; 1971 White Paper and 105, 107, 114-15; 1972 Act and 28, 135-6, 156-8, 164-5, 169-70, 172, 173, 185
electoral system 15, 23-4, 47, 93, 110, Appendix; passage of 1972 Act and 23-4, 128, 130, 134, 141, 144, 148, 153, 156, 162, 164, 166-9; *see also* wards

Subject Index 201

environmental health 33, 67, 99
European Communities Act 1972 139n, 154

finance 38-9, 41, 46, 184; audit 140, 146; rates 56, 82, 92
fire service 33, 52, 64, 137
food and drugs, *see* consumer protection
Fulton Report (1968) 16, 70, 178
functions 24, 25, 26, 33, 36, 37
functions, allocation of; RCLGE 63-4, 67, 68, 69, 71, 80, 84, Appendix; 1970 White Paper 86-7, 92, Appendix; 1971 White Paper 107-8, 109, 112, 114, 129, 130-1, Appendix; 1971 Welsh proposals 126, 127; 1971 Bill and 1972 Act 135-6, 137, 142-3, 145, 146, 148, 150-4 *passim*, 156-7, 158, 161, 162, 169-73, 184-5, 186-7, Appendix; other proposals 47, 77-80, 101-4; *see also* under individual services

general elections, effect of 16, 20, 60, 71-2, 74, 77, 86, 96, 99-100, 125, 177-9, 181-2, 188-9
general review areas, *see* Local Government Commission (1958-66)
government departments 33-4, 35, 39, 47-8, 56-7, 70, 71; *see also* central-local relations *and* under names of individual departments
Greater London, *see* London
Guardian, The 42, 53, 63, 71-2, 73, 83, 102, 125, 182

health, *see* environmental health *and* national health service
Herbert Commission, *see* Royal Commission on Local Government in Greater London
highways 46, 49, 171, 185, 187; RCLGE and 64, 67, 80, 87-8, 102, 103; 1971 White Paper and Bill 130-1, 135, 136; passage of Act 25, 28, 137, 145, 150, 156, 157, 171-3, 185, 187
Home Office 48, 56-7, 113, 167-8
House of Commons 16, 20, 63, 96-7, 104n, 112, 125, 126, 129-30, 141-2; *see also* Local Government Bill *and* Members of Parliament
House of Lords 98, 190n; *see also* Local Government Bill

housing 42, 46, 56, 88, 99, 158; allocation of 33, 52, 67, 76, 85, 107, 108, 130, Appendix
Housing Finance Act 1972 139n, 141, 154, 161

Institute of Education (London) 46
Institute of Housing Managers 58
Institute of Local Government Studies (Birmingham) 41
interest of public in local government 47, 82-3

joint committees 70, 167, 169; proposed by Senior 69
Justices Clerks Society 148, 154

Kilbrandon Report, *see* Commissions on the Constitution

Labour Government (1964-70) 16, 19, 20, 26, 32, 55, 60, 71-2, 73-4, 77, 91-2, 99-100, 119-25 *passim*, 1970 White Paper 34, 72, 84-5, 86, 88 92-3, 95, 99, 104, 107, 114, 179, 185, 188-9, Appendix; reactions to White Paper 93-6, 98, 100, 101, 102, 112
Labour Party 19, 29, 42, 55, 72-3, 74, 76, 79, 84, 95, 120, 126, 189; reactions to 1971 proposals 111-12, 136, 137, 138-9, 140, 146-7
Liberal Party 73-4, 81, 97, 120, 125
Libraries 33, 56, 137; allocation of 64, 67, 126, 135, 145, 150, 157, 171, 184-5, Appendix
Library Association 148
loan sanction 26
Local Authority Conditions of Service Advisory Board (LACSAB) 156
local authority associations, *see* associations
Local Authority Social Services Act 1970 51
local councils, *see* parishes
Local Government Act 1958 16-19, 56, 79, 117, 134, 146n, 177, 181
Local Government Act 1966 38-9
Local Government Act 1972 15, 21, 28, 127, 144, 154-9, 165, 166, 168, 169-73 *passim*, 185, Appendix
Local Government Bill 1971 133-6, 145, 156, 162, 173, Appendix; Second Reading 136-9, 140, 187; Committee Stage 136, 139-49, 150, 152, 164n,

Local Government Bill 1971, *cont.*
183-4, 185; Report and Third Reading 140, 144, 149-53, *passim*; House of Lords 140, 144, 149-50, 151-3, 158, 170, 184, 186
Local Government Boundary Commission (1945-9) 23, 36, 37, 39, 46, 69, 117
Local Government Boundary Commission (1972) 107, 113, 128-9, 132, 134-5, 144-6 *passim*, 148, 161, 162-6, 168
Local Government Commissions (1958-66): for England 16-19, 21, 23, 39, 46, 59, 76, 106, 117, 119, 146n, 177, 181; for Wales 117, 118, 119
Local Government Operational Research Unit (LGORU) 57
Local Government Staff Commission 70
London, local government in 29, 46, 70, 71, 110, 128; politics of reform 29, 72, 86, 87n, 112, 118, 177; problems of new structure 108, 155, 167-8; excluded from RCLGE 36-7; RCLGE Report and 64, 69; *see also* Royal Commission on Local Government in Greater London
London Government Act 1963 56, 112, 139

Magistrates Association 148, 154
Mallaby Committee (1964-7) 38, 53, 54
management structures 46, 53, 54, 109n, 110, 180; excluded from RCLGE 38-9; *see also* Bains Committee *and* Maud Committee
Maud Committee (1964-7) 38, 40, 53, 54
mayors 88, 166
Members of Parliament 21, 82, 114, 155, 177, 180-1; and RCLGE 72-3, 74, 79, 88; and 1970, 1971 proposals 96-7, 112-13; and passage of Bill 131-2, 136-8, 143, 150, 161, 186-7; attitude survey 147-9
metropolitan areas 49n; RCLGE and 45, 49, 64, 66, 70, 71, 88, Appendix; reactions to RCLGE Report 71, 73, 76-7, 78, 79, 80-1, 84, 86-7; 1970 White Paper and 84, 86-7, 92, 93, 94, 98, 182, Appendix; 1971 White Paper and 104, 105, 106, 107, 110, Appendix; 1971 Bill, 1972 Act and 132, 133n, 146, 154, 157, 167, 185, Appendix; rejected in Wales 124-5

metropolitan districts 50n; RCLGE and 52, 64, 66, Appendix; reactions to RCLGE Report 76-7, 80-1, 87; 1970 White Paper and 92, 93, Appendix; 1971 White Paper and 104, 107, 109, Appendix; 1971 Bill, 1972 Act and 113, 132, 133, 137, 144, 146, 156, 161, 168, 169, 186, Appendix; proposed functions of 52, 64, 80-1, 87, 93, 107, 137, 142, 146, 154, 156; *see also* metropolitan areas
Ministry of Education, *see* Department of Education and Science
Ministry of Health, *see* Department of Health and Social Security
Ministry of Housing and Local Government 16, 40, 44, 72, 85n, 99, 118, 177; evidence to RCLGE 33n, 46, 58; *see also* Department of the Environment
Ministry of Transport 33n, 46; *see also* Department of the Environment
municipal boroughs, *see* non-county boroughs

National and Local Government Officers Association (NALGO) 22, 33, 153
National Association of Parish Councils 64, 81, 141
National Farmers Union 138
national health service 26, 29, 52, 83, 177n, 187; RCLGE and 37, 47, 47n, 49-51, 52, 53, 56; 1968, 1970 proposals for 37, 50, 51, 93, 94, 115, 158
National Health Service Reorganisation Act 1973 50n, 187
national parks 37, 55, 153
National Union of Teachers 22
neighbourhood councils, *see* parishes
New Society 83, 110n
new towns 87, 163
non-county boroughs 65, 76, 79-80, 81, 101, 108, 126, 144, 165-6, 171, 172; *see also* districts
non-metropolitan counties, *see* shire counties
non-metropolitan districts, *see* districts
number of councils: old structure 21, 32, 117; RCLGE proposals 66, 67, Appendix; 1970 White Paper 85, 92, 93, 182, Appendix; 1971 White Paper 105, 107, 129, Appendix; 1971 Bill, 1972 Act 133, 146-7, 150, 151, 163-4,

Subject Index 203

number of councils, *cont.*
165, 186, Appendix; Welsh proposals 118, 120, 121, 123, 125, 126, 146-7, other proposals 76-80 *passim*, 103, 112

officers 60, 148, 150, 153, 156, 158; transfer of 162, 170
ombudsman, local 25

parishes 32; evidence to RCLGE 45, 64-5; RCLGE Report and 65, 66, 68, 85, Appendix; reactions to Report 71, 73, 78, 81, 83, 85; 1970 White Paper and 92, 95-6, 98, Appendix; 1971 White Paper and 110, 112, 126, Appendix; 1971 Bill and 134-5, 136, 144, 148, 155; 1972 Act and 161, 162, 165-6; 173, Appendix
parks and recreation 65, 67, 130, 157
Parliamentary Commissioners 72
party politics and reform 18-19, 71-2, 189-90; boundary issues 18, 42, 55, 72, 83, 113, 127, 135, 139, 178-9, 189; parties and the RCLGE 54-5, 71, 72-5, 109, 178-9, 179-80; parties and the 1972 Act 112-13, 132, 138-41, 147, 154-5, 186; in Wales 124, 125-6, 127, 147; *see also* general elections, effect of
passenger transport 20, 33-4, 46, 55, 64, 99, 157; 1968 changes 48-9, 49n, 51, 60; allocation of 64, 67, 80, 103, 135, 150, 157, Appendix
planning, town and country: old structure weaknesses 18, 33-4, 37, 42, 46; RCLGE and 33-4, 37, 46, 49, 55, 64, 65, 67, 69, Appendix; reactions to RCLGE Report 80, 87, 94, 102, 103, 125; 1971 White Paper 107, 108, 131, 186; passage of 1972 Act 135-6, 137, 138, 142, 145, 152-3, 156; new structure 25, 28, 145, 152-3, 157, 169-70, 171, 173, 185, Appendix
Planning Advisory Group (1965) 49n
police 33, 56, 57, 58, 64, 67, 137, 141, 145, 148, 153; 1966 changes 48, 53
Police Act 1964 48
Police Federation 148, 153
polytechnics, creation of 52
population size, *see* size of authority
Prescot Town Football Club 33n
press, admission to meetings 25, 154, 155

professional associations 15, 22, 28, 33, 75, 82, 145, 148, 156
public health, *see* environmental health

rate support grant 38-9
rates, *see* finance
recreation, *see* parks
Redcliffe-Maud Commission, *see* Royal Commission on Local Government in England
Redcliffe-Maud Committee (1973-4) 153
refuse service 67, 187; 1972 Act 28, 126, 137, 149n, 150, 157, 171, 173, 184-5, Appendix
regionalism 33; Regional Economic Planning Councils 41, 52-3, 65, 70; RCLGE and problem of 36-7, 41, 52-3; RCLGE Report and 65, 68, 87, Appendix; reactions to RCLGE 70, 73, 81, 87, 96; issue shelved 92, 184, Appendix; *see also* city regions *and* Commission on the Constitution
Reorganisaion of Central Government (White Paper 1970) 109
research 32, 43-5, 56-8, 59, 65, 83, 87
road safety 171
roads, *see* highways
Royal Commission on Local Government in England (1966-9) 15, 18, 20, 22, 28, 29, chapter 2, 182; evidence to 22, 32-5, 41, 48, 56-9 *passim*, 64-5, 67, 70, 71, 81, 88, 93, 121, 178, 183; membership of 19n, 20, 35, 38, 39-43, 60, 178; research for 32, 43-5, 56-8, 59, 83, 87; terms of reference 23, 26, 35n, 36-9, 46, 50, 51, 58, 59, 88, 113-14, 119, 178, 180; Report contents 23-4, 25, 26, 50-2, 53, 56, 58-9, 63-7, 70, 71, 182-3, Appendix; Senior's Report 24, 29n, 37, 47, 51, 52, 56, 63, 66, 67-9, 70, 184, 188; response to Report 24, 25, 69-84, 91-2, 96, 101, 104-5, 107, 111, 113, 178-9, 187-8
Royal Commission on Local Government in Greater London (1957-60) 20, 23, 32, 39, 44, 46, 60
Royal Commission on Local Government in Scotland (1966-9) 83, 114, 121
Royal Commission on Pollution 91
Royal Commission on the Police 48
Royal Commission on Trades Unions and Employers Associations 44

royal commissions, value of 31-2, 60, 119, 177-8, 181-3
Rural District Councils Association (RDCA) 21, 101-2, 121, 125, 163-4; evidence to RCLGE 34-5, 38; reactions to RCLGE Report 25, 44, 74n, 78, 79, 84, 94; passage of 1972 Act 24, 130-1, 134, 142-3, 144, 156
rural districts 74n, 75-6, 106, 108, 164, 172

Scotland 52, 114, 121, 166
sewage, *see* water and sewage
shire counties (1972 Act): proposed 1971 104-7, 109, 125-6; reactions 110-11, 112; 1971 Bill and passage 127, 133-4, 143-4, 146-7, 157, 186
size of authority (population) 55-9; old structure 18, 46, 56, 117-18; RCLGE members and 40, 42, 47; evidence to RCLGE 22, 34-5, 48, 51, 56-7, 58; research for RCLGE 44, 45, 56-8, 59, 87-8; RCLGE proposals for 23-4, 51-2, 56, 58-9, 63-4, 65-8; reactions to RCLGE Report 25, 78-80, 87-8, 101-4; Governments prevent debate 59, 85, 93, 94, 105, 109, 182-3; reactions to 1971 proposals 107, 132, 137; passage of 1972 Act 151, 153-4, 157-8, 185; non-metropolitan districts 105-6; 128-9, 163-5; urban parishes 165
social services 50, 56, 58, 76, 132, 145; Seebohm Report 52, 58; allocation of 34-5, 52, 64, 67, 80, 130, 137, Appendix
Sound Broadcasting Act 1972 139n, 154-5
special review areas, *see* Local Government Commission (1958-66)
Standing Conference on London and South East Regional Planning 65
Statutory Instruments 70, 113, 161
Sunday Times, The 63, 92n

terms of reference: of Local Government Boundary Commission (1945) 23, 36; of Local Government Boundary Commission (1972) 129, 162-3, 165; of Local Government Commission (1958) 16, 18, 23, 36, 117; of RCLGE (1966) 23, 26, 35n, 36-9, 46, 113-14, 119, 178, 180; Wales 117, 119
Times, The 63, 82, 83, 85

timetable for reform: of RCLGE 32, 59-60, 178, 182; of Labour Government 1969-70 71-2, 93; of Conservative Government 1971 98-9, 109-10, 113-14; in Wales 121-3, 125, 126; passage of 1972 Act 128, 129-30, 132, 133, 136, 139-40, 150, 153, 162; of Boundary Commission (1972) 162-3, 168; local elections 167-9; guidance on functions 170, 171-2; general legislative problems 54-5, 126, 131-2; *see also* general elections, effect of
town and country planning, *see* planning
Town and Country Planning Association 142, 148
town-country separation, principle of 27, 33, 35, 47, 81-2, 106, 120; criticised 19, 33-4, 46, 104, 124; rejected 55-6, 63-4, 67, 71, 105, 124-5
Town Planning Institute (Royal) 18, 75, 131, 142
town status 144, 166
traffic management 20, 156
transport, *see* passenger transport
Transport Act 1968 48, 50-1
Treasury, The 26, 70

unitary authorities: proposed by RCLGE 25, 26, 52, 53, 63-7, 69; reactions to 73, 76-81 *passim*, 84-8, 93-4, 97, 99, 179, 182-3; rejected 1971 104-6, 109-10, 140, 146; Wales 124-5, 182
Urban District Councils Association (UDCA) 21, 25, 102, 104, 121, 125, 163-4; evidence to RCLGE 34, 35, 38, 44, 57; reactions to RCLGE Report 78, 79, 80, 81, 94; passage of 1972 Act 135, 140n, 142-3, 144, 150, 156
urban districts 21, 65, 75-6, 106, 108, 126, 144, 165-6, 171-2

Wales 114, chapter 5, 135, 149, 161, 162, 165, 182; proposals for reform 20, 114, 118, 120, 123, 124-5, 125-6, 133, 146-7, 184-5; Welsh Council 120-1, 123, 125, 127, 146; Welsh Office 29, 113, 114, 119, 120, 123, 124, 126, 185
wards 23-4, 111, 130, 144, 164, 166-9; *see also* electoral system

water and sewage 26, 37, 55, 67, 115, 158, 161, 187
weaknesses of old structure 19, 46-7, 74-5, 104-5, 117, 122, 176, 181, 190
weights and measures, *see* consumer protection
Welsh Nationalist Party 53, 120, 125